第 一 辑

语言哲学研究

主编 钱冠连

YUYAN ZHEXUE YANJIU

Volume **One**

The Forum on the Philosophy of Language

高等教育出版社·北京
HIGHER EDUCATION PRESS BEIJING

图书在版编目(CIP)数据

语言哲学研究. 第1辑：汉、英/钱冠连主编. —北京：高等教育出版社, 2010.11(2012.7 重印)

ISBN 978-7-04-028701-1

Ⅰ.①语… Ⅱ.①钱… Ⅲ.①语言哲学—文集—汉、英 Ⅳ.①H0-53

中国版本图书馆 CIP 数据核字（2010）第 209781 号

策划编辑	贾巍巍	责任编辑	谢 森	封面设计	刘晓翔	版式设计	刘 艳
责任校对	谢 森	责任印制	尤 静				

出版发行	高等教育出版社	咨询电话	400-810-0598
社　　址	北京市西城区德外大街4号	网　　址	http://www.hep.edu.cn
邮政编码	100120		http://www.hep.com.cn
印　　刷	三河市华润印刷有限公司	网上订购	http://www.landraco.com
开　　本	787×1092　1/16		http://www.landraco.com.cn
印　　张	11.75	版　　次	2010年11月第1版
字　　数	243 000	印　　次	2012年7月第2次印刷
购书热线	010-58581118	定　　价	25.00元

本书如有缺页、倒页、脱页等质量问题，请到所购图书销售部门联系调换
版权所有　侵权必究
物 料 号　28701-00

《语言哲学研究》编委会

顾问委员会

主　任　涂纪亮（中国社会科学院）
　　　　江　怡（北京师范大学）
委　员　（按姓氏音序 in alphabetical order）
　　　　Maria Baghramian (University College Dublin, Ireland)
　　　　陈　波（北京大学）
　　　　陈嘉映（首都师范大学）
　　　　季国清（美国洛杉矶 东方文化形态研究院）
　　　　王　路（清华大学）
　　　　张志林（复旦大学）
　　　　朱志方（武汉大学）

编审委员会

主　编　钱冠连（广东外语外贸大学）
副主编　王　寅（四川外语学院）
编　委　（按姓氏音序 in alphabetical order）
　　　　陈章云（北京外国语大学）
　　　　成晓光（东北师范大学）
　　　　杜世洪（西南大学）
　　　　韩　红（对外经济贸易大学）
　　　　黄　斌（重庆大学）
　　　　黄华新（浙江大学）
　　　　黄会健（浙江工业大学）
　　　　霍永寿（广东外语外贸大学）
　　　　蒋运鹏（德国海德堡大学）
　　　　孔明安（中国社会科学院）
　　　　李洪儒（黑龙江大学）
　　　　廖美珍（华中师范大学）
　　　　林允清（北京航空航天大学）
　　　　刘利民（四川大学）
　　　　隋　然（首都师范大学）
　　　　王文斌（宁波大学）
　　　　文　旭（西南大学）
　　　　周　频（上海外国语大学博士后流动站）

执行编辑　（按姓氏音序 in alphabetical order）
　　　　　　杜世洪（西南大学）
　　　　　　霍永寿（广东外语外贸大学）
　　　　　　梁瑞清（暨南大学）
　　　　　　王爱华（中国成都 电子科技大学）

总 策 划
　　　　　　贾　巍（高等教育出版社）

前　言

中西语言哲学研究会将《语言哲学研究》作为我们发表研究成果的论集。

《语言哲学研究》以研究西方语言哲学和中国哲学为基础，倚凭此基础，发展出各种风格、各种进路的语言哲学。

西语哲，一般地说，包括（1）英美分析传统意义上的语言哲学（analytic philosophy of language）；（2）欧洲大陆阐释性传统的语言哲学。分析哲学是西方哲学在20世纪初叶产生的一种哲学运动、方式、风格或潮流。

为何我们今天还要研究西方语言哲学呢？最直接的理由是：第一，西语哲天然地、几乎无孔不入地为语言研究提供了并将继续提供营养与智慧。哲学要"计算"的主要是智慧，是人类对世界事物的规律的看法，是哲学家对哲学家的看法（即这种思想对那种思想的看法），而不是彻底回答与解决了多少难题。第二，对于过往的历史，其价值往往见诸后世，甚至久远者更珍贵。第三，不要说近五十年的西方哲学经典中语言哲学为数不少，就是在当代，以语词说事（关于世界之理）的哲学名著和名篇，还时有出现。第四，我们的研究，不仅止步于专门梳理西语哲的营养与智慧，尤其考虑应该怎么生发新枝、开新花。

近年来语言学界对语言哲学研究热衷起来，其意义重大，影响深远。但同时需要解决的问题是对语言哲学界定的泛化。研究对象的泛化最终会拖慢一个学科的发展。有学者认为，对语言作深层次的思考，就是语言哲学。我们的看法是，就算对语言作了深层次的思考，如果这个思考的最终结论达至语言学的道理，即词语的形式、意义、功能及其运用的，简言之，从语言叩问语言自身者，仍算语言学研究。现在我们试图用极为简单明确的语言概括出两者的总体区别：从语言入，从世界出或从思想出，谓语言哲学。从语言入，从语言出，谓语言学。

所谓"从世界出"，即达至了世界一束[世界、实在、对象、实体或虚体、事物、是、存在（the world, reality, object, entity, thing, being, existence）]的道理；所谓"从思想出"，即对思想进行思考（参见冯友兰："思想我们的思想"《中国哲学史》第2页）。

两者区别，除了上述理论目标（最终从哪里出来）不同之外，还在概念体系、理论建构、主要研究方法与学术品质诸方面，亦存某些扞格（当然也有联系）。以上这样划界，显然不在于分出两者的高下与贵贱，因为两者都旨在为人类文明带来积极的思考。

对于《语言哲学研究》未来的定位，我们的考虑是，既然承认西方哲学根据它自身的ontology 与 epistemology两个阶段及形而上学传统发展出来了分析哲学（凭借哲学的语言性转向[the linguistic turn]），为什么我们就不能试一试结合中国哲学与汉语文化语境发展出自己的语言哲学呢？因此，我们重视以汉语为语料，发展出我们目前还无法预料的某种新的语言哲学来。我们既要奉行"拿来"主义，也不妨实行"拿出"主义——我们中华民族的子孙们也要向世界奉献出我们自己的智慧。

人人都在世上以不同的方式言说并影响着世界。我们希望，将不自觉地影响世界的过程变为自觉地与负责地影响世界的过程。

愿我们的民族与社会更为和谐，更为进取。《语言哲学研究》会在这个和谐且进取的社会里继续着自己的言说。

《语言哲学研究》编辑部
2010-6-30

The Inaugural Statement on

The Forum on the Philosophy of Language

The China Association for the Philosophy of Language (CAPL) takes *The Forum on the Philosophy of Language as* journal of the association.

On the basis of research in Western tradition of philosophy of language (henceforth PL) and Chinese philosophy, *The Forum* aims at developing a multifaceted approach to philosophy of language.

PL, in its broad sense, includes (1) the Anglo-American philosophy of language in the analytic tradition, i.e. analytic philosophy of language; (2) the European Continent's PL in the hermeneutic tradition. Analytic philosophy is a philosophical movement which, with a distinctive style, developed in the beginning of the twentieth century and has become the dominant philosophical tradition in UK, USA and many countries of the European continent.

What are the reasons for studying PL today? And what exactly can we learn? The most immediate reason is that PL has provided and will continue to provide insight into and understanding of language for linguists. It has also had a pervasive influence on linguistic research in the West. What philosophy contributes is not so much an ultimate solution to any puzzle, but clarity and understanding. Analytic philosophy offers a methodical and scientific way of looking at the development of ideas, issues and events, as well as a broader perspective and overview of the research carried out in different traditions. Next, the value of a historical event tends to be shown in its long-term consequences. Moreover, the more ancient the event is, the more valuable it is. Third, in the present age, there appear from time to time some philosophical masterpieces discussing in linguistic terms theories of how things are. Additionally, there have been quite a few philosophical classics on PL in the past 50 years. Finally, we shall not confine ourselves to explaining what the PL has already covered; rather we aim to develop PL in China in ways that would be appropriate to our linguistic and historical context.

The fact that the linguistic circle in China has shown great interest in PL is of great significance and has far-reaching consequences. At the same time, the problem to be urgently addressed is that the scope of philosophy of language is too wide and broad. We are fully aware that giving too wide a range to a research subject could clip the wings of the subject and forestall its development. Some scholars hold that any thought on language, if expressed on a profound level, could be regarded as philosophy of language. Our belief, however, is that, even though one's thought on language is on a profound level, such a thought still remains linguistic, if the eventual conclusion of it concerns nothing else than linguistic forms, meaning and functions and their applications. Now, let us sum up in a terse and telling way the global discrepancy between the two: the research approach whose entrance is in linguistic terms but whose exit is in the world or in any thought may be regarded as philosophy of language; by contrast, the research approach whose entrance is in linguistic terms and whose exit is also in linguistic terms is linguistic.

By "exit in the world," we mean that philosophers eventually could arrive at arguments concerning the cluster of "the world"[1] including reality, objects, entities, and existence. By "exit in any thought," we mean that philosophers are eventually "to think on their thoughts."[2]

In addition to the different theoretical goals (i.e. the different exits) mentioned above, the differences between PL and linguistics lie, further, in their conceptual tools, theoretical structures, main methods of research, as well as academic qualities. Such a demarcation of the two is not intended to distinguish the high from the low or the complex from the simple. For the two have both resulted in positive thoughts for human civilization.

As to the orientation of this journal, we believe that, Western philosophy has developed the analytic tradition, through "the linguistic turn," by relying on specific epistemological and metaphysical grounding. We, on the other hand, would try to develop a novel kind of philosophy of language which would rely on Chinese philosophical traditions and the cultural context of the Chinese language. For this reason, we would rely heavily on the data available from the Chinese language, in the hope of developing a new kind of philosophy of language. When pursuing "importism," we would also aim to put "exportism" into practice. The reason for the two -isms is very simple: the offspring of the Chinese nation should offer wisdom to the nations all over the world.

Everyone in the world talks about the world and tries to influence it in novel and original ways. We hope that we will turn the process of exerting unconscious influences on the world into the one of achieving a conscious and responsible impact on it.

May our nation and society be in more harmonious development as it keeps forging ahead. The journal of CAPL will aim to go on saying about the world in its own way.

From the editorial board of the journal
2010-6-30

---

[1] "The cluster of the world" was proposed by Qian Guanlian in "The Philosophy of Language: Its Dissemination and Further Development in the Circle of FLS in China", in *Foreign Language Research*, Harbin, China, 2008.2, P.1.

[2] Feng Youlan, *The History of Chinese Philosophy*, Beijing: Peking University Press, 1996, 2nd edn. p.2.

目 录

● 意义与指称   1

人自称、人被称与物被称   钱冠连   1
假装、连环假装与"假装假装"——从奥斯汀和
     陈嘉映谈起   杜世洪 赖成彬   9
现象不可说的认识论问题   梁瑞清   19
引语的不确定性——语言哲学研究系列之三   王爱华   28

● 语言●思维●实在   39

主客主多重互动理解模式（SOS）：理论建构与语料实证   王 寅   39
Sophism of the School of Names: Linguistic Path toward
     Rationalism in Traditional Chinese Philosophy   刘利民   51
解析语言逻辑哲学难题   黄 斌   72
语言思维、语言模块与语言进化   成晓光   88

● 西方语言哲学梳理与开掘   102

Chomsky on the "Ordinary Language" View of
     Language   林允清   102
罗素论存在   蒋运鹏   144
由分析悖论引发的意义理论思考   黄会健   156

● 语言哲学与教学实践   165

"西方语言哲学"与外语学科博士研究生理论创新能力的
     培养   霍永寿   165

●《语言哲学研究》稿约   174

● 意义与指称

人自称、人被称与物被称

广东外语外贸大学外国语言学及应用语言学研究中心　钱冠连

提　要：本文首先观察了汉语"我"（的）丰富的变体这一自关心现象，并设置"人自称—人被称—物被称"三元并存范畴，其意义在于：（1）彰显人对自身生存状态的自关心，人自称的高度复杂性使我们认识了人的高度复杂性。（2）彰显人对自身生存状态的自关心、对他人生存状态的他关心、对物的他关心之间的差异。这一差异，不仅提示人自称对语言的复杂诉求终归可以看成是人对自己的优先彰显，还顺便地解释了 Frege 关于"呈现方式与认知内容"所不能解释的人自称的（超）多名（多变体）现象。（3）研究"我"变体可与海氏的"此在"相呼应。"'我'是此在的本质规定性"。在 Being and Time 里，人的优先地位是以海氏的阐释方式实现的，在汉语里，是以人自称的方式实现的。人自称正是在进行"对自己存在的解说"！

假如某物在特定语言中的指称方式多有变体，该物的"存在和出场"比他物得到更多张扬。人对世界一人一事的称呼与描述，其实是以自己的眼光干涉其中的。

关键词：人自称；人被称；物被称；"我"变体；自关心

1. 导言：本文的理论取向

说哲学的分析潮流早已结束，说"形而上学已经恢复了它（在哲学中）的中心地位"[1]，都威胁不了本文的研究进路。因为这个进路是：后语言哲学的思路。后语言哲学与经典语言哲学的相同在于：（1）从语句入（**in linguistic terms**）；（2）从世界出（达至世界与思想）。

后语言哲学区别于经典语言哲学的特点在于：（1）吸取西语哲（分析传统和欧洲传统）的营养，但不炒作它的老问题，而是节外生新枝。（2）生出什么新枝呢？从日常社会生活中寻找一个一个具体语言问题，从词语分析（形而下）找入口，从世界与人的道理（形而上）找出口，管住入口与出口，但是让选题与风格多样化。（3）重视汉语语境，实现西语哲本土化。

---

[1] 参见斯特劳森《个体：论描述的形而上学》，苏珊·哈克总序一，中国人民大学出版社，2004第1版。

2. 正文：

针对 a = b（The Morning Star is the Evening Star）这样的同一性（identity）之中的不同，Frege 提出了呈现方式（the mode of presentation）与认知内容（cognitive content）的两点不同。循此两点不同，他指出涵意并不就是指称（Frege，1952），寻此两点不同，也可以解释一物两名甚至三名（见下文）现象，但不能解释本文所发现的人自称的（超）多名（多变体）现象。补上这个漏洞是产生本文的直接推动力之一。

一则流传在海外华人中的笑话，即"洋人求学记"，作为本文主要语料：

有一个老外为了学好汉语，不远万里，来到中国，拜师于一位国学教授门下。第一天老外想挑一个简单词汇学习，便向老师请教英语"I"在汉语中应该如何说。

老师解释道：

（在）中国……，当你处在不同的级别、地位，"I"也有不同的变化，就像你们英语中的形容词有原级、比较级、最高级一样[1]。

比如，你刚来中国，没有地位，对普通人可以说："我、咱、俺、余、吾、予、侬、某、咱家、洒家、俺咱、本人、个人、人家、吾侬、我侬"。

如果见到老师、长辈和上级，则应该说："区区、仆、鄙、愚、鄙人、卑人、敝人、鄙夫、鄙躯、鄙愚、贫身、小子、小可、在下、末学、小生、不佞、不才、不材、小材、不肖、不孝、不类、走狗、牛马走、愚小子、鄙生、贫生、学生、后学、晚生、晚学、后生晚学、予末小子、予小子、余小子"。

等到你当了官以后，见到上级和皇帝，则应该说："职、卑职、下官、臣、臣子、小臣、鄙臣、愚臣、奴婢、奴才、小人、老奴、小的、小底"。

见到平级，则可以说："愚兄、为兄、小弟、兄弟、愚弟、哥们"。

见到下级，则可以说："爷们、老子、大老子、你老子、乃公"。

如果你混得好，当上了皇帝或王爷，则可以说："朕、孤、孤王、孤家、寡人、不榖"。

如果你不愿意当官，只好去当和尚、道士，则应该说："贫道、小道、贫僧、贫衲、不慧、小僧、野僧、老衲、老僧"。

最后一点必须注意，一旦你退休了，便一下子失去了权利和地位，见人也矮了三分，只好说："老朽、老拙、老夫、愚老、老叟、小老、小老儿、老汉、老可、老躯、老仆、老物、朽人、老我、老骨头"。

上面一百零八种"I"，仅为男性的常用说法。更多的"I"明天谟解。

老外听了老师一席话，顿时冷水浇头，一个晚上没有睡好觉。第二天一大早便向老师辞行："学生、愚、不材、末学，走。"退了房间，订了机票，回国去了。

任何一个说话人可用"我"（第一人称）指称自己，即把自己当作一个世界对象来指称。这便是人自称。关于词汇"我"的意义的理论（即专名理论）认

---

[1] 此笑话作者以汉语中的"我"与英语中的形容词的三级比较，不妥。

为，"词汇'我'是一个逻辑上的专名（或者"罗素式的单称词"，Alessandra，2007：94），即一个直接命名说话者所认识的对象的词汇。……'我'是这个特定主体的一个专名。这一观点的困难在于，即便我们承认我知觉到一个作为经验主体的自我，还是不清楚我怎么知道这个自我就是我自己"（尼·布宁、余纪元，2001：822）。本文不拟讨论这个逻辑专名的困难，只是指出，上述"不清楚我怎么知道这个自我就是我自己"的情况，在汉语的人自称中似有不同：汉语中人自称的多种变体表明，似乎人还是模糊地意识到，我知道这个自我就是我自己。

物被人称，即**物被称**，即事物的名字，与人自称形成了对立。既然是任何一个说话人，"我"所指称的对象就是暂时的、变动不居的（Quine，1960：173）。每换一个人自用"我"于己，指称的对象就换一次。这种"自我中心特称词"（egocentric particulars）（Russell，1940：116），它们的外延与讲话者及其时空位置有着相对性，并有赖于说出它们时的语境。"它们会影响包含有它们的命题的真，因为这样的命题不能有恒常的真值。可以说它们有外延而无内涵"（尼·布宁、余纪元，2001：286）。但是，我们会发现，汉语中"我"的变体中除了有所指即外延之外，还有内涵。

正是因为"我"变体中每一个有了内涵，才有了这篇论文所讨论的问题。

汉语从古到今出现了大量的"我"的替换词（即变体，以下简称"我"变体），它们可能吓退一个现代初学汉语的外国人，却大受几千年汉语母语使用者的欢迎，这说明了一个问题：在称呼我自己时，仅"我"这一基本词（字）不足以介绍我。猜想其原因，恐怕是"我"还不足以张扬人性，不能给出社会身份与身价、社会地位与等级的种种附加信息。

以上语料表明，在下面各种情况下，人自称（本文只涉及汉语使用中的男性）怎样使用丰富多彩的"我"变体：面对普通人的时候；见到老师、长辈和上级时；自己当了官以后见到上级和皇帝时；见到平级时；见到下级时；自己当上了皇帝或王爷时；自己当了和尚、道士时；一旦我失去了权利和地位时；如此等等。

这一切都是为了增加"我"出场（我存在）的凸显度。这是出于人对自身生存状态的自关心的需要。

窃以为，汉语"我"变体是支持英美语言哲学家所谓的"第一人称优先性"（preferential first person）的最有说服力的证据。从认识论的角度来说，人自称相对于物被称的优先性，普及到一切人称对（一切）物称的优先性，反映了人类在认识世界的过程中基本上遵循着由己及人、由人及物的循序渐进的认知路径。

在使用"我"之前，我只是不被人注意地存在着。"我"名我，我便出场与现身了。"我"才能使我自己出场与现身。我曾经有这样的思想："我们以言说使世界中的一物（实体或虚体）现身的同时，也使自己在世上出场或现身。……人在世上的出场比物的出场更具有意义。只有人的出场才使物的出场成为可能"（钱冠连，2005：卷首语）。这是第一个阶段。

第二个阶段，用上"我"变体时，我的出场便带上了种种凸显度。超大量的**"我"变体将原来隐匿的人性需求（张扬出社会身份与地位）凸显地、隆重地公开出来。**

本文对汉语里人自称的高度凸显与张扬的观察结果，与海德格尔"关注人的现实性，即一个真实的人的存在或生存到底是怎样的？这个问题具有哲学上的优先性"（Heidegger, 1999）简直是不谋而合。在汉语的人自称超丰富表达里，我们读出了海氏所谓"一个真实的人的存在或生存"状况。海氏的详细解释是："对自己存在（everyday Being-one's-Self）的解说使我们得以看见我们或可称之为日常生活（everydayness）的'主体'那样的东西，即常人（the "they"）"（Heidegger, 1999: 149-150，着重号为本文作者所加）。他所说的"常人"不是本真生存的人，而是非本真生存的人。但是，我们这里的人自称正是在进行"对自己存在的解说"！他又说："这个谁是用我自己、用'主体'、用'自我'来回答的"（Heidegger, 1999: 150）。请注意"我自己"、"主体"及"自我"都是可以回答"谁"的[1]，"我自己"、"主体"及"自我"在日常用语里便是本文所强调的人自称的种种变体。窃以为，人自称就是反省的"我"的意识，用海氏的话说便是 reflective awareness of the "I"（Heidegger, 1999: 151）。他又说，"'我'这个词只可领会为某种东西的不具约束力的形式标记"（Heidegger, 1999: 151-152）。

从上面的这些阐释看来，研究"我"变体的重大意义在于能与海氏的"此在"相呼应。"我"是此在的本质规定性。海氏不无暗示地说，"如果'我'确是此在的本质规定性之一，那就必须从生存论上来解释这一规定性"（Heidegger, 1999: 152）。他意在提示，"我"是此在的本质规定性（the "I" is an Essential characteristic of Dasein）。在 *Being and Time* 里，人的优先地位是以海氏式的阐释方式实现的，在汉语里，是以人自称的方式实现的。人自称正是在进行"对自己存在的解说"！

人自称情况，因时不同，因地不同，因文化不同，当它与张扬人性的种种附加信息相交时，就变得高度复杂起来。不同的附加信息，用于不同的"我"变体。

这与物被称的情况非常不同。最明显的不同在于，人自称之并列之名非常之多，物被称并列之名少了许多。一物一名，这是非常普遍的情况。一物两名者较少，如"番茄"与"西红柿"。一物三名者也较少（参见下文）。

这一多（人自称并列称呼多）一少（物被称并列之名少），使我们发问：物被称为何少了许多？

一物两名或三名之间，正如 Frege 所指出，其表达方式与认知内容彼此是有区别的（Frege, 1952）。一物如 Venus，清晨出现的时候，人们叫它 The Morning Star，晚间出现的时候，人们称它为 The Evening Star。Frege 指出了这两个名字（后来罗素称之为"摹状语"）的极为重要的两点区别：一是这两个名称的呈现方式（the mode of presentation）不同，二是认知内容（cognitive content）也不同。我增加的例子是一物三名，如有一物，它是块状粗根植物，汉语使用者可以根据它的形状像挂在马脖子上的铃铛叫"马铃薯"，根据它从南美

---

[1] 这句话需要交待的术语太多，原句如下：The question of the "who" answers itself in terms of the "I" itself, the "subject", the "Self."

洲进口中国，它又叫"洋芋"，根据它形如黄豆且埋在土里故叫"土豆"。这样的三个词表现了三种不同的呈现方式与认知内容。我以为，一物两名或三名的区别，是不同地域之人根据指称对象的物理性状的不同感知而定名的，也只需要物理性状就可以完成对物的区分性指称。而物理定性是外在的，是固定的，根据物理性状定名与定多少名，相对容易把握。

也就是说，一物多称的低概率是源于对事物物理性状的认知可脱离语境性较大，或说语境依赖性小，即语境敏感度（Context-sensitivity）低（这一思想得益于梁爽提醒）。然而，以"我"变体名我时，我的物理性状不变也无须涉及，但我作为人，其人性张扬与社会性状却必须顽强地、细微地涉及。"我"的种种变称传达出不同的社会性状（在此是社会身份如级别与地位）。"在下"、"卑职"、"为兄"和"哥们"、"爷们"、"朕"、"贫道"、"老朽"以不同的呈现方式与认知内容显示出不同的社会身份的贵贱与色彩。人性与社会性状是内在的、多样的，据此定名与定多少名，相对地说，不容易把握。也就是说，人自称的众多变体源于语境敏感度高，即语境依赖性大，可脱离语境性为零。这是人自称超多名现象的内在驱动力之一。

我自称对人性张扬与社会性状的要求的无限性与模糊性，与物被称对物理性状的要求的有限性与明确性，是前者复杂多变与后者简单少变的原因。这是两者一多一少的内在驱动力之二。

两者一多一少的内在驱动力之三，人们为了减少呼叫的记忆负担，物体与事物的名字要尽量少，这才符合语言的经济原则。如果物被称之名也像人自称那样多，语言体系就会膨胀到人们无法承受的程度。这一点和梁瑞清（2008）提出的语言地图说有相通之处。这是物被称时并列之名在竞争中淘汰多、存活少的重要原因。可是，为了凸显人性与社会性状，在人自称这一个项目上（毕竟是少数），即使牺牲了语言的经济原则也是值得的，因为一个项目上的膨胀总量也不会大到人们受不了的程度。这是人自称时并列之名的竞争中淘汰少、存活多的重要原因。

两者一多一少的内在驱动力之四，**并列称呼或名字之间的竞争与淘汰结果，取决于一个称呼与名字所体现出来的呈现方式与认知内容是否能被另一个称呼与名字取代**。"中国"与"中华人民共和国"同时共存着，"马铃薯"、"洋芋"与"土豆"三名共存着，它们谁也没有淘汰谁，原因在于它们各自凸显了竞争对方无法取代的呈现方式与认知内容。但是，毕竟物被称的多名之间，决定竞争的优胜劣败的因素少而明确，容易导致凡是能被取代的名字都被淘汰掉了。

物体并列名称被淘汰的第五个原因是，对物体的认知修改或纠正（不是取代）进程快（这一思想得益于王爱华），而人自称涉及自抬自高的利益，这种修改几乎不愿发生。而人自称并列名称之间，诸种竞争方无法取代的因素多到难以计算，只好让许多变体共同存活。不过，汉语中的人自称（如前所引语料）随着时代的推移，既淘汰了一批旧称呼，也产生了一些新称呼，这方面的情形本文不予讨论。贵称、自抬、自高自己是为了获取尽量多的利益与声名，贱称、自谦、自贬、自揶也是为了最终保护自己的利益与声名，这或许是中国文化中特有的道德上的自谦观生长与发展的理由。人的天性倾向于斤斤计较于社会地位与等级，于是加在名字上的隐匿信息随之增加，并列的称呼减不了多少，只能接受。

从以上人自称的超多名现象产生的五种驱动力来看，都不是呈现方式之不同与认知内容之不同所能解释的。

以上的分析，大致上可适用于"你"或者"you"，"他"、"她"或者 he/she 第三人称的情形。这种情形恰好就是"人被称"。在"人自称"与"物被称"之间的对立，插入一个'人被称'（这一思想得益于梁爽），形成一个"三元并存范畴"即"人自称—人被称—物被称"，分三方但不对立，可以应和由己及人、由人及物的循序渐进的认知路径。这个三元并存范畴体现了人对自身生存状态的自关心、对他人生存状态的他关心、对物的他关心之间的差异。

但是，各种语言特别是汉语中，似乎人被称（第二、第三人称）的社会身份的隐匿性信息变体却没有"我"名我时那样的多。原因在于：（1）人自我膨胀之心总是多于膨胀别人之心；（2）可能在于我更了解、更能认知自我，对他人的了解和认知是间接的、后一步的，所以称呼方式相对少一些（这一思想得益于王爱华）。

必须对物被称的情况作一重要补充：用以指称一个对象的语词，其变体越丰富，其（主动或被动地）凸显度越高。这可能是一条对人自称、人被称和物被称都适宜的规律：**假如某物在特定语言中的指称方式多有变体，该物的"存在和出场"比他物得到更多张扬。**

最后，汉语"我"变体的丰富与浓烈的自关心是否具有普适性？西语的"自关心"如果有，应该以什么为标记？须知西方人也跟我们一样是十分复杂的。但是，如果这个东西不具有普适性，那么导致汉语"自关心"的特殊根源在哪儿（这个讨论得益于刘利民、梁瑞清的提问）？我以为，这个问题可以变换成如下的问题更为方便：如果汉语"我"变体的丰富与浓烈的自关心不具有普适性，可不可以断言它是一个文化问题而不是一个真正的哲学问题呢？我的回答是：不可以。因为：（1）"我"众多变体是指称，我自身是指称的对象；（2）这一切都是为了增加"我"出场（我存在）的凸显度；（3）汉语中，人自称的特别丰富与物被称的相对少量，无疑体现了人的认知规律——先识己后识物。根据这三点，足以断言，汉语"我"变体的丰富与浓烈的自关心是一个真正的哲学问题，但其中杂有地域文化现象（也许汉语文化更加怂恿人自称的超大量出现）。

3. 结论

设置"人自称—人被称—物被称"三元并存范畴的意义在于：（1）彰显人对自身生存状态的自关心，人自称的高度复杂性使我们认识了人的高度复杂性。（2）彰显人对自身生存状态的自关心、对他人生存状态的他关心、对物的他关心之间的差异。这一差异提示，人自称对语言的复杂诉求终归可以看成是人对自己的优先彰显，这是不能以 Frege 所提出的呈现方式之不同与认知内容之不同来解释的。（3）研究"我"变体可与海氏的"此在"相呼应。"我"是此在的本质规定性。在 *Being and Time* 里，人的优先地位是以海氏式的阐释方式实现的，在汉语里，是以人自称的方式实现的。人自称正是在进行"对自己存在的解说"。

假如某物在特定语言中的指称方式多有变体，该物的"存在和出场"比他物得到更多张扬。人对世界一物一事的称呼与描述，其实是以自己的眼光干涉其中的。

参考文献

Alessandra T. 2007. *Philosophy of Language A—Z*. Edinburgh: Edinburgh University Press Ltd.
Frege, G. 1952. On sense and reference. In P. Geach & M. Black (eds.), *The Philosophical Writings of Gottlob Frege*. Trans. Max Black. Oxford: Blackwell.
Heidegger, M. 1999. *Being And Time*. trans. John Macquarie & Edward Robinson, China Social Sciences Publishing House, Chengcheng Books, LTD. Reprinted from the English Edition by SCM Press Ltd. 1962.
Quine, W. V. O. 1960. *Word and Object*. Massachusetts: MIT Press.
Russell, B. 1940. *An Inquiry into Meaning and Truth*. London: Jorge Allen and Unwin.
梁瑞清，2008，"语言地图说"，《外语学刊》（3）。
尼·布宁、余纪元编，2001，《西方哲学英汉对照辞典》。北京: 人民出版社。
钱冠连，2005，《语言: 人类最后的家园》。北京: 商务印书馆。

通讯地址: 510420 广东外语外贸大学外国语言学及应用语言学研究中心 <qianguanlian@163.com>

The Calling-oneself-one, the Referred-one and Referents of Something
Qian Guanlian

Abstract: The paper discusses, first of all, the phenomenon of I-focus-my-attention-on-myself in terms of the enormous variants of "wǒ" in Chinese (as "I" in English), then, sets up a triadic category of the calling-oneself-one (the variants of "wǒ") — the referred-one (the second and third person) — referents of something. The significance of the triadic category lies in that (1) The category explicitly displays that man focuses his attention on the existence state of his own and that the high complication of the calling-oneself-one enables us to recognize the high complication of man himself; (2) The category explicitly displays discrepancy between man's attention on the existence state of his own, man's attention on that of others, and man's attention on things. Such a discrepancy not only indicates that the complex appeal of the calling-oneself-one to language should be taken eventually as a preferentianl display for man-himself, but also may explain in passing the phenomenon of (extremely) enormous variants of "wǒ" in Chinese which may not be explained in terms of "the mode of presentation and cognitive content" proposed by Frege; (3) The variants of "wǒ" in Chinese and Heideggerian Dasein may echo each other. The "I" is an Essential Characteristic of Dasein. In *Being and Time* the preferential position of man is achieved by means of Heideggerian hermeneutics, while in Chinese it is done by means of the calling-oneself-one. The calling-oneself-one is, hereby, nothing but the explication of Being-one's-self.

If reference of a thing in a specific language has a large variant, the being or presence of the thing becomes much more explicit and open than others. As a matter of fact, names and descriptions given to a person or a thing have to be interfered by human eyesight.

Keywords: I-focus-my-attention-on-myself; the calling-oneself-one; the referred-one and referents of something; the variants of "wǒ"

假装、连环假装与"假装假装"[1]

——从奥斯汀和陈嘉映谈起

西南大学 杜世洪   昆明理工大学 赖成彬

提　要：哲学家奥斯汀开启了"假装"的概念考察工作，我国学者陈嘉映先生对此做了转述与补充，而且就"假装"话题还主持了两次讨论。然而，从二人的书面论说和陈先生主持的讨论看，奥、陈二人对"假装"的论说并未厘清事关假装的几个根本问题。本文以此为出发点，分析了假装的复杂性，总结出了假装的种类、假装的特性、构成假装的四个必要条件以及假装与无法假装的界限，最后断言我们能"连环假装"，但始终无法"假装假装"。

关键词：假装；特性；条件；界限；连环假装

1. 假装考察的缘起

日常语言哲学家奥斯汀的"假装"（Pretending，以下简称奥文）一文最初发表于1957年，后来收编在 J. O. Urmson 和 G. J. Warnock 编辑的奥斯汀的《哲学论文集》（*Philosophical Papers*）里，于1961年由牛津大学出版社出版。虽然这篇文章本身在中国读者里并不起眼，但是它所讨论的主题及现象却一直游荡于我们的生活。因此，对假装的研究应该得到必要的重视。陈嘉映先生对奥文作了转述，并对假装做了一定的思考。陈嘉映先生撰文"我们怎么假装"（以下简称陈文）首先发表于2004年，后来又收编到他2005年出版的学术文集《无法还原的象》里，而且，陈先生以假装为话题，还在华东师范大学主持过两次讨论。应该说，这是对假装进行哲学考察的一项开启工作。

然而，我们在仔细阅读奥文和陈文之后发现，二文对假装的考察耐人寻味。在对二人的论说进行玩味时，我们发现对假装的考察还有许多空白，还有许多意犹未尽之处。这正如陈文结尾所说："关于假装，还有更大的问题要问。"从陈文这一论断出发，我们打算追问以下几个问题：我们假装什么？假装有什么样的特性？假装与无法假装的分界在哪里？我们能够做"连环假装"，但根本无法"假装假装"。

---

[1] 本文获"教育部人文社会科学研究项目"（项目编号09YJA740091）与"西南大学博士基金"（项目编号SWU080926）资助。

2. 我们假装什么？

陈文的标题"我们怎么假装"肯定了我们能够假装，那么我们能够假装什么呢？在思考这个问题前，我们先就问题的核心词语假装在英语和汉语里的使用情况做点说明。

从用法上看，英语里的假装 pretend 作为动词，稍加成分调整或补充后可以与名词、形容词、形容词短语、动词不定式、不定式进行时等连用，而且动词 pretend 本身可以有时态、语态的形式，有名词形式 pretence。现代汉语中的"假装"，虽然在形态上没有英语的 pretend 那样变化多端，但在用法上基本一致，而且汉语的"假装"本身可以在句法中占据动词、名词甚至形容词和副词的位置。因此，为了不把问题引向语言纠缠的歧路，我们讨论的中心不在两种语言的形式差别上，而始终借助"假装"一词来考察人类社会中的假装现象。

从生活经验看，我们会发现有形形色色的假装。如：假装生气、坚强的养路工假装快乐地活着、被追击的小偷躲到锯木厂里假装锯木头、诸葛亮吊孝而假装悲伤、南郭先生假装吹竽、反映上海女人生活图景的影片《假装没感觉》、2005年10月昆明十位个体老板假装乞丐在街上行乞、外语课堂上并未听懂的学生却跟人一起哄笑以示听懂了的假装领会、周瑜为诱使蒋干中计而假装睡着了、前些年为了打假的青岛人王海假装消费者南来北往以及《美国语言之旅》的作者每当遇到世人给他讲古怪的方言时就系统地发出一些怪音而假装应答等等。这么多的假装，粗略地看都属一丘之貉——假装而已。它们真的一样吗？奥文和陈文都明确说明，其实假装并非都一样。既然假装并非都一样，那么它们的不一样究竟表现在哪里呢？

在不知道事物的本质的情况下，我们只能依靠它们的表象来做考察。实际上，对表象的考察也是对本质的间接或直接分析。根据上述假装的表象情况，我们发现假装可以分为四类：（1）假装一种行为；（2）假装一种状态；（3）假装一种身份；（4）假装一种情绪。

我们假装一种行为，那行为可以是即将发生的，也可以是正在进行的，还可以是对已发生的行为进行弥补性假装。假装的行为看上去很真实，甚至行为本身就是实实在在的。如南郭先生吹竽、跟着同学一起哄笑的学生、发出系统怪音而假装说外番话等。

假装一种状态就是做出一副姿态，显示自己已经达到某个层次，而实际上假装者还并未达到。如：假装睡着了；假装大醉；在脖子上戴个套狗项圈那么大的黄铜链而假装阔气；假装不痛以及假装殷勤、真诚等。

假装一种身份比较复杂，显示出来的身份自然是假的，但行为本身却不必是假。如：躲到锯木厂假装木工锯木头的小偷；假装消费者的王海；假装乞丐的真正行乞等。假装一种身份可以是长期的，也可以是短期的。无论长短，假装一种身份就是选择一种本身不属于自己原有生活方式的生活形式。

假装一种情绪，很直接。我们可以假装生气，假装很开心，假装很忧愁、悲伤等。根据奥文和陈文，这类假装似乎应该有限度，超过限度就可能不是假装了，尤其是假装生气更应该有限度。

身份、行为、状态和情绪都可以假装，假装似乎极具魔力，在我们生活中忽左忽右、忽上忽下地出现，似乎与我们的真实情况形影不离。至此，我们不禁要问：假装究竟从哪里来的呢？为什么古往今来我们的生活中都有假装？看来我们有必要先弄清假装的特性问题。

3. 假装有什么样的特性？

也许有人会说："我一辈子都不假装。假装与我无关。"如果真有一辈子都未假装过的人，我们应该庆幸，不妨把这种人称为龙德君子。在这样的龙德君子那里，假装属异物，并非出自人的本性。这话有几分道理，但未必就是真理，因为假装并不随龙德君子的"与我无关"而真正烟消云散。假装就算能从龙德君子那里消失，但绝不会从整个社会生活中消失。我们如此断言，势必会引发一个思考：假装究竟是异物还是人之本性？假装到底有什么样的特性呢？

3.1 假装是意识活动

如果说假装本来是独立于人而存在的异物，那么假装必定有其自然属性。倘若假装有一种使假装成其为假装的自然属性，那么除人之外宇宙万物就应该有假装的存在。对这一断言，我们可以从动植物那所谓的假装现象来证实。一经证实，这一断言就不会被当作纯粹的空话。不少动物会假装，这已被人们熟知。那么植物会假装吗？生长在澳大利亚的"赤罗"兰花能够假装雌性黄蜂来诱骗雄性黄蜂。捕蝇草常以假装的欢迎姿态来诱捕小昆虫。

既然我们注意到了动植物的假装现象，那么我们能不能从它们的假装中测量出某种自然属性呢？这属性具备规定性，它规定假装之所以为假装。虽然限于目前的研究，我们无法从科学的角度来证明有无这种属性，但是我们可以从哲学思辨的角度来考察假装究竟是人的外在之物（即异物）还是人的本性之物。

从动植物那里，我们勉强证实了前面的观点，宇宙中除人以外的他物也有假装。相对于他物而言，人也是他物，那么人有假装乃情理之中的事。假设龙德君子所谓的假装属异物这个观点成立的话，那么现在的焦点问题就是，人的假装究竟是不是受外界感染、后天获得的呢？要回答这个问题就得从考察人的假装与他物的假装是否相同入手。

植物的假装可以还原成生物化学和物理学的东西，不过我们最好把这一科学知识悬置起来，重点考察人的假装是否与动植物的假装相同。按龙德君子的标准，他一生都没有假装过，他好比假装没有侵袭到的净土，然而相对于他这方净土而言，他人、他物却受了假装的污染。以此类推，假装相对于人来说肯定是异物、是外在的了。如果说假装源于外界这一论断是真的话，那么我们就可以推出人类的假装就应该与动植物的假装相同,至少有亲缘关系,这就出现了两个漏洞:其一,植物那所谓的假装根本就是人为标签,是人凭主观而认为那并无意识的植物有意识活动的假装。其二,如果假装有外源的话,那么假装就有如感冒病毒,会不停寻找受体与宿主而进行代间和代际复制与传染。既然假装象流行病毒一样,那么为什么龙德君子不会感染呢?就是偶尔感染了假装病毒的非龙德君子们为什么不会永远假装呢?有什么东西在控制假装的发作与不发作呢?对这里的矛盾进行仔细思考,我们只会得出结论说人的假装与意识有关,即人的假装是受意识支配的。我们如此断言,自然有理据可考。

神经心理学研究成果表明,意识的物质基础是人脑的神经元。一切意识活动都可还原成神经元的活动。人脑拥有的神经元数目巨大,数以百亿计,而且神经元与神经元之间还有数百亿的相互关联的"壁标(somatic marker)",神经元活动越复杂意识活动就越复杂,但神经元活动并非一生下来就很复杂,要经过一定的发展期。在对人类行为研究过程中,教育学家和心理学家都发现,一岁半的婴儿就会假装了,而且假装意识在婴儿中很普遍。这些发现说明,假装受意识支配,而且龙德君子幼小时会假装,而长大成人后却不假装,这就是因为意识在控制着假装与不假装。也正是因为假装受主观意识支配,所以非龙德君子的普通人才会有时假装而有时不假装。

讨论到这里,问题随矛盾的出现而变得明朗起来。按前面所说,假装是外在之物,人和动植物都有假装,而且应该同样或同源。这里预设的命题就是,假装并不是意识的东西,因为植物并无意识,动物的单维度简单意识也不同于人的多维度的复杂意识。这里出现的矛盾就是假装属于非意识与属于意识之间的矛盾。这个矛盾反证出人的假装属异物、外在之物的观点是站不住脚的。

于是,我们只能维护前面的断言——假装是人类大脑内在的意识活动,这是假装的特性之一。而且,我们平常只能在假装的表象层面上感觉到假装,也只能在表象层面上声言假装是别人的假装,自己没假装。然而,从意识的本质角度看,我们可以说假装是每个人的,每个人都具有假装的能力,而且假装的可能性大小与表象会因人而异。

既然每个人都可能假装,那么假装有无共同的本质特性呢?回答这个问题,实际上就是要回答假装本身究竟是公共的还是私有的?如果是公共的,假装本身就具有共相;如果是私有的,假装本身就只能以殊相形式而普遍地表现出来。这里要注意,我们说每个人都可能假装,并不等于说假装一定有共相。

3.2 假装是个人意向与私有的心理经验

我们知道三角形的内角和等于180度这一自然属性规定了三角形之所以为三角形。我们由此也曾幻想有一种像三角形这一属性类似的自然特性来规定假装的存在。然而,对于假装而言,这仅是一种幻想而已。不论假装现象多么普遍,但绝不等于假装本身具有一种可测的具有普遍性的自然属性。假装的表象可以被观察到,但假装本身作为一种个人的意识活动却无法被直接测量出来,甚至很多时候，我们还无法感知到别人在假装。

动词意义下的假装好像在明确地告诉我们假装就是动作，然而假装绝不只是肢体行为和具体的实践活动。假装是意识活动，是个人在意识中形成的一种企图或预先程序，这就是个人意向。个人意向与现象学的"意向"类似，但"不同于现象学的意向性"。个人意向只有假装者本人才清楚，因为意向是别人看不见的。因此，我们很容易误以为假装就是一种看得见的行为或状态。实际上，假装在很多情况下是没有属于它自己的特定的表象行为的。老板假装乞丐在街上行乞，那乞讨行为属于真正的行乞行为。小偷假装木工的锯木行为是真真切切的锯木行为。假装听懂了而应声哄笑，那笑声听起来还是笑。从这样的事例可以推断，假装只能被假装者本人完全感知，旁人只能感觉到假装的表象。旁人即便判断出假装来，也无法像假装者本人那样真切地感受到假装本身所带来的心理经验。在这个意义上说，假装就是个人意向与个人的私有心理经验，假装不具有共相。这是假装的特性之二。

既然假装是个人的意向与私有心理经验，那么假装在本质上不可能具备普遍性。即便是同一个人对同一事情进行第二次假装，其所得的两次心理经验不会完全相同。对某事，所谓的"你也能假装，我也能假装"并不是说，你我有同样的心理经验，而是说我们各自都能假装，而假装在表象上可能相似，但更多的时候连表象都相差很大。

既然假装是假装者个人意向的体现，是个人的心理经验，那么假装行乞时的心理经验与真正的乞丐的心理经验就绝对不同。打假的王海买到假货的心理感受绝对不是一个真正的消费者买到假货的心理感受。既然假装与真实在心理经验上存在巨大的差异，那么我们要问，现今社会的一切假装究竟能在多大程度上经验到事实的真相呢？

假装虽然能够带来独特的心理经验，但我们认为，假装并不是为了获得真实经验知识，假装本身就是做给人看的。这样，假装似乎注定不具备神圣性了。不过，有的假装也会导致一些神圣，例如教师利用假装来诱导学生上进。假装本来很容易被看成是只有假装者本人才能受益的事，现在看来，有些假装还是能让别人受益。它毕竟是属于人性的东西，既不具备超自然的能力，又要受制于人性本身的局限。于是，什么能够假装，什么无法假装自然而然就有了界限。

3.3 假装依附于活动而现身

在讨论能够假装与无法假装的界限之前，我们需要谈谈假装的另外一个特性。前面说，假装既是个人内在意向又是个人私有的心理经验。这里预设了一个前提，假装如果不以某种活动表现出来，假装就只能永远处在意识的襁褓里，甚至无法成型。在还没有成型的假装的时候，你即便公开宣称你在假装，也不会有假装。为什么呢？首先，假装本身要求秘而不宣；其次，假装必须依附于某种活动才能现身。这就是说，作为个人意向与私有经验的假装是无形的胎儿，它在意识里发育却必须通过某种活动来达到成熟。我们之所以能够感觉到或认识到假装，就是因为假装具有表象形式，而假装的表象形式就是假装赖以进行的活动。虽然假装必须依附于活动，但是假装并不固定在活动中。说假装并不固定有两层意思：其一，假装可以显现到活动里，又可以从活动中隐退；其二，同一假装可以出没于不同的活动。

4. 假装与无法假装

奥文和陈文都在批判假装与真实之间的模糊界限论时，指出假装应该有限度：真实与假装之间的界限和假装的时限。我们认为，奥文对模糊界限论的批判不得要领。首先，奥文没有认识到把假装与真实看成是一个连续体的两端的错误所在。认为在假装与真实之间有一个模糊的界限就错误地预设了假装与真实处于同一个连续体的两端。我们认为，假装与真实并不是两个对立的等值体，假装与非真实，或者非假装与真实，并不构成逻辑等式。比如：假装锯木头并不是非真实锯木头，假装锯木头确确实实在锯木头；另外，假装的情绪与真实情绪、假装的状态与真实状态、假装的身份与真实身份、假装的行为与真实的行为等，它们都是离散的、非连续性的。

模糊界限论的错误还在于，把假装本身与假装表象混为一谈。我们说假装本身是个人意向与心理经验，对同一个意向与心理经验来说，它的表象却可能是这样或那样的行为、状态。作为表象的行为或状态本身并无真假与对错之分，所以也就不必甚至不可能从表象中去划清界限。

真正需要划出的界限是能够假装与无法假装的界限。在讨论界限之前，我们先看看假装之所以为假装必须具备的条件是什么。

奥文说，假装称得上是假装，下列条件必须得到满足：有某种事或事物，而且是公开的；假装者正在做那事；假装者的实际行为。对此，陈文概括说，假装"一般有以下两个成分：（1）借以进行假装的活动；（2）被遮掩的实际情形"。我们发现这只是从假装的基本成分的角度做了说明，还不是假装之所以为假装的构成条件。

我们发现，假装之所以为假装必须满足四个条件。（1）保密条件：个人意向秘而不宣。（2）成分条件：包括人的成分、意向成分和表象成分。人的成分包括假装者、接受假装的核心对象和外围对象，外围对象不是必须的。意向成分包括假装意向与真实意向；假装意向是一种直接意向，是假装者需要接受对象感觉到的意向，是一定要实现的意向；而真实意向常常是间接的，是假装的目的，假装者不希望接受者感觉到，是要掩盖的意向；真实意向可能与假装意向同时实现，也可能晚于假装意向实现；需要注意的是，没有真实意向就没有假装意向。表象成分就是假装者借以假装的活动与行为方式，可以直接观察到；一般，表象成分不会单一出现，而是多种成分复合起来承担表象的任务。（3）过程条件：假装必须在完成后才能成为假装；一个完整的假装是假装者通过表象成分把假装意向公然地显示给接受对象，以便掩盖同时发生的真实意向或者为延后的真实意向的实现做准备，或者为提前暴露了的真实意向做弥补。（4）能力条件：假装意向和表象成分必须是假装者可以控制的与操纵的，超出假装者控制与操纵能力的意向与表象成分是不可能进入假装活动的。

根据这四个条件，我们把奥文中的魔术师表演锯活人和陈文的拍摄电影时的假装情景排斥在假装以外，因为这两种情况都未满足保密条件。生活中的假装不会让接受对象预先知道假装要发生。我们可以把变魔术和拍电影、演戏中的假装称为表演性假装。要注意的是，表演性假装可以成为真正假装（或叫生活性假装）的表象成分的。

用这四个条件去衡量，我们能够分清什么能够假装、什么无法假装。现在我们可以说明为什么有些东西人们从来不去假装。从宏观方面看，我们从来无法假装宇宙，无法假装山川、河流、海洋、湖泊等；而从微观上讲，我们无法假装病毒、DNA片段等；从参与假装情况来看，我们的个体无法假装群体，如我一个人无法假装四个人在打麻将，虽然我可以依次表演四个人打麻将的表现。为什么呢？因为这些东西都是假装者个人无法控制或操纵的客观现实。

我们可以控制我们的行为，但我们对一些状态延续性行为本身无法假装。有谁能假装摇头？又有谁能假装不摇头？发出一串怪音我们便可假装说外语，但我们不能对说与不说的动作本身进行假装。你已经在说话了，你能假装不说或假装在说吗？

有些瞬间动作一旦完成后就会保持一种状态或改变一种状态，我们对此也无法假装。你举起手后，你能假装不举手或假装举手吗？你不能假装站着也不能假装坐着。你睁大眼睛后，你不能假装睁大眼睛，也不能假装紧闭眼睛。你闭牢眼睛后也是这样。

对这些你不能假装的，除了它们是你无法控制的以外，还有一个本质原因就是，这些动作本身既不传达意向也不掩盖意向，它们是分解了的表象成分。不过，它们可以作为表象成分去完成其他的假装活动。因此，对汉语句子"他假装举手说他没去看电影"的理解，我们既不能把他的"举手"看成是假装的，又不能把"说"看成是假装的。《广西商报》2000年2月21日上有这样一句话，"她用手摸口袋，发觉钱不见了！她马上推醒覃某追问，覃某假装摇头说不知。"这句话里面的假装摇头又做何理解呢？简单地说这样的句子不符合汉语语法，这是不负责任的隔靴搔痒。摇头确实无法假装，但可以作为表象成分参与假装。

对一些状态，我们可以假装，但我们却无法假装它们的对立状态。你可以假装醉，因为你还清醒，但是，你无法在大醉中假装不醉或假装清醒。你可以假装睡着了，但你无法在睡着了的时候，假装未睡着。周瑜可以假装在做梦而计弄蒋干，但他却无法在做梦时假装不做梦。这类无法假装的道理在于，在这些状态下，你的意识已经不听使唤，而且，这时，你没有要遮掩的真实意向，也就没有假装意向了。

假装的表象成分可以被同一个假装者重复，但无法被其他不知就里的假装者进行原样假装。被警察追击的小偷甲逃到锯木厂里假装锯木头，他可能是站着的；而小偷乙假装锯木头，却可能是坐着的，或者站的位置不一样，或者小偷乙逃到这里干的是别的什么，就是没有假装锯木头。假装的表象成分只能模仿，却无法假装。

　　无法假装的肯定还不止这些，我们不必一一列举。能够假装与无法假装的界限就在于假装的四个条件能否得到满足，四个条件缺一不可。需要强调的是，假装意向是真实意向的派生物，而且假装意向一定要显示给接受对象的，而真实意向是一定要遮掩的。一旦真实意向显示出来，让接受者知道了，假装就原形毕露了。在身份假装中如果假装者的真实意向永远被悬置起来，一直不显示，那么该假装就永远不会终止。

5. "假装假装"有无可能？

　　陈文说："我们不仅会假装，而且会假装假装。"这一断言听上去很有道理，但不可避免地会引人追问："我们怎么假装假装呢？"陈文虽然没就怎么假装假装给出指令般的说明，但实实在在地给出了两个例子。甲例说："我假装打你一拳，可这一拳打得很重，你不禁怀疑我心怀怨恨，假装打你是一种伪装。"我们用假装必须满足的四个条件来分析，首先就会遇到一个问题：这个例子满足保密条件吗？"我"该不该预先让"你"知道"我"要假装打"你"呢？"我"又是怎么让"你"知道的呢？假设这个例子满足了保密条件，秘而不宣，那么，"我"秘而不宣的真实意向是什么呢？"我"的真实意向是真正打"你"呢还是假打"你"一下？如果是假打"你"一下，为何还要假装呢？于是，这里的真实意向是真打才合情理，而用来掩盖的假装意向就是不让"你"知道"我"要真打。那么，怎么掩盖呢？那就是让"你"预先知道"我"要假打"你"了，注意这里就宣布了要假打，而这种宣布本身却成了这次假装的必要的表象成分，这种表象成分与打结合起来，就完成了一次假装。这个例子里只有一次假装，并没有所谓的假装假装。它与其他假装不同点在于它以宣布了的假打为假装意向，并以此来掩盖真打。

　　陈文中乙例说："演员张三对李四怀恨在心，于是借拍摄之机狠扇李四的耳光。"我们认为这里并不涉及假装，因为，剧本要求张三打李四的耳光，如果要求假打，张三就该假打，如果真打了，那是张三篡改了剧本；如果要求狠打，自然就无话可说了。当然，按照道义，虽然剧本要求狠打，张三也应该假装而敷衍地打才够哥们义气，这就是说张三有选择假装打李四的道义责任。结果是张三在宣布了要假打的情况下，却狠狠打了李四，在这个意义下，这个例子就与甲例类似，问题落在保密条件与成分条件中的意向成分与表象成分上了。

　　陈文的这两个例子反映出的是假装的复杂性，但这种复杂的假装终究成为"假装假装"。其实，复杂的假装还可能有连环的形式，即"连环假装"。

6. 我们可以"连环假装"却无法"假装假装"

2006年10月17日在陈先生主持的非正式"学术会饮"哲学活动过程中，假装话题再次在华东师范大学引起了激烈讨论。陈先生试图捍卫他原先的观点，即我们可以"假装假装"。在陈先生的启发下，L博士称找到了"假装假装"的例子，说有一化妆品公司被某消费者告上了法庭，控诉理由是该公司推出的化妆品"A套和B套必须配合使用才能保证效果"的广告在误导消费者，即该公司的广告在误导过度消费。于是，那充当消费者的原告振振有词，特别强调说她只用了公司的A套化妆品就达到效果了，根本不需要什么B套。L博士说这就是"假装假装"的典型例子，是公司找人充当消费者假装控告公司，而公司也假装在认真接受控告，其结果无论胜诉还是败诉，获利方肯定是公司。

我们认为这个例子仍然不是"假装假装"，只不过是"连环假装"而已，因为用构成假装的四大条件来衡量，那消费者的假装控诉与公司的假装接受控诉属于在同一个真实意向驱使下，各自彰显不同的假装意向来达到共同的目的——让消费者相信该公司的化妆品效果好。这种"连环假装"有它本身的复杂性，同一个真实意向由不同的实施主体用不同的假装意向来完成。

有趣的是，F博士虚构出另外的一个例子，说某公司有一职员为了巩固自己在公司的地位或者捍卫自己的某种权利抑或是出于别的某种目的，自己给领导写匿名信，而那匿名信里尽量巧妙地突出自己的某些优点，以希望得到领导的赏识。F博士称这里就有"假装假装"，首先那匿名信是假装的匿名信，其次，那匿名信的控告也是假装的，控告是假而暗地宣传自己为真。其实，这里仍然是连环假装而已，里面只有一个真实意向——为假装者自己牟利，那虚假的匿名信并不虚假，它充当了假装的道具而已。只不过，这种假装者特别奸狡，违背常规地炮制出匿名信来以使自己获利。说他违背常规，其实不然，因为一切恶的东西本身就不按常规（比如道德常规）行事，不守规矩就是恶人的规矩。于此看来，假装问题并不简单。

值得注意的是，陈文断言"我们可以假装假装"，却对"假装假装假装"表示疑问。陈文说："可是，我们也能假装假装假装吗？为什么不能？"对此，结合前面的讨论，我们认为我们连"假装假装"都不能，又怎么能够进行"假装假装假装"呢？我们无法假装假装，原因在于假装假装不能满足成分条件，即假装假装没有自己的接受对象与属于自己的真实意向。陈文的乙例按假装分析时，也只是一个层次上的假装。即张三相对于其他人来说在假装打李四，而对李四来说并没有假装。假装是在双边关系的单向道上进行的，即从假装者到假装的核心接受者，任何涉及三边关系及以上的例子都可还原成在其中某一双边关系中的单向道上的活动。

7. 结束语

2005年10月中山大学逻辑学教授鞠实儿先生在华东师范大学做报告时说：

"一个东西如果是简单的,如果它又是普遍的,如果又是人们不知道的,那么这个东西一定是重要的。"假装普遍,但我们对假装的了解往往停留在表象层次上。如果我们说对假装的考察很重要,这未免会有王婆卖瓜之嫌。对此,奥斯汀说得好,重要的是在于求真。陈嘉映先生在对假装进行考察的求真路上指引了方向,断言"还有更大的问题要问",这不但给鞠实儿教授的话做了注解,更重要的是他把我们的思维引向没有躁动与喧嚣的无声处。

在考察了假装的类别、特性、能够假装与无法假装的界限以及我们无法假装假装之后,我们大胆沿着陈先生的思路问一个大问题:"假装作为一种意识究竟是先验的呢还是经验的?"这无疑是一个牵涉到许多哲学问题的问题。不过,无论是对这个问题接受与反对,只要不是马虎打发,都会对假装的深入考察带来建设性观点。正如波普所说:"我可能错,你可能对,结果是我们都更加接近了真理。"

参考文献

Austin, J. L. 1961. Pretending. In J. O. Urmson & G. J. Warnock (eds.), *Philosophical Papers*. Oxford, UK: Oxford University Press, 251-271.

陈嘉映,2004,我们怎么假装,《中文自学指导》(1):40-42。

陈嘉映,2005,《无法还原的象》。北京:华夏出版社。

丁一岚,2002,《假装没感觉》——一幅上海女人的生活图景,《当代电影》(4):95-96。

通讯地址:400715 西南大学外语学院 <dushihong2008@126.com>;650024 昆明理工大学 <luvachan@hotmail.com>

Pretence, Double-Pretence, and Pretence of Pretence
— A Supplementary Remark on Austin's and Chen's Analysis of Pretending

DU Shihong　　　　LAI Chengbin

Abstract: J. L. Austin has initiated a study of pretence and his idea about pretence has been crystallized into an English philosophical paper *Pretending*, which has been translated and extended in Chinese by Chen Jiaying, who has presided over two debates on pretence. However, both Austin and Chen have failed to offer a complete picture of the study of pretence. Specifically, several essential problems in this regard remain unnoticed. In carrying on their study, this paper provides a deep insight into pretence by framing the types of pretence, the nature of pretence, the necessary conditions for pretence, and the demarcation between the possible pretence and the impossible pretence. This paper claims that we are capable of making a pretence and double-pretence, but unable to make a pretence of pretence.

Keywords: pretence; nature; condition; demarcation; double-pretence

现象不可说的认识论问题[1]

暨南大学外国语学院　梁瑞清

提　　要：感觉经验的私人性似乎在逻辑上同时蕴涵了不可说性和不可知性。本文在浅析几种关于私人性的哲学观点的基础上，提出了经验网络假说，认为感觉经验的现象属性虽然是弱式不可说的，但对于他人来说依然是可知的。该假说也表明，我们没有必要，也不可能构建所谓的私人语言来言说感觉经验的现象内容。

关键词：现象不可说；私人性；经验网络假说

1. 引言

不可说似乎与不可知论有着天然的联系，这是因为语言在我们的认知活动中扮演着重要的角色。如果说感觉经验的现象属性具有不可说性（梁瑞清，2006，2008a，2008b），那么它是否也具有不可知性呢？对这个问题，哲学界一般有两种观点。第一种观点是否定该问题的前提，即认为感觉经验的现象属性不是不可说的，因此也不是不可知的。第二种观点是承认感觉经验的现象属性既是不可说的，也是不可知的。而这两种观点的争论焦点又在于感觉经验的私人性：前者否认感觉经验的私人性，并进而否认感觉经验的不可说性和不可知性，后者则反其道而行之。本文在讨论这两种观点的基础上提出，感觉经验的现象属性虽然是弱式不可说的，或者说是言不尽意的，但在一定程度上却是可知的。同时，我们还将考察与这个问题密切相关的私人语言论证，认为没有必要也不可能构建一种所谓的私人语言来言说感觉经验的现象属性。首先，让我们从上述争论的焦点入手来分析私人性这一概念及其相关的几种哲学观点。

2. 私人性的种种困惑

毫无疑问，私人性是感觉经验的主要特征之一，这主要是因为某一特定的感觉经验都必定有一个特定的经验主体。一方面，经验的主体性会使得对某一感觉经验的感受在很大程度上因人而异，从而使得该感觉经验对不同的经验主体具有不同程度的现象效果（梁瑞清，2007）。另一方面，经验的主体性又会导致未经历某一特定感觉经验的"他人"无法确切地理解该感觉经验的现象属性，从而

---

[1] 本研究为2009年度教育部人文社会科学研究青年基金项目"'言不尽意'的哲学解读及其语义分析"（项目批准号为09YJCZH005）的阶段性成果。

使得它对经验主体来说具有私人性。如果我头痛欲裂,但我不告诉你我的痛觉经验,而是表现如常,那么你一般不会知道我的头很痛,因为任何知识都是基于某种证据的,不管这种证据是直接的还是间接的,是语言证据还是行为证据。在缺乏语言证据(因为我没有告诉你我头痛)和行为证据(因为我表现如常)等间接证据,同时也缺乏亲身经历的直接证据的情况下,你当然不能让我确信你知道我头痛的事实。但是,私人性涉及的其实不是这种知道如此这般的陈述性知识(knowing-that / declarative knowledge),而是一种知道如何这般的程序性知识(knowing-how / procedural knowledge)。

关于私人性的一种哲学观点是唯我论。唯我论者认为,只有"我"才是可知的唯一实在,因此"我的"经验只有我知道,从而在认识论的意义上具有私人性。当然,唯我论者并不是想否定你在掌握证据的情况下可以知道我头痛欲裂的这样一个事实,而是想说,即便你掌握了充分的语言证据或行为证据,你也无法知道我是如何头痛欲裂的。换言之,唯我论者否认的不是陈述性的知识,而是你不可能知道我的头痛究竟是一种怎样的痛法之类的程序性知识。因此,在唯我论者看来,"我的"感觉经验的现象属性由于具有私人性从而对他人来说是不可知的。下面关于私人性的讨论都是在这个意义上来进行的。

一些早期的语言哲学家也持有类似的思想,如 Frege 曾经指出,"任何其他人都不具有我的痛。有人可能会因此而同情我,但我的痛还总是属于我,而他的同情也总属于他。他不会具有我的痛,我也不会具有他的同情"(Frege, 1956; Hallet, 1977: 333)。这说明,在 Frege 看来,他的痛只有他自己知道,别人是不可能知道的。也许正是在 Frege 的影响下,Russell、早期 Wittgenstein 和逻辑经验主义者在这个问题上都不同程度地采取了唯我论的立场,只不过他们很少使用唯我论这个标签,而是把它命名为感觉材料理论或现象论(phenomenalism)。但究其实质,无论是感觉材料理论,还是现象论都可以说是唯我论的变种。按照Ayer的说法,"现象论者总是认为,任何物理实体的确认都应该基于感觉材料来进行分析"(转引自Bunnin & Yu, 2001: 743)。所谓的感觉材料通常被看作我们大脑中的心理图像或印象,是我们赖以感知世界的媒介,而心理图像或印象又通常被认为是经验主体私人的所有物。因为感觉材料具有私人性,所以命名感觉材料的语词同样具有私人性。Russell 或许正是因此才认为,逻辑专名应该"在很大程度上对某个说话人而言是私人的"、"不能进入另外一个说话人的语言"(转引自 Candlish, 1998),以至于他最终认定只有"这个"或"那个"才是真正的逻辑专名,因为它们并不指称任何特定的物理实体,而是指称某种私人的感觉材料。同样,对维也纳小组的成员(如 Carnap)来说,记录命题或经验命题具有特殊的认识论地位,因为它们描述我们的直接经验,从而可以被完全证实。

中期 Wittgenstein 也认为,只有采用第一人称、现在时态的经验命题(如"我有……"、"我感觉……"等)才是真正的基本命题,因为我们可以直接通过内省或参照当下的经验来证实或证伪它们。但是,和逻辑经验主义者不同的是,他注意到句(1)和句(2)是两种不同的命题:

（1）I have [a] toothache.
（2）I have a matchbox.

句（1）是经验命题，而句（2）则是一个假设（hypothesis）。一方面，我们可以谈论没有主人的火柴盒，但却不能有意义地谈论没有主人的牙痛；另外一方面，所有权是可以转让的，我可以将我的火柴盒转让给你，但不能将我的牙痛转让给你。因此（1）中的"我"并非指称某个所有者，甚至可以用一个存在句型（3）将其消除掉（Wittgenstein，1975）。

（3）There is [a] toothache.

这样，通过否定"我"在经验命题中的所有者身份，Wittgenstein 将被唯我论者认为是唯一实在的"我"悬置起来，一定程度地驳斥了唯我论思想。

后期 Wittgenstein 从另外一个角度对唯我论进行了批评。他认为句（4）这种说法既是错误的，又是毫无意义的（Wittgenstein，1986: 246）。

（4）I *know* I have a pain. / 我知道我有痛。
（5）I have a pain. / 我有痛。
（6）I *doubt* I have a pain. / 我怀疑我有痛。
（7）He knows I have a pain. / 他知道我有痛。

首先，句（4）中的"我知道"完全是多余的，因为（4）和（5）的意思完全一样，而且在日常语言中，除非是开玩笑我们一般不会说"我知道我有痛"，也不会问"你知道你有痛吗？"其次，"我知道"、"我怀疑"和"我相信"等都是构成句子的算子（sentence-forming operator），只有在能够使用其他算子的时候，我们才能够说"我知道……"，而我们不能说（6），因此我们也不能说（4）（参考Hacker，1972: 245）。这意味着，在经验命题前增加"我知道"这样的算子在逻辑上是非法的。唯我论认为"我知道我有痛"，但是根据Wittgenstein的分析，恰恰相反，我们不能说（4），却可以说（7）。

如上所述，唯我论的要害在于声称只有他本人知道自己的感觉经验，从而使得他心知识（other-knowledge）或第三人称知识（third-person knowledge）成为不可能。Wittgenstein 的目的正是希望通过批评唯我论使我们能够合理地宣称这种知识，但我们认为他的批评依然不能令人满意。第一，把经验命题中的"我"解释为不具有所有权，从语义的角度来看是不经济的，因为我们必须为这类命题中的"我"设定一个特别意义，但这样一来又将不可避免地滑向唯我论。同时，我们也可以用一个存在句型来消除掉（2）中的"我"，从而模糊掉（1）和（2）之间的区别。第二，Wittgenstein 认为句（4）中的"我知道"不仅是多余的，而且是非法的。然而，这一观点可能导致我们不能对第一人称知识（first-person knowledge）做出合理的宣称。一方面，虽然"知道"和"怀疑"确实有着相似的用法，但是人们一般不会对第一人称知识产生怀疑。我通常不说"我知道我有痛"，那是因为我从不怀疑自己有痛的感觉。当然，这并非说明第一人称知识就是不可错的（infallible），只是说明如果有人追问或怀疑我是否知道自己有痛的话，我可以说"我知道我有痛"。如例（8）所示，在一定的语境中，在经验命题前面增加"我知道"这样的算子既非多余，也不是非法的。

（8）（一个父亲和他八岁的女儿路过麦当劳。女儿正在换牙，想吃冰淇淋，要求父亲给自己买一个。）
父亲：你不是牙痛吗？
女儿：**我知道我牙痛**，但我就是想吃冰淇淋嘛。

在这里，女儿当然不是在开玩笑，而是在实施一个真诚的请求。同理，如果我不能说"我知道我有痛"，我当然也不能说"我知道我有一个可爱的女儿"、"我知道我的名字是 LRQ"，等等。因此，如果 Wittgenstein 的冗余论成立的话，那么我们不仅不能声称知道自己的感觉经验或私人经验，而且也不能声称知道其他的、一般不被认为是私人的信息，从而使所有的第一人称知识都无法做出宣称。

3. 经验网络假说：私人性困惑的破解

我们注意到，唯我论所否认的并不是他人不可能知道他有某种感觉经验的陈述性知识，而是相关的程序性知识。Wittgenstein 的批评着眼于陈述性知识，因此还不足以彻底地驳斥唯我论。实际上，当唯我论者说只有他自己知道自己的感觉经验时，他想说的是，即便听话人掌握了充分的语言证据和行为证据也不可能知道他所经历的感觉经验的现象属性或现象内容。在我们看来，唯我论的错误在于它使用了"只有"这样一个表示唯一性的副词。正因为这个副词的使用，才使他人无法知道"我"的感觉经验，或者使"我"无法知道他人的感觉经验，最终导致我们无法宣称第三人称知识。

事实上，当我们在日常语言中说"只有我知道我的痛"时，我们并没有包含他人在掌握了足够的间接证据后依然完全不知道我的痛的意思。比如说，我头痛去看医生，向医生描述我的痛时，如果只有我知道我的痛，那么作为他者的医生就不可能知道我的病症，也不可能为我治疗。更多的情况下，我们是想表达，我对自己所经历的感觉经验有更直接、更深切的体会和认识，我（第一人称）的知识相对于他人（第三人称）的知识具有优先性，因为我有最直接的证据。这就是说，在类似的语境中，"只有"其实并非表示唯一性，毋宁说是一种宣示第一人称优先性的夸张说法，它并不表示第三人称知识是完全不可能的。

那么，第三人称知识又是如何成为可能的呢？我们认为，它是建立在各种直接证据和间接证据的基础之上的，其中间接证据又包括语言证据和行为证据等。如果你也有头痛病史，你当然能够知道我头痛时的现象属性；即便你没有这一直接证据，你也可以结合自己其他的疼痛经验和我给予的语言证据和行为证据，对我的头痛经验有所了解。虽然基于间接证据的第三人称知识不如基于直接证据的第一人称知识那么确切，但否认第三人称知识显然有悖于我们的常识。

从更深层次讲，第三人称知识的可能性还在于这样一个事实：我并不是独自生活在这个世界上的。在我们看来，整个社会是一个巨大的人文网络（钱冠连，2002），而我们对于社会和世界的经验又可以分为人类经验、社团经验和私人经验，它们组成了一个经验网络（the Web-of-Experiences Hypothesis），其中私人经验处于最核心的地位，人类经验处于最外围，而社团经验介于两者之间。但是，私人经验并不会因为其私人性而不被他人理解，因为大部分私人经验可以转化为社团经验，并进而成为人类经验的一部分。私人经验之所以可能（但不是必然）转化为社团经验，又是因为我们生活在同一个世界中，有着大致相同的神经属性和社会属性，从而对世界的感觉经验也大致相同（梁瑞清，2006）。

4. 私人语言论证与现象不可说

如前所述，唯我论及其现代版本现象论从感觉经验的私人性出发，推断表示感觉经验的语言也应该具有私人性。它认为，如果自然语言不具备这一特征，那么我们应该构造出一种理想语言，以便能完全地描述具有特殊认识论地位的感觉经验，同时也便于"将关于物理对象的陈述"还原为这种语言（Russell，1962）。这种理想语言其实就是一种私人语言，因为在这种语言中，逻辑专名"在很大程度上对某个说话人而言是私人的"、"不能进入另外一个说话人的语言"（Russell，1919，转引自Candlish，1998）。Schlick甚至明确指出，"即使我愿意，我一定也不能够传达关于我的感觉的信息。"在此情况下，"我们的自然语言将不再是万能的，因为在它之外一定还有一种私人语言以供我们思考我们的所感"（Schlick，1949: 404-405，转引自Hallett，1977: 311-312）。Ayer（1940: 57）则主张构造一种"感觉材料语言"来取代自然语言，而中期Wittgenstein（1975）也曾宣称要构造一种"现象学语言"，以表达他认为是本质的感觉经验，但是到了后期，他开始对包括他本人在内的现象论者进行彻底的批判。著名的"私人语言论证"就是在这样的背景下提出来的。围绕"私人语言论证"出现了许多肯定的或否定的回应（如Ayer，1986；Cook，2001；Hacker，1972；Kripke，2001；Rhees，1986；陈嘉映，2003；江怡，1999；徐友渔，1994），限于篇幅，本文无法展开，随后的讨论主要基于Wittgenstein本人的观点。

在后期Wittgenstein看来，私人语言具有如下特征：（1）该语言中的语词指称的是只有说话人才知道的对象；（2）这些对象就是说话人的直接感觉（或感觉材料）；（3）他人不可能理解该语言，因为指称直接感觉的语词只能为说话人所理解（Wittgenstein，1986: 243）。很明显，私人语言论证的靶子正是现象论者所主张构建的理想语言。在自然语言中，我们有时自言自语，给自己提问题、下命令，有时为了某种特别的目的设计出只有极少数人能明白的语码，但这些都不属于私人语言的范畴，因为自言自语用的还是自然语言，即便是密码也并非只有说话人才能听懂。那么，只有说话人明白的私人语言是否具有存在的可能性呢？Wittgenstein 从语义的角度排除了这种可能性。

Wittgenstein 认为，如果唯我论者声称只有他自己知道指称某一私人感觉的语词，那么他将无法确定该语词的意义。首先，我们不能像命名外在对象那样用明示定义（ostensive definition）的方法来指称私人感觉，因为明示定义无法保证私人感觉语词意义的连贯性。外在对象是公共可观察的，而私人感觉不是。我看到一只甲虫，并将之命名为"甲虫"，然后不管在什么情况下都可以用"甲虫"来指称它。但私人感觉就像装在盒子里的甲虫，你以为盒子里面一定有个甲虫一样的东西，但实际上可能什么也没有。其次，我们也不能诉诸记忆来确保私人感觉语词的意义不变，因为对私人感觉的记忆随着时间的变化可能模糊，甚至消亡。由于我们无法确定私人语言中语词的意义，因此这样一种语言的存在就成了问题。退一步说，即使唯我论者能够确定私人感觉语词的意义，别人也不可能理解，因为他声称只有他自己知道该语词的意义。如果别人碰巧能理解其意义，那么，该语词就不再是私人的了。从这个角度上来说，不可能存在私人语言。

在 Philosophical Remarks 的另外一处（1975: 610），Wittgenstein 请读者描述一下咖啡的芳香。他承认，我们确实很难用自然语言对咖啡的芳香进行穷尽性的描述，但我们从来不缺乏这方面的描述。钱冠连（2002：212）也指出，豆腐乳的味道是"说不全"、"说不准"的。为什么呢？诚然，正如 William James（转引自 Wittgenstein, 1986: 610）所说，"我们的词汇不够"，但我们为什么不能引入新的词汇？如果引入新的词汇，那么情况又会怎样呢？Wittgenstein 虽然没有说可能发生什么样的情况，但是我们可以设想，如果我们引入足够多的词汇，以便穷尽性地描述我们的感觉经验，那么，我们的语言将会变得非常累赘。如果我们同意现象论者的观点，尝试去构建一种全新的理想语言，那么，这种语言最终将变成私人语言，以至于除了构建者之外谁也不能理解。在此，我们也可以发现，现象论者其实是认为我们的感觉经验是词汇不可说的，因此才会有构建理想语言的形而上学冲动。实际上，我们不能也不应该将这种现象内容的不可说性归咎于词汇的缺乏，因为再丰富的词汇也无法将之穷尽。

如果说感觉经验的现象内容在这种意义上是不可说的，那么是否意味着存在私人语言呢？从 Wittgenstein 的论述中我们可以发现，"私人语言"这一概念本身其实是对"语言"一词的误用。如果一种语言只有说话人自己明白，那它根本就不能算是一门语言。这也就是说，语言的本质在于相互理解性（mutual understandability）。直觉告诉我们，相互理解必然牵涉到不同的语言使用者以及语言使用者相互接受的规则，而规则不在于意见上的统一，相反，在于语言使用者"生活形式"的高度统一。

我们说感觉经验在某种弱的意义上是现象不可说的，或者说是言不尽意的，但并非完全不可说，也并非不可知。实际上，我们的自然语言中充满了非常丰富的感觉话语，这些感觉话语使我们相互之间谈论感觉经验成为可能，而且是可以相互理解的。因此，感觉话语谈论的虽然是私人经验，但不是私人语言。也正因为如此，Wittgenstein 的私人语言论证不能作为现象不可说的证伪。首先，感觉话语的指称并非只有说话人才知道，因为根据经验网络假说，即使是从未经历过相应感觉经验的听话人也能基于间接证据对之有所了解，虽然这种理解可能是不完整的。其次，当我使用某一感觉话语的时候，他人亦能明白，否则我们将无法交流我们的感觉经验。

更重要的是，语言地图说（梁瑞清，2008b）告诉我们，语言和世界以及我们对世界的经验是不对称的，也不可能是完全对称的，否则我们将不得不背负沉重的语言包袱，而这样一个沉重的语言包袱不利于语言的习得和理解，从而不利于人类的进化。因此，我们不必如现象论者那样主张构建一种所谓的"感觉材料语言"或"现象学语言"，相反，我们应该满足于日常语言中已有的感觉话语。实际上，现象论者和物理论者由于其还原论的承诺都犯了同样的错误：现象论者试图把关于物理世界的陈述还原为感觉材料语言或现象学的语言，而物理论者则试图将关于感觉经验的陈述还原为物理语言。诚然，感觉话语依然无法穷尽感觉经验的现象属性，但是它们具有指示作用，为我们理解他人的感觉经验提供了语言上的线索。只要听话人将说话人所产出的感觉话语和自己的背景知识以及亲身经验整合起来，运用移情等理解模式，依然可以大致地理解说话人所经历的感觉经验的现象属性及其感觉话语的现象意义。因此，对我们来说，既不可能存在私人语言，也没有必要去构建一种理想化的私人语言。

5. 结论

感觉经验的私人性似乎在逻辑上决定了其现象属性或现象内容同时具有不可说性和不可知性。但是，在对几种关于私人性的哲学观点（特别是后期Wittgenstein的相关论述）进行分析之后，本文提出了经验网络假说，认为感觉经验的现象属性虽然是弱式不可说的，但对于他人来说依然是可知的，从而使得我们在宣称第三人称知识的同时，可以合法地宣称第一人称知识。该假说也表明，我们没有必要，也不可能构建所谓的私人语言来言说感觉经验的现象内容，因此Wittgenstein著名的私人语言论证不能构成现象不可说的证伪。

参考文献

Ayer, A. J. 1940. *The Foundations of Empirical Knowledge*. New York: The Macmillan Company.
Ayer, A. J. 1986. Can there be a private language? In S. Shanker (ed.), *Ludwig Wittgenstein: Critical Assessments* (Vol. 2, pp. 239-248). London: Croom Helm.
Bunnin, N. & Yu, J. Y. (eds.). 2001. *Dictionary of Western Philosophy: English-Chinese*. Beijing：People's Publishing House.
Candlish, S. 1998. Private language. *The Stanford Encyclopedia of Philosophy* (Winter 1998

Edition), Edward N. Zalta (ed.), URL = <http：//plato.stanford.edu / archives / win1998 / entries / private-language />.

Cook, J. 2001. Wittgenstein on privacy. In A. P. Martinich (ed.), *The Philosophy of Language* (4th ed., pp. 514-530). Oxford: Oxford University Press.

Frege, G. 1956. The thought：a logical inquiry. *Mind* 65, 289-311.

Hacker, P. M. S. 1972. *Insight and Illusion*. Oxford: Clarendon Press.

Hallett, G. 1977. *A Companion to Wittgenstein's "Philosophical Investigations."* London: Cornell University Press.

Kripke, S. 2001. On rules and private language. In A. P. Martinich (ed.), *The Philosophy of Language* (Vol. 4, pp. 531-544). Oxford: Oxford University Press.

Rhees, R. 1986. Can there be a private language? In S. Shanker (ed.), *Ludwig Wittgenstein: Critical Assessments* (Vol. 2, pp. 249-260). London: Croom Helm.

Russell, B. 1919. The philosophy of logical atomism. *Monist* 28, 495-527.

Russell, B. 1962. *An Inquiry into Meaning and Truth*. Baltimore: Penguin Books.

Schlick, M. 1949. On the relation between psychological and physical concepts. In H. Fiegl & W. Sellars (eds.), *Readings in Philosophical Analysis* (pp. 1949). New York：Appleton-Century-Crofts.

Wittgenstein, L. 1975. *Philosophical Remarks*. New York: Barnes & Noble.

Wittgenstein, L. 1986. *Philosophical Investigations* (G. E. M. Anscombe, Trans.). Oxford：Basil Blackwell.

陈嘉映，2003，《语言哲学》。北京：北京大学出版社。

江　怡，1999，《维特根斯坦》。长沙：湖南教育出版社。

梁瑞清，2006，"说不出"及其现象意义，《外语学刊》130（3）：20-25。

梁瑞清，2007，咖啡的芳香：论感觉经验的不可说性。广州：广东外语外贸大学博士论文。

梁瑞清，2008a，感觉句子的意义三分说与翻译的限度，《暨南学报》30（2）：104-109。

梁瑞清，2008b，语言地图说，《外语学刊》142（3）：7-12。

钱冠连，2002，《汉语文化语用学》。北京：清华大学出版社。

徐友渔，1994，《"哥白尼式"的革命》。上海：三联书店。

通讯地址：510632 暨南大学外国语学院<john_lrq@163.com>

The Epistemology of Phenomenal Ineffability
Liang Ruiqing

Abstract: It seems that the privacy of sensory experience logically entails its ineffability and unknowability. The present paper, based on a tentative analysis of some philosophical views on privacy, ventures a Web-of-Experiences Hypothesis, arguing that sensory experience, though phenomenally ineffable in a weak sense, is still knowable to other minds. The hypothesis also suggests that it is neither necessary nor possible to construct an alleged private language to talk about the phenomenal content of sensory experience.

Keywords: phenomenal ineffability; privacy; the Web-of-Experiences Hypothesis

引语的不确定性——语言哲学研究系列之三

电子科技大学外语学院　王爱华

提　要：本文探讨了语言哲学对引语的多种诠释，在此基础上提出了引语指称的"不确定性"观点。该文旨在引起国内学界关注西方语言哲学家对引语的不乏深刻的诠释，以期深化我们对引语的认识和研究。

关键词：引语；引语源；指称；不确定性

1. 序言

引语（quotation）是最难，但也是最有趣的语言哲学问题之一。它是一种语言的明达[1]表征（linguistic metarepresentation），涉及对另一个语言表达式的语形或语义等属性的表征问题。本文将表征另一语言表达式的成分称为引语，将被表征的语言表达式或思想，称为引语源（the original quoted expression）。如例（1）：

(1) "Aristotlehas" nine letters.

"Aristotle"是引语，Aristotle是引语源。根据引语源是否可归属于某言语使用者，Eun-Ju Noh（2000）将引语分为两类：纯引语（pure quotation）和转述语/思想（reported speech / thought）。纯引语，也称为提及（mention），是对抽象的语言形式或命题的表征，引语源不归属于某一言语使用者，如例（1）的Aristotle不属于某人所说的言语，因此属于纯引语。转述语/思想是对某人（包括说话人自己）话语和思想的表征。这类引语又可分为直接引语、间接引语和自由引语。还有一种引语叫混合引语（mixed quotation），指的是引语源同时被使用（used）和提及

---

[1] 关于meta-前缀的汉译问题，参看王爱华（2006，"论明达语言性及明达语言维度观"，《外语学刊》，第3期，2-11）。有些学者将它译为"元"，这不但不能对应meta-，还无情地误导了汉语读者。因为"元"在汉语里有"起始"（如"元旦"谓一年之始，"元年"谓帝王即位第一年，又如"元初"等等）与"核心"（如"元老"谓核心成员，"元恶"谓首恶，"元气"谓最基本的生命力）的含意。而meta-的意义不仅不是"元"，而且还是above, beyond, behind, 即"在上"、"在外"、"在后"，就是不在"中心"！于是就有了"上阶"、"下阶"、"后续成分"、"衍生物"、"发展物"，甚至"工具性"（如钱冠连，2003）的意思。所以，不分语境地将meta-、metalanguage译成"元"、"元语言"，一到了具体的语境中，怎么看怎么别扭。作为尝试，我们将其译成"明达"，对meta采取音译的形式，不过不排除"明达"还有"明晰与达致"的意义。这样，"明达语言"就使对象语言明晰与达致起来。由此，"明达"成了纯粹中性概念，它不与任何一个（在上、在下、在外、在后）固定地联系起来，但是一旦到了具体语境，meta-就会选择一个合适的意义。

（mentioned）的表达式。"使用"是主要特征，而"提及"是次要特征（Eun-Ju Noh, 2000: 20）。如例（2）：

（2）小燕说生活"对穷人来说很艰辛"。

例（2）中的"生活'对穷人来说很艰辛'"是混合引语。它与纯引语不同在于其引语源有归属（"生活'对穷人来说很艰辛'"这个话语归属于小燕）。它也不同于转述语，因为它的引语源有一部分被提及。

对上述引语现象的研究在国外多见于语言哲学、认知语言学、语用学和文体学著述。国内对引语的认知分析（彭建武，2001；冉永平，2002；张荣建，2007等）、语用分析（方向红，1998；张荣建，2000；等）和文体分析（申丹，1991；徐赳赳，1996；辛斌，1998等）较多。遗憾的是，国内对引语的哲学研究几乎没有，而哲学对语言的研究恰恰是深刻的，很多语言哲学研究课题相继成为语言学研究的源头。本文试图对引语的哲学研究作一些探讨，并提出自己的观点，以期深化国内对引语的研究。

2. 引语的哲学诠释

发端于20世纪初的西方语言哲学的两个中心话题是语言的"意义"和"指称"。这两个话题的背后有一个基本假定：意义以真（truth）为基础，而"真"表达了语词和世界之间的关系（何英玉，1999；李洪儒、孙赫杰，1999；吕公礼，1999）。像引语之类的语言现象关涉的是语言本身，不与世界直接挂钩，所以在真值演算中引起诸多困难。对其研究显然就具有了重要的哲学意义。Cappelen & Lepore（2007）认为引语是最难、最有趣的语言哲学话题之一，是逻辑和语义学必须面对的话题，涉及指称（reference）、索引（indexicality）、隐含语境（opaque context）、语义学与语用学划分等重要语言哲学论题。

西方哲学界对引语的研究源于Frege（1999），之后，对引语的关注与日俱增。围绕引语，语言哲学家都在试图回答以下三个问题：

第一，在一个引语中，是什么成分在"指"（refer）？
第二，引语如何"指"（refer）？
第三，引语"指"（refer）的是什么？

这三个问题实质上就是关于引语的指称和意义问题。对这三个问题的不同回答，就形成了不同的哲学引语理论，如，**专名论**（the proper name theory），**描述论**（the description theory），**指示论**（the demonstrative theory），**去引用论**（the disquotational theory）和**使用/同一论**（the use / identity theory）等。评价这几个哲学引语观的合理性是看它们在解答上述三个问题的同时是否很好地解释了以下几个公认的引语基本特征（Cappellen & Lepore，2007）：

特征1，引语中，共指（co-referential）语词或同义词不能互换保真，这就是引语的不透明性（opacity）。例如，（3）与（4）的bachelor 和 unmarried man

同义，但两句的真值却不一样，（4）的真值为假：

(3)"Bachelor" has eight letters.
(4)"Unmarried man" has eight letters.

特征2，引语不能被量化，因为带引号的表达式不具备变元（variable）性质。例如，（3）不可能量化为（5）：

(5)(∃x)("x"has eight letters.)

因为引号内的x指的是字母表中的第24个字母，而不是一个变元。

特征3，我们可以引用怪字、怪符号等，也就是引语源不受任何语言词汇的限制。

特征4，引语与它自身的语义值存在特殊的紧密关系，其语义值包含于引语之中。

特征5，理解引语就等于有无限能力去理解和生产无限多的引语，也就是引语在自然语言中具有能产性（productive）。

特征6，引语源可以同时被使用和引用，也就是上文提到的混合引语。

根据上述三个问题和六个特征，下文将重点考察五个哲学引语观的合理性（参见Cappellen & Lepore，2007）。

专名论源自Quine（1940）和Tarski（1933）。此论认为引语是引语源的非结构（unstructured）专名。每一个引语就是一个单词，其构成部分就像单词的音节，与整个陈述句无逻辑关联，就像单词 letter 中 let 与整个陈述句"John" has four letters 无逻辑关联一样。由此看来，专名论认为，引语中执行"指"功能的是整个引语（包括引号和引语源），它以专名的方式指，但指什么？专名论必然难以回答。

专名论可以解释引语特征1—3：引语不能互换保真，是因为替换专名中的构成成分，犹如用cat替换 cattle一样（cat 当然不能代替 cattle）；引语不能量化是因为引语是一个单个语词，不具有变元性质；允许新引语创造，就像自然引语能允许新词创造一样。但是专名论无法解释引语基本特征4—6。例如，如果引语是专名，而专名缺乏语义结构（semantic structure），这就无法确定如何生成和理解新引语。要理解，我们得像学新词一样去学习每一个引语。因此，无法解释特征5。另外，根据特征4，引语和引语的语义值（semantic value）之间有着特殊的紧密的关系，那就是引语的语义值包含在引语中，而根据专名论，引语"Cicero"与其语义值 Cicero 的关系就像语词 Cicero 与其所指对象的关系那样具有任意性。专名论也无法解释混合引语（特征6），因为，如果引语是专名，引号内的表达式就没有语义结构，我们就无法将引语表达式切分，进而形成例（2）那样的混合引语。

Geach（1957；1970）在专名论的基础上提出了描述论，为的是保证"表达式的被引用系列总是被引用表达式的系列"（a quoted series of expressions is always a series of quoted expressions）。描述论保留了引语是专名的基本思想，增加了"基本单元"（basic units）这一概念。Geach认为任何语言都有一组基本单元，比如，字母、单词等，如果引语源的基本单元数量为一个以上，那么这个引语就被看作是对基本单元的并列描述。于是（6）就可以描述为（7）：

（6）"bachelor" has eight letters.
（7）"b"-"a"-"c"-"h"-"e"-"l"-"o"-"r" has eight letters.

例（7）中的"-"表示并列，而每一个引语是基本单元"字母"的专名。描述论所处理的似乎只不过是一个有限的基本单元集。通过有限的单元集可以生成无限的引语，因此，引语就具有了潜在的能产性（productive）（解释了基本特征5）。但是由于描述论是基于专名论的，所以无法克服专名论的所有缺陷。

Davidson（1979/1985）在批判专名论与描述论的基础上提出了引语指示论。指示论有三个基本要点：a）引号有指示（demonstrative）或索引（indexical）功能，用以指称引号内表达式的形状（shape），参见（6）与（9）的对比，因此引号可解读为"其例示在这儿的表达式"（the expression a token of which is here），参见例句（6）、（8）；b）引号内的表达式不指称任何东西；c）引号可以被改成文字，将引号内的东西从句中移开，因为引号内的东西不发挥语义功能。所以，（6）就可以改写为（8），因为（6）的逻辑结构是（8）：

（6）"Bachelor" has eight letters.
（8）Bachelor. The expression of which this is a token has eight letters.

指示论是20世纪语言哲学中关于引语的最有创见性的理论。它至少有4个优点：a）解释了特征5：掌握了引号的指示功能，就等于拥有了运用无数引语的能力，因为能被我们指示（demonstrate）的东西是无限的；b）较好地解释了特征1，即引语的不透明性。比如，（6）和（9）中的bachelor和unmarried man虽然语义相同，但形状不同，所以两句引号所指对象不一样，其真值就必然不一样，正如（10）与（11）两句中，如果this所指内容不同，两句的真值不可能相同一样。原因很简单，我们没有理由认为引号指示不同对象的两个句子有相同的真值：

（6）"Bachelor" has eight letters.
（9）"Unmarried man" has eight letters.
（10）This is mine.（this指一把斧子）
（11）This is mine.（this指一支笔）

指示论的另一个优点c）可很好地解释混合引语（特征6）。根据指示论，引号内的表达式在整个句子中没有语义功能，那么该表达式的任何部分都可以被引号指示，成为"引语之箭的靶子（the target for the arrows of quotation）"（Davidson, 1979/1985: 90-91）。d）可以解释为什么引语是无限的：新引语的产生并不比语言中的新词的产生神奇，因为能被指示的东西是无限的，那么能被引用的东西也是无限的（解释了特征3）。

指示论的问世引来无数争议。指示论最明显的缺点归结起来有三：a）如果指示论是正确的，那么（6）的引语"Bachelor"有可能指示别的东西，如，an apple,因为,根据指示论,(6)的逻辑结构是(12):

(6) "Bachelor" has eight letters.

(12) Bachelor. The expression of which this is a token has eight letters.

(12)包含有一个指示词 this,而指示词的基本特点是具有语境不确定性,可以用来指示任何可指的东西。在给定的语境中,什么被指示取决于说话人,所以(12)完全有可能被用来指示an apple。显然(6)不可能指示an apple。b)存在关联性麻烦。根据Davidson,引语是通过指称一个表达式的例示(token)来间接指称一个表达式。而表达式可以是形状(shape)或模式(pattern)。问题就在于任何例示会有无限多的形状或模式。那么我们怎样能从一个特定的例示推及到一个唯一的类呢?c)指示论无法解释没有引号的引语:引号有指示功能,那么没有引号的引语应由什么来执行指示功能呢?

由于指示论太复杂,Richard(1986)提出了相对简单的去引用论。他的理论有一个"理查德去引用图式"(Richard's Disquotational Schema),简称DQR:

DQR:对任意表达式E,左引号(lq)加上表达式 e 再加上右引号(rq),指称 e(Richared, 1986: 397)

由此看来,引语的语义值就是引号内的表达式(Ludwig & Ray, 1998: 163, note 43)。根据去引用论,引语不是专名、描述语或指示语,而是能将一个表达式变为论元(argument),并给其赋值的功能算子(functors)。

去引用论可能是最简单、最自然、也是最显明的引语理论(Ludwig & Ray, 1998: 163)。其DQR图式简单,不需要我们对句子表层结构作复杂假设,这显然是对指示论的改进或批判。另外,去引用论还有如下优点:a)引号之内的表达式有语义值,因此,"bachelor"和"unmarried man"有不同的语义值,由此解释了引语的不透明性(特征1)。b)引语作为"功能"算子,将一个表达式影射到自身,于是揭示了引语与引语源之间的特殊紧密关系,那就是"同一"(特征4)。去引用论的最大缺点是不能解释混合引语:如果引语是指称引号内的表达式,那么用 John 来命名表达式"has a certain anomalous feature",(13)应该与(14)描述了同样的事,表达了同样的命题:

(13) Quine said that quotation "has a certain anomalous feature."

(14) Quine said that quotation John.

根据DQR,(13)和(14)不但应有相同的命题,还应有相同的逻辑形式。这显然不对。另外,去引用论显然不能解释无引号的引语。

同一/使用论由Washington(1992)首次提出,其中心思想是引语由起标示作用的引号和用于"提及"功能的被引用表达式构成,所有表达式一旦被放入引号内,都具有了"提及"功能,引语的指称与被引用表达式本身同一,也就是,被引用表达式提及自身。

由此看来，引号的基本功能只是标示，表明引号内的表达式是提及，而不是作常规外延性使用。但是引号不做"指"这个行为，引号没有指称功能，在引语中作指称功能的是表达式本身。因此，在"Aristotle" has nine letters这句话中，是 Aristotle 而不是引号指称 Aristotle。因此引号没有真正的语义功能，他们只不过是标示手段，一个派生物。那么无引号的提及也是一种引用性运用，如，Man is a noun中的man就是无引号的引用性运用。（可是在一般情况下，Man is a noun这一句子被判为错，这就是中国古代先秦名家"白马非马"论的诡辩来源。）

同一/使用论有三个优点：a）解释了新符号的引用问题（特征3），凡能被提及的（包括新符号在内），都可以被引用；b）解释了引语与引语源的关系问题（特征4），被引用的表达式与所指对象的关系紧密，有时是同一，有时是例示；c）解释了引语的创造性问题，提及的能力是无限的，所以引用的能力也是无限的（特征5）。

同一/使用论的缺陷也十分明显：a）引语与提及关系如此相关联，那么如何区分二者？这需要进一步解释。b）无法解释混合引语现象。

综上所述，五种哲学引语观对引语的"指"、"如何指"和"指什么"三个问题给予了不同的回答，其中不乏深刻的道理。但没有一种引语观能全面合理地解释引语的6个基本特征。追究其根源，本文作者认为，这主要是由于五种引语观只是耽留在引语本身的结构上来考察引语的指称和意义，并倾向于认为引语的指称具有确定性，所指的就是引语源的形状或表达式。其实，引语作为一种言语现象，只考察其自身的结构是不够的，我们还必须将其与引语使用者和语境结合起来考察，才能揭示引语运作的本真。

3. 引语指称的不确定性

基于上述五种哲学引语观的缺陷，本文作者根据Quine（1960）指称的不确定性论题（the thesis of indeterminacy）和Strawson（1950）的说话者指称论（speaker theories of reference），提出引语指称的不确定性观点，认为引语的"指"、"怎么指"、"指什么"都具有不确定性，以期能合理地解释引语的6个基本特征。

3.1 指称的不确定性论题

Quine（1960: 26-79）在讨论翻译的不确定性问题时，首先讨论了指称的不确定性（indeterminacy of reference），有时又称指称的不可测性（inscrutability of reference）。Quine著名的gavagai例子意在说明：这种不确定性在原则上是不可能澄清的东西，因为指称具有以下三个基本特性（Quine, 1973: 89）:a）异常多变性（vagaries），其中包括含糊、歧义及不透明性，这样就增加了判断所指的难度。b）"指称对象"有时是神秘莫测、极难把握的。这就涉及到指称的一个本体论特征，即相对性。c）Quine用

"本体论相对性"一词是想说：指称总是相对于某种"背景语言"而言，我们只能将某个指称相对于其"背景语言"提出问题，而不是以绝对方式提出问题，指称才能显示意义，这个深刻的却常常被人忽视的前提，Quine 称之为"本体论的承诺"。因此，要确定一个语词的指称对象，必须排除绝对性，承诺它处在某种赋予意义的"背景语言"中，包括情境描写、行动描写、意向描写、因果描写等本体性质的条件或前提；脱离使指称显现的"相对性背景语言描写"，对指称显然无法确定。而指称本身证明是行为上不可测知的。指称的不可测知性观点不是关于我们认识的局限性的陈述，而是一个应该承认的形而上学的事实（陈波，1998：134）。

3.2 引语指称的不确定性

Quine 的指称不确定性论题讨论的是语词与外在对象之间的关系，不涉及指称对象是语言本身的引语之类的语言事实。但 Quine 所讨论的指称的异常多变性、指称对象的相对性和背景语言性等特征表明引语源是一个充满矛盾、冲突、歧义、模糊、含混、不确定的指号集。而引语本身也是一个语言表达式，其指称同样具有Quine所说的三个特征，因此同样是一个充满不确定性的指号集。由于引语源和引语有着直接而紧密的关系，引语源和引语的双重不确定性使引语指称的不确定性更为错综复杂。这种错综复杂的不确定性为引语使用者赋予了主体性地位。引语使用者的主体性地位体现为刘宓庆（2001：52-53）所说的三个特征：主导性、主观性、主体能动性。引语使用者的主导性表现为以自己的意识、意向、目的为前提或主导来理解、阐释和表征引语源，处处伴随着一种"自我权威感"。指称的三个特征，特别是背景语言性意味着不同的语言对刺激的反应在指称上不可能相同，在这种情况下，引语使用者对引语源的指称的取舍具有主观性，即引语使用者有以自己的意志、意向、目的为轴心的倾向。在引语使用中，引用使用人对引语源的语词与其作为个体所领悟到的语境相对照，领会语词的具体意义，对抽象意义进行"分析性假设"，以便做出引用选择。这种"领悟"和"假设"是引语使用者的主体能动性发挥的结果，而这种主体能动性是建立在整体主义基础之上的。

引语使用者的这种主体性地位决定了引语的"指"和"怎么指"具有不确定性。在引语使用中，引语使用人的主导性、主观性和主体能动性表明，引语本身（不管是引号，引语源，还是引号和引语源构成的整个表达式）无所谓"指"，是引语言说者在具体语境中，根据自己的意志、意向、目的，用引语来执行"指"。正如日常语言哲学家Strawson（1950）的说话者指称论（speaker theories of reference）所说，不是名称在"指"，而是说话人在具体语境中用名称执行"指"，在这个"指"的行为中，说话人的信念和意图尤为重要。那么解释引语的"指"和"怎么指"至少要考虑三方面的内容：引语本身具有的约定（比如，引语与引语源有直接的联系）；说话人的意向、信念、意志、目的等心理特征；具体的引语使用语境。这三方面在本质上都具有不确定性：说话人的心理特征和语境不确定性主要表现在它们必然因人、时间、地点而异；引用本身具有的约定性，比如引语与引语源的关系的不确定性直接由Quine所说的指称的异常多变性、指称对象的相对性和背景语言性以及说话者指称的不确定性所规定，因而无需证明。

引语与引语源的关系的不确定性实质上就是引语"指什么"的不确定性。既然引语"指什么"的不确定性不证自明，下文我们将主要探讨引语"指什么"的不确定性的种种表现形式。在探讨之前，我们首先考察引语的指称与引语源之间的相互关系。

关于引语的指称与引语源的关系问题，我们赞同前面讨论的五种哲学观，认为引语的指称与引语源有直接的联系，但我们认为这种直接的联系不是五种哲学观所说的那种简单的"同一"或"形状（shape）等同"，而是相似（resemblance），即引语的指称和引语源之间有某种共同的特征或属性。这种共同特征或属性可以体现在语音、语形、语义、逻辑或命题、概念、文体等方面。根据Wilson（2000）的观点，语音、语形或文体上的相似是明达语言性的（metalinguistic），语义、逻辑或命题、概念上的相似是解释性的（interpretive）。例如，在直接引语（15a）中，引语与引语源之间，在形式或语言上的相似性更突出，因而属于明达语言性相似；在间接引语（15b），（15d）中，语义或逻辑上的相似性更突出，应该属于解释性相似。而在（16）中，即使Descarte不会说英语，引语"a thinking substance"指称的也不可能是一个英语表达式，而应该是语义。因此（16）属于解释性相似。混合引语（15c）既运用了明达语言相似也运用了解释性相似。而对思想的引用属于典型的解释性相似。同一性（identity）是一种特殊的相似，引语的指称与引语源同一，表明它们在每一语境中共享所有的隐含，包括知觉、语言、逻辑、文体等隐含。

(15) a. Mary said to me, "You are neglecting your job."
b. Mary told me I was not working hard enough.
c. According to Mary, I am "neglecting" my work.
d. Mary was pretty rude to me. I am neglecting my job!

(16) In one of the greatest philosophy books ever written in Latin, Descartes said that man "is a thinking substance."

不难看出，上文的五种哲学引语观只论及了引语指称与引语源的明达语言性的相似性，而没有考虑它们之间的解释性相似。依据引语的指称与引语源的相似关系，我们将引语的"指什么"的不确定性归纳为三类：

第一，明达语言性层面的不确定性。

(17) (Pointing to the script "Boston" on the blackboard) Look at "Boston."

例（17）中，同一个明达语言性的引语"Boston"可以指称a)—d) 等不同的对象：

a) 指Boston的语音特征，比如Boston的两个音节；

b) 指Boston的形状特征，比如，Boston的6个字母；
c) 指Boston的语法特征，比如，Boston是一个名词；
d) 指由Boston这个例示（token）所表达的不同的类（type）。

在具体语境中，到底指哪一个，要随引语使用者的目的、意识、意向等心理状态而定。

第二，解释性层面的不确定性。如果引语的指称与引语源在解释性层面上关联的话，间接引语（18）的指称可作三种解释：指称的是引语源的话语、思想或命题，因为话语、思想、命题都涉及与引语源的内容相似。

(18) It is false that John can speak Chinese.

如果（18）的引语的指称是引语源的话语或思想，那么引语源"John can speak Chinese"就归属于某人。如果（18）的引语的指称是引语源的命题，那么引语源"John can speak Chinese"就不归属于某人。这种不同的引语指称和引语源归属会直接导致对（18）的不同理解。如果引语的指称是有归属性的话语或思想，那么（18）就有一个隐含意义，那就是说话人不赞同说"John can speak Chinese"这句话的人的观点，由此也隐含了（18）的说话人与引语源说话人之间的社会或人际关系。如果（18）的引语的指称是没有归属性的抽象命题或信息，那么就没有上述两个隐含了。

第三，引语的指称是明达语言性的，还是解释性的？有时难以确定。请看例子（19）。

(19) A：飞猴病了。
B1：A说侯飞病了。
B2：A说飞猴病了。

假如B1和B2知道"飞猴"指的就是侯飞这个人，那么B1的引语指称一定是解释性的，因为它指的是A的内容。而B2的引语的指称更具明达语言性，特别是"飞猴"二字，因为B2的引语不但表征A的内容，还表征了"飞猴"的语言形式。但是，如果B2的听话人不知道"飞猴"指的是"侯飞"这个人，他很有可能将B2解读为是对A的纯解释性表征。如果B2的听话人知道"飞猴"指的是："侯飞"这个人，他也知道B2知道这个信息，那么他会将B2的"飞猴"解读为明达语言性的。

当然，我们主张引语指称的不确定性，并不意味着引语的指称是完全无法把握的。我们认为，对不确定性的讨论本身就预先假定了确定性。至于人们是如何在引语指称的不确定性中把握其确定性，本文作者倾向于认同Wittgenstein（1953/1999）的语言观，即有意义的且不引起歧义的语言始终坐落在生活形式（forms of life）之中。在生活形式中的引语，必然随着语境关联、交际双方的语用推理和语用充实，而具有显明而确定的指称。对这一论题的探讨留待另文讨论。

最后要交代的一个问题是：我们以上的引语观能否很好地解释引语的6个基

本特征呢？回答是肯定的。a）可以解释特征1，即引语的不透明性。因为引语指称与引语源的关系是明达语言性的或解释性的相似，不是等同。并且这种相似关系具有不确定性，随语境、引语使用人等因素变化，所以共指语词和同义词不能互换保真。b）可以解释特征2，即引语不可量化。引语指称与引语源相似，而引语源本身是一个具体表达式，不是一个变元，所以不能量化。c）能解释特征3、特征5和特征6。在引语使用中，由于说话者具有主导性、主观性、能动性等主体地位，所以能对任意符号，包括奇异符号进行引用（特征3）；有无限能力去理解和生产无限多的引语（特征5）；能同时对引语进行提及和使用（特征6）。d）解释了特征4：即引语与引语源有紧密的关系，那就是相似。

参考文献

Cappelen, H. & E. Lepore. 2007. Quotation. *The Stanford Encyclopedia of Philosophy*. Edward N. Zalta (ed.), URL = http: //plato.stanford.edu / archives / spr2007 / entries / quotation /.

Davidson, D. 1979/1985. Quotation. *Inquiries Into Truth and Interpretation* (pp. 79-92). Oxford: Oxford University Press.

Geach, P. 1957. *Mental* Acts. London: Routledge Kegan Paul.

Greach, P. 1970. Quotation and Quantification. *Logic Matters*. Oxford: Basil Blackwell.

Frege, G. 1999 .On Sense and reference. In M. Baghramian (ed.), *Modern Philosophy of Language* (pp. 6-25). Washington: Counterpoint.

Ludwig, K. & G. Ray. 1998. Semantics for opaque contexts. *Philosophical Perspectives* 12, pp. 141-166.

Noh, E.-J. 2000. *Metarepresentation. A Relevance-Theory Approach*. Amsterdam:John Benjamins.

Quine, W. 1940. *Mathematical Logic*. Cambridge, Mass: Harvard University Press.

Quine, W. 1960. *Word and Object*. Boston: The MIT Press.

Quine, W. 1973. *The Roots of Reference*. La Salle, Illinois: Open Court.

Richard, M. 1986. Quotation, grammar, and opacity. *Linguistics and Philosophy*, 9, pp. 383-403.

Strawson, Peter F. 1950. On referring. *Mind* 59, pp. 320-344.

Tarski, A. 1933. The concept of truth in formalized languages, In Tarski(ed.), *Logic, Semantics, Metamathematics*. Indianapolis: Hackett.

Washington, C. 1992. The identity theory of quotation. *Journal of Philosophy*, 89, pp. 582-605.

Wilson, D. 2000. Metarepresentation in linguistic communication. In Sperber, D (ed.), *Metarepresentations: A Multidisciplinary Perspective*. New York/Oxford: Oxford University Press.

Wittgenstein, L. 1953/1999. *Philosophical Investigations* (G. E. M. Anscombe, Trans.). Beijing: China Social Sciences Publishing House, Chengcheng Books Ltd.

陈 波，1998，《蒯因哲学研究：从逻辑和语言的观点看》。北京：生活·读书·新知三联书店。
方向红，1998，引语的语用环境试析，《烟台大学学报》（哲学社会科学版）：（4）：92-96。
何玉英，1999，指称理论中的照应问题《外语学刊》（2）。
李洪儒，孙赫玉，1999，认知链条上词的主义与指标对象，《外语学刊》（1）。
李　勤，1999，俄汉不确定/确定范畴比较，《外语学刊》（4）。
吕公礼，1999，真实准则的哲学认识论背景及理论逻辑模式，《外语学刊》（4）。
刘宓庆，2001，《翻译与语言哲学》。北京：中国对外翻译出版公司。
彭建武，2001，语言转述现象的认知语用分析，《外语教学与研究》（5）：360-366。
冉永平，2002，元表征结构及其理解，《外语与外语教学》（4）：15-18。
申　丹，1991，对自由间接引语功能的重新评介，《外语教学与研究》（2）。
辛　斌，1998，新闻语篇转述引语的批评性分析，《外语教学与研究》（2）：9-14。
徐赳赳，1996，叙述文中直接引语分析，《语言教学与研究》（1）。
张荣建，2000，书面语和会话中的引语分析，《外国语》（2）：42-47。
孙华建，2007，英语引语的多视角分析，《重庆师范大学学报》（哲学社会科学版）（2）：104-107。

通讯地址：610054 电子科技大学外国语学院 <wang_diana2003@yahoo.com.cn>

The Indeterminacy of Quotation
Wang Aihua

Abstract: This paper explores various philosophical interpretations of quotation, on the basis of which, a view of indeterminacy of quotation's reference is put forward. The paper is meant to arouse attention to the western philosophers' deep study of quotation in hopes of deepening our understanding of and research on quotation.

Keywords: quotation; original quoted expressions; reference; indeterminacy

● 语言●思维●实在

主客主多重互动理解模式（SOS）：
理论建构与语料实证

四川外语学院　王寅

提　要：西方哲学在研究认识和理解时主要遵循了"单向（从感性到理性，或从理性到感性）"或"双向（主客互动，主主互动）"的运思模式，均存在理论解释上的困惑。我们根据体验哲学提出了"体验性普遍观"，并基于此进一步提出"主客主多重互动理解模式（SOS）"，可望弥补"单向"和"双向"留下的问题。同时，我们还以同一首《枫桥夜泊》的40篇英语译文为例作出了论证。

关键词：体验哲学；体验性普遍观；主客主多重互动；理解

1. 序言

哲学主要研究存在（自然）与思维（人）的关系。语言哲学则是通过分析语言以解决哲学这一老问题（Baghramian, 1999: xxx）。钱冠连（2007）基于此提出中国后语哲，强调"从语言分析入手，从形而上学出来"的研究策略，刘利民、李洪儒、隋然、杜世洪、王寅等也沿此思路作出了论述，这对我国语言学界同仁颇有启发，可望开创一条新的研究进路。本文基于这一思想，通过分析同一首唐诗《枫桥夜泊》40篇英语译文的语言，来论证我们提出的SOS理解模式[1]。

2. 对传统理解模式的反思

自古希腊以来，哲学家们就在思考存在与思维、理解与自然之间的关系，不断地追问What is the world? What is the man?，并基于其上演绎出各种其他问题。对这些问题的解答必然涉及"感性与理性"、"存在与思维"、"客观与主观"之间的关系，这已成为西方2000多年哲学史中长期争论不休、永不衰败的话

---

[1] 本文部分观点曾发表于《哲学动态》2009年第10期"主客主多重互动理解"一文和《外语教学与研究》2008年第3期"认知语言学的'体验性概念化'对翻译主客观性的解释力——一项基于古诗《枫桥夜泊》40篇英语译文的研究"一文中。

题。人们围绕它也提出了很多不同的认识模式或理解模式：诸如传统哲学的单向观，现代哲学所主张的主客互动双向观，后现代哲学所倡导的主主互动双向观等，现将他们的主要观点依据"方向性"作如下简要梳理：

（1）单向运思模式：从感性到理性（即从客观到主观，存在到思维），或者从理性到感性（即从主观到客观，思维到存在），在语言研究和翻译理论中分别出现了强调作者（作者中心论、作者的独白）和文本（文本中心论、文本的独白）的倾向。

（2）主客互动模式：皮亚杰沿着施莱尔马赫、狄尔泰、杜威、梅洛·庞蒂等阐述的互动思想，在批判单向模式的基础上正式提出"主客互动"模式，意在强调主体与客体之间的互动关系。

（3）主主互动模式：后现代哲学家认为在主客互动过程中人的主体性地位还没有得到应有的重视，且不能解释人与人之间是如何得以有效协商和沟通，因而提出了"主体间性"以强调人与人之间的互动。

3. SOS理解模式：强调多元因素互动

我们曾依据体验哲学的基本原理提出了"体验性普遍观（Embodied Universalism）"和"体验性概念化（Embodied Conceptualization）"，认为人类的范畴、概念、思维和语言之所以具有一定的普遍性，是因为我们面对一个相同或基本相同的客观世界，且人具有相同的身体结构，器官又有相同的功能，这才是形成人类部分共识的基础，这一观点与乔姆斯基所倡导的"先天性普遍观"相对。但人类识解世界的方法不全然一致，这就导致了范畴概念和语言表达上的差异，因此人类的理解必定具有"概念化"性质，但是Langacker又过分强调其主观性和动态性等特征，而忽视了概念化的经验基础和相对确定性，我们拟将其修补为"体验性概念化"，以弥补其不足。

表1 哲学研究中的方向观

传统（古希腊194/0s）	自 然	人	单向运思模式
	感 性	理 性	
	存 在	思 维	
	客 观	主 观	
现 代	互 动		主客双向模式
后现代	主体间性		主主双向模式

在"单向观"的关照下，人们往往采取以偏概全的思路，要么像经验论者那样，过分强调从感性到理性（或从存在到思维）的方式；要么像唯理论者那样，过分强调从理性到感性（或从思维到存在）的方式，这两种认识论都常以一方面而掩盖另一方面。Lakoff & Johnson（1980，1999）以及 Lakoff（1987）把西方哲学研究中的感性主义和理性主义都归结为"客观主义（Objectivism）"，因两者都认为

客观地存在一个独立于人的外部世界，在其背后存在一个绝对真理，我们就应当不遗余力地将其寻找出来，但两种认识论在寻找方式上存在根本性差别。

对经验论者来说，经验是人们一切知识或观念的唯一来源，我们关于世界的全部知识来自我们的感知，完全是由感觉能力所建构的。说到"经验"，理当包含人的因素，但经验论者并没有真正研究"人是什么"，而且还强调追求绝对真理时当排除人的主观因素，从而将研究目标导向了科技理性（或叫工具理性、科学主义）的进路。

对唯理论者来说，只有先天具有的推理能力才能向我们提供关于真实世界的知识。谈及"理性"，唯人有之，也理当包含人的因素，但唯理论者虽触及这一问题，却又过分强调排除人的感官经验，力图消解"个人偏见"和"价值污染"，竭力抛弃传统观念的干扰，建立了所谓的"笛卡儿范式（Cartesian Paradigm）"。

Lakoff 和 Johnson 在他们的论著中严厉批判了客观主义哲学理论，针锋相对地提出了"非客观主义（Non-objectivism）"，即"体验哲学（Embodied Philosophy）"[1]，参见王寅（2003）。现将他们对历史上哲学主流观点的反思概述如下：

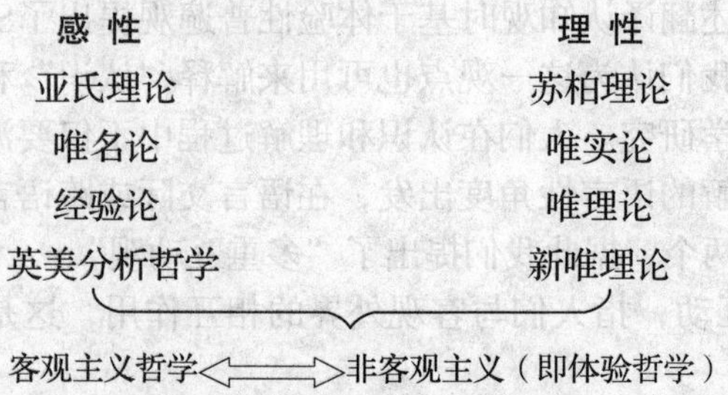

感 性	理 性
亚氏理论	苏柏理论
唯名论	唯实论
经验论	唯理论
英美分析哲学	新唯理论

客观主义哲学⇔非客观主义（即体验哲学）

图1 体验哲学对单向观的批判

皮亚杰等看出了传统认识论中两种单向运思模式的问题，并针对它们的误区提出了双向互动说，这是一大进步。但他的互动论又过于模式化和简单化，仅论说了主体与客体两要素之间的互动，而忽视了其他重要的相关因素，特别是在语言交际过程中这一模式更显得捉襟见肘：是作者与读者的互动，还是两者与文本的互动，抑或是两者与客观世界的互动，它们是如何互动的，这些都有待于进一步论述。我们认为，该模式也不足以描述解释、翻译和认知全过程，其间还要考虑到语句、文本、不同的语音、不同的书写等多重因素之间的互动问题。而且，对于皮亚杰来说主体与客体这两个要素好像具有同等作用，而从唯物论角度来说，客体对于主体的认识当具基础性功能。

---

[1] 我们认为，后现代哲学都持"非客观主义"立场，它包含很多理论和观点，Lakoff 和 Johnson 所提出的体验哲学仅是其中之一。在他们的论述中时而将两者等同起来。

后现代哲学又过于强调理解中的人本性（Humenism[1]）和主观性，似乎忽视了"主体间性"得以建立的经验基础，又将人类的认识和理解导向了另一个极端，忽视客观世界的基础性，抛弃人类理解的体验性，类似于空中楼阁而已。这一倾向也可从Langacker提出"意义等于概念化（Conceptualization）"观点可见一斑，他（1987：194）曾对这一观点细述如下："意义不是客观地给定的，而是（人为地）建构出来的，即便是那些描写客观现实的语言表达，其意义也是这样。因此，我们不能通过纯粹描写客观现实来解释意义，而只能通过描写认知性的例行常规（指认知加工），正是它构成了人们对现实和意义的理解。语义分析的主观方面就是人们的概念化，我们所关心的结构，就是一个人通过主动地认知加工强加在他的心智经验之上的结构"。

他尝试用"概念化"来解释意义和人类的理解，也算是一种独创，但从其论述可见他过于强调概念化的动态性、人本性、主观性和识解性，显然是打上了后现代哲学观的烙印。人们难免会发出这样的疑问：主体之间的理解基础是什么？笔者基于唯物主义和体验哲学将其修补为"体验性概念化"，顺着这一思路我们就不难发现，后现代哲学观所倡导的"主体间性"解构了理解的体验性和客观性，淡化了人们得以相互理解的认知基础。

我们曾在论述翻译认知观时基于体验性普遍观提出了SOS理解模式，经过一段时间的思考，我们认为这一观点也可用来解释"认识"和"理解"，也同样适用于语言学和文学研究。人们在认识和理解过程中不仅要涉及主体和客体这两个要素，特别从理解的语言性角度出发，在语言交际或跨语言交际时，相互作用的要素就不能仅是两个，据此我们提出了"多重互动观"：

（1）主客互动，指人们与客观外界的相互作用，这是得以形成部分共识的基础；

（2）主主互动，指交际过程中双方之间的相互作用、协商和理解；

（3）人语互动，指语言交际时必然要包括人与文本、语音、文字等之间的互动；

（4）客语互动，指文本与客观外界在人作用下的互动；

（5）语语互动，指人在跨语言理解时，当需考虑源语言和目标语之间的互动。

因此，我们认为，人们在理解和翻译过程中主要涉及上述五重互动关系，其间既有主客互动，又有主主互动，以及主客与语言的互动，更重要的是几者的有机整合。

我们经过对"单向运思、主客互动、主主互动"的反思，提出"主—客—主"三个关系项中的体验基础，与原来的理解模式有本质的差异，且又强调了"多重互动"这一重要因素。

---

[1] 笔者主张将后现代哲学中的"人本观"译为"Humenism"，将其中的 man 改为复数men，以示区分。由于传统的和现代的人文主义主张在形而上学的理论框架中追求统一的、普遍的、抽象的人性，且将其作为客体来观察和描写，此处用humanism可反映出这一立场。而后现代人本观反其道而行之，认为不存在统一和普遍的人性，人与人之间存在很多差别，应考察具体的生活世界，且让其自身自我呈现，因此当用复数的men，译作Humenism更妥。

4. SOS理解模式的论证

大多后现代学者主要从理论角度论述了理解的人本性和差异性，接受了理解的阐释学立场。特别是德里达解构主义中的关键词"延异"，正可对这一观点作出清晰说明：由于文本在空间上发生了变异，在时间上出现了延伸，作者与读者会处于不同的空间和时间，因此各人对同一文本的理解就会有不同。这一理论自有可取之处，至少可让我们从另外一个角度来认识"理解"。但我们也发现，很少有学者提供语料库以佐证，据此我们不仅提出了SOS，且还尝试运用语料作实证性支撑。

笔者收集到同一首唐诗《枫桥夜泊》的40篇英语译文，它们正可反映出这40位作者的不同理解。我们在阅读译文时明显有一个感觉，各位作者都在认认真真地理解着原诗中的各种含义，且都在努力将这些含义转译出来。尽管他们的理解和翻译有所不同，但其主旨并没有改变，这是毋庸置疑的事实。例如，各位译者译的都是"枫桥"，没人将其随意修改为"廊桥"、"蓝桥"、"康桥"等，更没人将"枫桥夜泊"改译为"廊桥遗梦"、"蓝桥魂断"、"康桥别了"等等，他们都是在张继所设定的圈圈中作有限的不同识解。各篇译文的表述虽不尽相同，但这些译文的内容都没能跳出张继所描述的主题，译者们都在努力体验着张继所体验的经历，理解着张继所描写的场景和境界，这也完全证明了体验性概念化中的"体验性"含义。选词和译法上的差异，正说明了识解的差异，以及语言表达的丰富性和多样性，不足以说明理解和翻译的自由性和放纵性。

人们对同一现实世界进行不同方式的概念化就会产生不同的认知结果。因此，读者与作者之间的理解就不可能完全相同，不同读者对同一文本会有不同的解读和翻译，此乃常情。后现代哲学思潮正是从这一点出发来否定文本和话语具有稳定不变的意义。但长期以来，有些学者仅只被动地接受了这一观点，以为"主观性"本来就是主观的，有很多不确定因素，不可能有一个统一标准，因而很少有人对其做出深入思考，着手系统分析不同读者理解同一文本究竟存在哪些差异，有哪些变化，是否很大，有何规律可循。很多人深感对其加以限制性描写难以下手，无从说起，因此大多国内外学者对翻译主观性仅停留在描写上，未见有何深入探究和理论阐述，更不见从认知角度做出认真解释。我们尝试运用认知语言学中的"识解观"来统一解释这些差异。

Langacker（1987, 1991, 2000）将"识解（Construe / Construal）"定义为：人们可用不同方法认识同一事态的能力，可分为5小项：辖域、背景、视角、突显、详略度。笔者曾与他本人讨论过多次，这些小项似有重复，且在不同论著中有不同表述，他也很坦率地承认了这一点。我们拟将"辖域"和"背景"合并，且按照逻辑关系将它们按顺序排定：（1）确定不同辖域（Scope）；（2）择用不同视角（Perspective）；（3）突显不同焦点（Salience）；（4）定位不同精细度（Specificity）。这四点不仅是形成概念体系、语义结构和语言表达的必经之路，也是理解和翻译中不可或缺的基本认知方式。

第（1）项表明讲话人认识事态时先要确定一个大致范围或辖域，主要将论述哪一方面的事情，涉及哪些背景知识。第（2）项则是在辖域范围中确定认识的视角，确定参照点或切入点。第（3）项则在前两项的基础上进一步作入微和聚焦处理，择其相对于背景而言更为突显的部分来论述，因为人们不可能将场景中所有信息都全盘托出。第（4）项表明对聚焦部分的认识可采取"从详"或"从略"的方式来论述。在这4项微观过程中，转喻机制起着关键作用，识解过程主要遵循着"从面到点、以点带面、用部分指代整体"的机制。下文将以此为主线来建构理解主观性的理论框架，并结合《枫桥夜泊》40篇英语译文具体解读翻译主观性。

4.1 辖域和背景

"辖域"指表达式所涉及相关经验和被激活的概念域配置，即理解一个表达式的意义或结构所需要的相关经验，并且需要另外一个或多个表达式的意义或结构作为背景，这与我们常说的百科性背景知识有关。这一识解因素在《枫桥夜泊》译文中主要体现在对以下词语的理解和翻译上。

1）译"泊"。对一个"泊"字的理解需要体验和想象当时的历史背景，涉及很多有关概念域。在我国古代乃至今天，小船的停靠很少用"锚"，多用绳子拴在河边的桩上，有这种生活体验或背景知识的人就不难理解此诗中"泊"的含义。在40篇英译中对其有以下5种译法：moor, anchor, stop, park 和 tie up，但它们的确切含意不同：stop 过于笼统，可指 put an end to 任何种类的运动或活动；park 主要指停"车"，tie up 仅指"拴绳子"这一动作，用部分代替整体的转喻方式来译"泊"。大部分译者选用 moor（用绳子系泊）和 anchor（抛锚停船），显然前者更符合张继诗中的"泊"，有32位译者选用它，占80%，这说明他们比用anchor的译者更了解当时的生活背景。

2）译"乌啼"。从译文语料库来看，"乌啼"都被理解和翻译成了"乌鸦的啼叫"，但乌鸦只在白天啼叫而夜里不啼，据此它有可能指地名"乌啼桥"，这句话的意思为"挂在天空的月亮正朝乌啼桥方向落下"。但这一解释并未被译者所接受，40篇译文大多没照此意来处理。还有一种可能，是否张继将猫头鹰或捕鱼的鱼鹰的叫声误认为乌鸦的啼叫，并以此建立"乌啼桥"和"乌鸦叫"之间的双关呢？

3）译"江枫"。有很多学者认为，"江枫"是指寒山寺附近的两座桥"江村桥"和"枫桥"，有不少译者将其处理为"江边的枫树"，或许这又是一个双关。

4）译"渔火"。主要有以下3种处理方法：

（1）译为"渔船上的灯火"：dimly-lit fishing boats, the lights of fishing boats, fishing boat's lights, boat lights。

（2）译为fishing lights, the fishing torches, the fishing lamps, fishing fires, fishing lanterns，似乎除（1）义外还可能理解为"为打鱼而设置的灯火"。

(3) 理解为"打鱼人的灯火"：fishermen's flares, a fisherman's lamp, the fisher's lights, fishermen's fires, fisherman moves with his torch，似乎上述两义兼而有之。

根据背景知识我们认为，第（1）类译法较妥，第（2）、（3）类译法没有前者明确，因为在我国没听说过渔民夜晚用油灯来吸引鱼。

5）译"寒山"。寒山寺得名是因为唐朝曾有一位叫"寒山子"的诗人住过那里，那么究竟当译为"Cold Mountain"还是"Han Shan"呢，这也是一个仁者智者之见的问题。总的来说，这是一篇以"寒"、"霜"、"愁"为背景构思而成的律诗，从场景中的"霜"、"寒"到心境上的"寒"和"愁"，顺畅而又自然，译作为突出这一意象直接说出"cold"也可起到点题的效果。但值得注意的是"寒山寺"不是指在"寒山"上的寺庙，如有一译者处理为"The monastery on cold mountain"显然有悖原意。

6）译"船"与"山"。在译文语料库中，"船"有译为 boat 和 ship 的，"山"有译为 hill 和 mountain 的，它们之间在语义上还是有差别的，一般说来，后者比前者要大。根据诗中的具体情况，用前者似为更妥。译文中用 boat 的有32例（用ship有3例，aboard有2例，sail和bark各1例，还有1例不见"船"），占83%。

用 hill 的有12例，仅占30%；用 mountain 有10例，占25%；大部分译者用拼音，有18例，占45%。

4.2 视角

有了描述范围和背景之后就当考虑从哪一个视角切入来观察问题，这涉及观察者与事体之间的相对关系，个人兴趣，语篇的人称，分句的语法主语等一系列问题。

张继原诗的总体视角（即论述的出发点）应为：作者本人在进京赶考落榜返乡途中路过苏州寒山寺，触景生情，有感而发。据此"对愁眠"的主语应是张继本人，确定了这一视角之后有利于准确理解和翻译整个诗篇。从译文语料库来看，对整个诗篇的视角有以下几种不同的处理方法：

（1）有19首译文选择了张继的视角，占48%，我们认为这是符合原意的。但我们也注意到了，不同的译者采用了不同的方法来体现这一视角，如有的用"I"，有的采用所有格"my"的方法来体现，如说成"ere my eyes"，"my uneasy eyes"，"my sleepless eye"，"my sleep"，"my troubled sleep"等。

（2）有的笼统译为"we"。

（3）还有用"旅行者"、"流浪者"、"访问者"、"乘客"、"陌生人"等来点明视角。有译者译为"the sorrowful traveler was sleeping"，将"对愁眠"的主语理解为"游客"。

（4）有的译文笼统地译为：the man in sad dream，但不知这里的 the man 究竟指谁？或许是在故意避开这个难题。

（5）有的译为"渔民"难以入眠，这似乎离原意较远。

（6）视角不明，有8篇译文处理为"渔火"、"渔船"，如：

"The bank maples and the fishing flares see a sleepless night."

"Few fishing-boat lights of th' riverside village[1]

Are dozing off in their mutual sad gaze."

汉语语句常省略主语，特别是诗歌，主语大多是略而不提，尽管原诗没有交代主语，但在大多情况下我们还是能找到被省略的成分，但这其中也不乏仁者智者的问题，这就给古诗英译提出了一道难题，择"谁"作主语？上述所列述的第（6）种视角不明的情况，其实也多多少少地有损原诗的意向和风格。

另外，原诗最后一句"到"的主语是什么？是"钟声"？还是"客船"？在译文语料库中绝大部分译者理解成前者，但也有1例取后者，译为：Amid the night toll arrives a boat up the stream。

4.3 突显

有了论述的范围和视角，就要考虑抓住场景中的哪一部分进行聚焦描述。人类有确定注意力方向和焦点的认知能力，语言表达在很大程度上要受制于注意力突显的原则。"突显"有多种含意和用法，直接反映了人们在主观上对某一事体感兴趣或最感兴趣的部分，本文主要从以下两个方面加以分析：

1）隐藏与突显。在译诗过程中必然要考虑到信息的取舍，有些信息可以隐藏，有些信息可以突显（这与详略度有关，参见下文），例如：

（1）原诗的"渔火"在有的译文中被译为"灯火"，隐藏了"渔"这一概念。而有8篇译文将没有明说的"渔民"也译了出来，也就是说，将原诗中隐藏的信息在译文中显露了出来。

（2）汉语句子可以没有主语，而英语的动词作谓语一般应有主语，这就涉及如何将汉语中隐藏的主语在英译中显露出来，这在古诗翻译中常是一个棘手的难题，如本诗中的"对愁眠"的主语究竟是谁？这个问题又与"视角"相关，参见上文。

2）突显运动过程的不同阶段。人们在描写一个运动事件时可以聚焦该运动的过程，或聚焦于运动过程的某一点，也可聚焦该运动的结果，从而形成了语言中的不同表达，这与 Ungerer & Schmid（1996：218）所论述的"注意窗（the Windowing of Attention）"密切相关。这一识解因素在我们的语料库中也有很多具体反映：

（1）译"月落"。原诗中的"月落"是指挂在西边天空中的月亮正在向下落去，还是已经落下了？这也颇有争议，但大多学者持前一观点，将诗句突显为"月亮下落运动的过程"，而有些译文将其译为"at moonset"，突显了运动的终点。

---

[1] 译文中"河边的村庄"是译者添加的内容，有可能被误解为"渔民就居住在附近的村庄里"。实际上，他们常以渔船为家，就住在渔船上到处游动。

（2）译"霜满天"。人们曾经疑问过究竟应是"霜满天"还是"霜满地"的问题。按照正常的生活经验，天上若"下霜"，应是地上霜。其实这两种说法分别体现了"下霜"的不同阶段，前者主要指下霜的过程（作者的想象），后者主要指下霜的结果。

（3）译"月落乌啼霜满天"。该句意为"挂在天空的月亮正在下落，有乌鸦在啼叫，天空正在下霜"，这三件事体线性排列，不分主次，体现为并列关系。若要在译文中反映这一含意，应将它们处理为并列成分较妥。但我们发现很多译者将其中的一项或两项置于主句，另两项或一项译为从句或短语，这就使得原诗并列的含意在英译中有了主次之分，自然也就突显了不同的内容。

（4）译"对愁眠"。它可指睡觉这一动作过程的不同阶段。在40位译者主体中有的将其理解为：

(a) 想入睡，感觉要入睡，如译为：Asleep I feel。

(b) 入睡过程，但还没睡着，如用 lie, keep me from sleep, sleepless night, keep me awake等。

(c) 入睡结果，如译为：fall into sleep, was sleeping 等。

(d) 深层入睡，如译为：in sad dream。

这些译文分别突显了同一动作"眠"的不同阶段。

按照经验，在那个背景和心境下的张继是难以入眠的，所以才看到或听到了诗中所描写的种种夜景，如"月落、乌啼、霜满天、江枫、渔火、寒山寺、钟声"等，因此将其理解为（b）更为合理。在艾克利等（1992）的《唐诗三百首今译》中将"对愁眠"理解为"忧愁难眠"，也是指"入睡的过程"。据此，若将其译为"入睡的结果"、"进入梦乡"就考虑得不很到位了。

（5）译"到"。原诗第4句的"到"显然是表示动作结果的，有24篇英语译文按此义处理，主要用reach（20篇），come（3篇），arrive（1篇），touch（1篇），hear（4篇），其余处理为"过程"或"不明显的结果"，如用了break, flow out to, flow afar to, towards us, forth to, down to, ring for me等。

另外，上文提到的"泊"是译成 tie up, 还是stop, moor, anchor, 这同样也涉及将"泊"理解为动作的过程或结果的问题。

过程与结果之间的互换，实际上也是一种转喻认知方式，用部分来代替整体或整体中的另一个部分。因此，译者对运动过程不同阶段的突显这一识解因素也可视为一种转喻认知机制。

4.4 详略度

突显与详略度是密切相关的两种认识方式，可聚焦某部分加以详细观察和论述，也可忽略某些其他部分只加以轻描淡写，这样人们就以不同的详略度来认识或描写一个事体，这一现象可能出现在语言的各个层面。这一情况在译诗过程中就具体体现为译者对原作中有关信息的增删处理。这里所说的详略度并不仅从用词量的多少来衡量，因为英语的虚词用量常多于汉语，这不是我们讨论的重点。

本文主要分析实意概念的详尽与粗略，如不同译者对古诗中的"对愁眠"就有不同详略程度的描写，我们从40篇译文语料库中摘出用"lie"对译的例子，并大致按照从略到详，从粗到细的顺序作如下排列：

I lie.
I lie in bed.
I sadly lie in bed.
I sleepless lie.
Facing sadness I lie.
I lie awake in sorrow.

这都体现了不同译者同对一个"对愁眠"作出了详略度不同的翻译。

又例"客船"在不同英译中也有不同的详略程度，为论述清楚起见，将它们大致从略到详分为两组：

(A) ？　　　　　（一译文未见"船"）
　　aboard, sail
　　the boat, my boat
　　the guestboat
　　the mooring boat
　　my boat from strange land
　　my lone boat moored nearby

(B) a traveler's boat, the mooring boat, the wanderer's boat, the visitor's boat, rover's bark, the roamer's boat, the sad and troubled napper's boat

将"客船"译为（B）类都不同程度地细化"客船"的含义，它们都是译者主体做出的较为详细的理解，尝试将张继当时的心境译出来，但译者用"流浪汉"似乎不很符合原意。

还有的译文将"月落"中的"月"译为"old moon"，似乎也比原文更为精细。

有一译文将"夜半钟声到客船"译为"out to the mooring boat the distant chimes of midnight"，其详细度远大于原诗，多出原文所没有的意义out, distant, chimes。

在另一译作中将"江枫渔火对愁眠"译为"the maples vague, the fishing lamps are blinking ere my eyes"将"对愁眠"这一主旨略而不译，详细度又明显小于原诗，因此该译文值得进一步推敲。

还有一译文将原诗首句中的前两项意义处理为：

The moon is setting in the west.
Crows are crying to their best.

为了凑韵，在译文中增添了原诗所没有的意象：in the west 和 to their best，译文显得更为细致入微。

另外，原诗仅4行，有的译者将其处理成6行，还有译为8行、9行、10行、11行，都是出于"更为精细"的考虑，空间上的拓展，时间上的延长，朗读时的从容，可更细致地展现原诗的含意。

上文通过40篇译文语句的分析，我们不难发现这40位译者对原诗的理解既有客观因素，也有主观因素，还有语言因素，它们具有主客主多重互动关系，正可说明 SOS 理解模式的解释力。40篇译文所反映出的理解或内容之所以近同，是因为译者与原作者张继具有基本相同的体验或认识，之所以不同是因为体验或认知上存在一定的差异所致，且这些差异都可统一在"识解"框架中作出合理而又统一的解释。

5. 结语

语言哲学的要义为通过分析语言解决哲学老问题，即"存在（自然）"与"思维（人、语言、理解）"的关系。本文通过同一汉诗 40 篇译文的分析旨在说明存在与思维（理解、翻译）的关系，这其中既有客观性，又有主观性，且具有多重互动关系。若仅遵循"单向（从感性到理性，或从理性到感性）"或"双向（主客互动，主主互动）"的运思模式，尚不能对其作出合理解释。我们根据体验哲学提出了"体验性普遍观"，并基于此进一步提出 SOS，可望弥补"单向"和"双向"，以及后现代哲学过分强调主体性的缺陷，突出了交际双方所能共同体验的客观因素（相同的客观世界，相同的身体构造，相同的器官功能），同时又将传统"互动论"修补为"多重互动论"，因为在语言交际中会涉及人与人、人与客、人与言、客与言等多重互动关系，在翻译时还要涉及言与言之间的互动，这可用同一首《枫桥夜泊》的40篇英语译文为例作出论证。

通过透析40篇译文，我们发现了人类理解的共通性（体验性），至于同一文本的不同表述（识解性），而不像持后现代哲学观的翻译理论家所认为的那样，可以漫无边际地作任意解释、随便翻译、放纵发挥。其实这 40 篇译文的翻译主体都是在一定的内容辖域内进行着有限的揣测和解读，都受制于"体验性"和"识解性"的约束，他们都在追寻张继当初的创作意图，都在体验和构想有关枫桥夜泊的可能场景，并尽量将其译得恰当和妥帖。

同一文本有若干不同译文，正可说明理解和翻译的主观性，这也表明后现代哲学对理解的论述不是空穴来风。但是提出问题仅是第一步，更重要的是对其作具体深入的分析和探讨，本文在这方面做了一点尝试。我们认为，"识解"可作为一个理论框架来分析理解和翻译的主观性。从40篇《枫桥夜泊》不同的英语译文来看，识解四要素基本可统一解释译者主观性在翻译活动中所体现出的主要差异，可望对理解和翻译中的主观性从理论上做出初步描写和探索。

参考文献

Baghramian, M. 1999. *Modern Philosophy of Language*. Washington, D.C.: Counterpoint.
Lakoff, G. & M. Johnson. 1980. *Metaphors We Live By*. Chicago: The University of Chicago Press.

Lakoff, G. 1987. *Women, Fire, and Dangerous Things*: *What Categories Reveal about the Mind*. Chicago: The University of Chicago Press.

Lakoff, G. & M. Johnson. 1999. *Philosophy in the Flesh — The Embodied Mind and its Challenge to Western Thought*. New York: Basic Books.

Langacker, R. 1987. *Foundations of Cognitive Grammar Vol. 1*: *Theoretical Prerequisites*. Stanford, California: Stanford University Press.

Langacker, R. 1991. *Foundations of Cognitive Grammar vol. II*: *Descriptive Application*. Stanford, California: Stanford University Press.

Langacker, R. 2000. *Grammar and Conceptualization*. Berlin: Mouton de Gruyter.

Ungerer & Schmid. 1996. *An Introduction to Cognitive Linguistics*. London: Longman.

艾克利、段宪文、王友怀，1992，《唐诗三百首今译》。西安：三秦出版社。

李洪儒，2001，从逻辑、哲学角度看句义理论的发展——"语句中的说话人音素"理论探讨之一，《外语学刊》（1）。

刘利民，2009，先秦名家在形容词语义中的哲学盘旋，《外语学刊》（5）。

钱冠连，2007，西语哲在中国：一种可能的发展之路，《外语学刊》（1）。

王　寅，2008，语言学新增长点思考之四：后语言哲学探索——语言哲学、后语言哲学与体验哲学，《外语学刊》（4）。

通讯地址：400031 四川外语学院 <sdwang@pub.sz.jsinfo.net>

Subject-Object-Subject Multiple-Interactive Understanding Model (SOS): Theoretical Construction and Corpus Support

Wang Yin

Abstract: Western philosophers are mainly concerned about cognition and understanding via unidirectionality (from perception to rationality, or vice versa) or bidirectionality (interaction between subject and object, or between subject and subject), which have left many problems unsolved. On the basis of Embodied Philosophy, we have proposed "Embodied Universalism," based on which "Subject-Object-Subject Multiple-Interactive Understanding Model (SOS)" has been developed, in the hope of solving the above-mentioned problems. The paper has also used 40 English Translations of one Chinese poem "Night Mooring by Maple Bridge" to support the new model.

Keywords: Embodied Philosophy; Embodied Universalism; SOS; understanding

Sophism of the School of Names: Linguistic Path toward Rationalism in Traditional Chinese Philosophy

Liu Limin Sichuan University

Abstract: This paper re-examines the "sophistic paradoxes" of pre-*Qin Ming Jia* (School of Names) and proposes that these are not paradoxes at all as they were labeled traditionally. Rather, they were metaphysical speculations on the nature of language meaning by way of language analysis. The propositions were in the past misunderstood partly because of the isolated feature of the classical Chinese language. But it was just this feature that started *Ming Jia* on their way towards philosophical reflection on questions of language meaning and certainty of knowledge.

Keywords: pre-*Qin Ming Jia*; philosophy of language; rationalism

This paper intends to re-examine the philosophical ideas of *Ming Jia*, or the School of Names, an active group of thinkers during the pre-Qin Chinese history of over 2,500 years ago, who were labeled "sophists" traditionally. Two reasons make this topic necessary.

First, for lack of historical data, the *Ming Jia* philosophical propositions have proved hard to understand, which has resulted in giving *Ming Jia* various contradictory labels, such as idealists (e.g. Hou et al., 1957: 419) vs. materialists (e.g. Liu, 1995) ; the only logicians in ancient China (Chan, 1973: 232) vs. "amateur logicians" but "notorious sophists" (Sun, 1987: 172); theoretical scientists (Li, 1998: 228) vs. falsity or a meaningless play of words (e.g. Liu, 2003: 300). The *Ming Jia* ideas need further exploration and explanation.

Second, the study of the *Ming Jia* ideas is very important for in-depth comprehension of classical Chinese philosophical thought. As Feng Yu-Lan has noted, *Ming Jia* were the only thinkers who had "purely theoretical interest" in ancient China, and a Chinese philosophy without *Ming Jia* would seem "all the more one-sided[1]" (Feng, 1994: 192). Feng's point is important because it is relevant to the question whether there is a Chinese philosophy; or rather, whether a philosophy in the western sense of the word is possible in classical China, given the characteristics of the Chinese language. Indeed, there does not

---

[1] Feng's original wording translated as "one-sided" here is "畸形, jixing," meaning "deformed, disfigured, handicapped, distorted" in Chinese.

seem to be a philosophy in the history of Chinese thoughts, if by "philosophy," we mean metaphysical speculations on "being as being." But should the absence of metaphysics in Chinese tradition be attributed to the features of the Chinese language? Is it possible for a philosophy in the western sense of the word to occur in the Chinese language environment? I shall argue that the Chinese language is no obstacle for the birth of metaphysical thoughts in traditional Chinese philosophy; and this idea is presented through a brief description of the characteristics of the Chinese language, followed by an illustration on why *Ming Jia* propositions were in fact representatives of the rationalistic philosophical speculation on the basis of those characteristics.

1. Characteristics of the Chinese language and its significance for philosophy

About the differences between the Chinese and European languages, Wang Li[1] has commented: "In terms of the structure of sentences, the western languages practice a rule of law, while the Chinese language, a rule of man." By "rule of law," he means that European languages attach great importance to the structural forms of language, with all those conjugations and declensions, such as the morphological changes of nouns according to gender, number and case and the changes of verb forms in terms of tenses and aspects. The occupation of syntax positions in a sentence by certain parts of speech and the relationships between different words in a sentence are all strictly and clearly defined. On the contrary, the Chinese language is characterized by "rule of man," because this language does not emphasize the structural form, with practically no morphological changes. The parts of speech in Chinese cannot be distinguished by the form and words of different grammatical categories are free to exchange in their use. As Qian G. L. (2002: 8) says, to understand a sentence in Chinese requires "intellectual intervention" and even pragmatic reasoning. That is, grammatical relationships in Chinese are inferred and not formally presented. Such great language difference does seem to have some serious philosophical implications.

First, there was no copula *to be* in the classical Chinese language. The earliest use of "是(*shì*, near equivalent of *to be*)" as a copula in Chinese was somewhere around 200—500AD (Wang, 2000: 401), about 5 or 6 hundred years after the birth of traditional Chinese philosophy. What is more, the copula *shi* in Chinese

---

[1] Quoted in Ma B. Y. Preliminary Study on the Difference Between Chinese and English, Foreign Languages, 1995(5).

is not as semantically rich as *to be* in European languages, *shi* merely serving the function of linking the subject with the predicate, unlike its counterpart "*to be*" in European languages that has the copula use, veridical use, and existential use, which proves to be essential for the rise of the core subject area of western philosophy: ontology. Since the Chinese language lacks the copula, "ontology" in the western philosophical sense of the word does appear impossible in Chinese philosophy (see Song, 2002 for detailed discussions).

Second, the noun in Chinese, as the other parts of speech, does not have morphological inflexions. One cannot tell by its form, whether a noun in Chinese is abstract or concrete, countable or uncountable, singular or plural. This lack of formal inflexion in Chinese is said to have prevented the Chinese philosophers from speculating on the issues of the "One" and the "many" and from generating abstract terms of universality, as it does not distinguish individuals but generally denotes "masses," orienting the Chinese philosophers towards a so-called "behaviorally nominalism"; western style metaphysical entities, such as the Platonic "idea" simply cannot occur, because the Chinese language does not provide the necessary devices for such thoughts (see Hansen, 1983 for detailed discussions).

Third, because of its structural flexibility, the Chinese language does not have a stipulation as to what part of speech can take the position of subject in a sentence. Nouns, verbs, adjectives can all be put to the place of subject of a sentence, whether they are true subject or not. About such syntactic features, Zhang (1995: 334-349) has claimed that with no morphological inflexions, the subject and the predicate of Chinese sentences can not be formally identified. Unlike the Greek language that channeled Aristotle to speculate on the ontological status of the subject, there is no such a linguistic facility conducive to the Chinese philosophers' attention to similar issues.

Thus, it seems that the Chinese language does lack important structural properties essential for the development of metaphysics. Ontology, as the study of "being as being," does seem impossible to be born in China, given the linguistic parameters imposed on Chinese thinkers.

However, I argue in this paper that the essence of ontology lies in metaphysical speculation on the nature of existence itself. Philosophy, at least in its more metaphysical end, is a reflection on the ultimately correct meaning of existence, and this reflection is not language-specific. When the Chinese philosophers come to the speculations on the correctness of the meaning of words we use, it is possible for the occurrence of rational speculation on what there is and what is true, only that the Chinese philosophy has to follow the path with the characters of their own language towards such a mode of metaphysical thinking. This path is what I call the "character-meaning-centered" reflection. This is so because a character is a name in Chinese. To reflect on the ultimately correct meaning of language, Chinese philosophers would have to engage themselves in speculation on the nature of names. With no formal inflexions, the names in Chinese for real objects and those for properties, relations and abstractions are all the same in form and usage. Granted that the names for real objects do have ontological status, it would be dubious that the same status can be given to those that don't denote objects and events that are real, for example the names for relations, properties, etc. It is true that the ancient Chinese philosophy was not knowledge-oriented and the issue of ultimate Truth was not on the philosophical agenda, but as we shall see next, Chinese philosophers like *Ming Jia* had already stepped on to the path of rational thought, at least partly because of the characteristics of the Chinese language which, with its lack of formal syntax, poses questions to the expression and understanding of ideas.

2. *Ming Jia* as rationalist thinkers

The pre-Qin Chinese philosophy, like classical Greek philosophy, attached great importance to language. The first large-scale debate on philosophical issues in the history of China was the famous "Debate on Names and Actualities,"[1] which lasted about two hundred years and involved all the then philosophical schools of thought. The Debate had as its central issue which was the relationship between words as names and things in actuality. It was in this great debate that *Ming Jia* came into being, with their strong and clear-cut rationalist standpoint expressed in their philosophy of language. There are several reasons why I refer to *Ming Jia* as rationalists engaged in the philosophy of language.

First, the speculation on language meaning itself was a necessary development of the Debate on Names and Actualities.

The Debate was initiated by Confucius, with his theory of "rectification of names." The motivation for this theory stemmed from Confucius' belief that language underlay all social and moral orders. In face of the turbulence of the then society and the reshuffle of the social structures and moral values, Confucius attributed the collapse of the old institutions and the chaos that followed to a discrepancy between names and actualities, or a divorce of names from what they should stand for. To say correctly is the prerequisite of to do correctly. To restore

---

[1] The great Debate is believed to have happened during the Period of Spring-and-Autumn (770—476BC) and the Warring States (475—221BC) in Chinese history, a period of social disturbances during which an atmosphere of relative freedom of thought and speech led to the birth of "a hundred rivaling schools of ideas" engaged in competition with each other.

the ideal social order of the good old times, Confucius proposed that we should first rectify the use of names. To him, the right meaning of a name should be what the name had had in the past ideal social situation. The meaning of a name existed *a priori* and it was compulsory that the actuality conform to the *a priori* semantic configuration of its name.

Contrary to Confucius, Laozi, father of Daoism, retorted that this rectification was impossible. In his only book, *Dao De Jing*, the first statement in the first chapter claimed: "The *Dao* can be reached in language, but the *Dao* that has been talked about in language, is not identical with the eternal *Dao*; the name can be named, but the name that has been named is not the constant name." Laozi thus created a highly abstract metaphysical entity, the *Dao*, which is the source from which everything in the world is generated and the ultimate law governing the change of everything. As such, the *Dao* is, to Laozi, the essence of all existence and the ultimate foundation of all meanings. By such a viewpoint, the meaning of everything rests with the *Dao*. The names that are used to say of actualities do not have a necessary connection with the actualities that are named, because the essential meaning of name is dictated by the *Dao*. The genuine *Dao* transcends, and constitutes the essence of, everything. Thus, it would be in vain to talk about rectification of names. It is *Dao*, rather than language, that determines word meaning. Rectification of names is not possible.

Another major school of thought against Confucianism was Mohism, especially the later Mohism. The later Mohists are now popularly accepted as the representatives of scientific thought in ancient China. A strong strain of empiricism was present in their ideas concerning names and actualities. The Mohists believed that the actualities were what existed physically out there, and names were just their linguistic labels. In the Mohist *Canon*, we find statements such as "What we use to talk are names, and what we talk about are actualities," "[we] use names to describe or imitate actualities" and so on. As to the criteria for evaluating the correctness of names, the Mohists proposed the theory of application and effect: "If what we say works, then we conclude that our saying is correct; if what we say does not work, then it is incorrect." Thus, to Mohists, actualities are of primary importance while names secondary.

There were many other schools of thought participating in the Debate, but in general the most influential and conflicting ideas concerning names and actualities included the above-mentioned Confucianism, Daoism, and Mohism. Such different ideas rose in the Debate on Names and Actualities, conflicting with each other, with no one successfully convincing the others. In this situation, it was inevitable that *Ming Jia* ideas would came on to the stage, because if the relationship between names and actualities was to be straightened out, it would be necessary for the philosophers engaged in the Debate to clarify what they meant by "name" and "actuality" in the first place. This means a task of speculation on the nature of the terms of "name" and "actuality" themselves that the philosophers were using. The meaning of names and the basis of the meaning thus became the vital issues the philosophers had to face up to and there just had to be someone to ask this question. The school of thought that did raise this question was *Ming Jia*. When the other schools of thought were concerned with the relationship between language and actuality, *Ming Jia* raised the question of language itself and they specialized themselves in speculating on language itself and the nature of meaning. Such a speculation had to be rational analysis, because there was no empirical way to verify an issue of such a nature.

Second, the criticism and repudiation of Ming Jia by the other schools of thought proved by a negative side that Ming Jia were doing philosophical speculation on language.

Soon after they made their ideas known, criticisms and repudiations from various major schools of thought were directed at *Ming Jia*. Yet almost all the criticisms, except those from the Mohists, were wide of the mark. This is because while *Ming Jia* were speculating purely on the meaning of names, the others were concerned with language and actuality; they were, in Carnap's phrasing, not in the same language framework. Both Confucianism and Daoism criticized *Ming Jia*, ideas from the perspective of secular social political and moral perspectives. Their criticisms were so vehement that they sometimes bordered on slander [1]. However, none of these criticisms attempted to diagnose and thereby repudiate, by the use of the same language logic as *Ming Jia* adopted, the places where *Ming Jia* could not justify themselves or were unable to make their sayings consistent.

The Mohists were the only thinkers who reacted to *Ming Jia* in the spirit of intellectual critique. But their criticisms were from an empirical perspective. For instance, when *Ming Jia* proposed "'Fire' is not hot" (meaning that the concept of "fire" as a language abstraction [*de dicto*] is not the same thing as fire in actuality [*de re*]), the Mohists countered that "'Fire' is hot, because the hotness is not just an experience within an individual, but is felt universally like when all feel under the scorching sun." Such criticisms from the Mohists, correct in its own right, were not valid contradictions against *Ming Jia* sayings, because *de re* and *de dicto* are issues of different nature. The Mohists were using the words ("*fire*" *etc.*) to discuss what they should stand for in actuality, while *Ming Jia* were mentioning the words to speculate on what they should represent as conceptual abstractions. Should *Ming Jia* have

---

[1] For instance, Xunzi actually condemned *Ming Jia* sayings as "worthless and no wiser even than chickens and dogs." Such criticisms were ideologically irrelevant, but they had a tremendous influence on the other people in their view concerning *Ming Jia*, which was also responsible for the governmental crash down on *Ming Jia* and other similar-minded thinkers later on.

been concerned with the relationship between names and actualities, their sayings would have certainly been nothing but nonsensical. But if they were concerned with the meaning of names *per se*, as they indeed were, that transcended physical actualities, their level of thought would be more metaphysical than that of the Mohists. Rather than contradicting *Ming Jia*, the viewpoint from the perspective of empiricism helped to foil the rationalist characteristics of *Ming Jia*' s metaphysical speculation on language.

Third, from sample records of the debate between Ming Jia and others, we can have a glimpse of the rationalistic tendency of Ming Jia. And what is left of Gongsun Long's essays demonstrate their language rationalism very clearly.

Here and there in the works of classical Chinese thinkers and historians, one can find record of the actual debate involving *Ming Jia* philosophers. Let's look at a record of such a debate in Zhuangzi's book (*Zhuangzi* Ch.17) between Zhuangzi himself and Hui Shi, a major *Ming Jia* thinker:

Zhuangzi and Hui Shi were one day promenading on the bank of River Hao.

Zhuangzi exclaimed: "*Look at the leisure way the fish swim! They are so happy.*"

To this, Hui Shi asked: "*You are not the fish. How can you be sure that the fish are happy?*"

Zhuangzi: "*You are not me. How do you know that I don't know the fish are happy?*"

Hui Shi: "*I am not you and therefore do not know what you know. It follows that you do not know the fish are happy because you are not fish. A matter of logical reasoning!*"

Clearly, Hui Shi was not interested in whether the fish were happy or not. What he pressed for was: what logical basis did Zhuangzi have for his proposition that the fish were happy. Hui Shi was not an empirical scientist, who probably might infer the state of emotion of fish by the observation of their behaviors and other external features. He was unmistakably inquiring into the certainty and the rational ground of the knowledge claim expressed in Zhuangzi's proposition. Such a tendency of rationalist thought was unique and rare among pre-Qin Chinese philosophers.

The most convincing evidence comes from Gongsun Long's 5 essays, of which three are his theoretical meditations: *On Name and Actuality* (名实论) and *On Reference* (指物论).

In *On Name and Actuality*, Gongsun Long began with the statement of "Heaven and earth, together with what they produce, are things." This is his standpoint of materialist realism, i.e., what are real out there are physical objects. Except this declaration, the rest of the essay is entirely concerned with his theory of the correctness of meaning of the names. What Gongsun Long was interested in is this: the existence of objects in actuality is one thing, but it is quite another to know about the objects by means of language; then how can we be sure that we are using language to know and to talk about the things correctly? He said: "The relationship between Name and Actuality, that is a matter of language use to express thoughts." Since language use was so important, Gongsun Long put forward his principle governing the use of language: "The sole criterion of correctness is the 'thisness' in this and 'thatness' in that (唯乎其彼此)."

This is where Gongsun Long's theoretical interest lies: the relationship between names and their true meanings, rather than that between names and things. His criteria for telling whether a name expresses a correct conceptual meaning should be rephrased as: "The true meaning of a name is the conceptual content of our thought. If we know that the 'thisness' is not in a 'this,' that is, the 'this' does not have an essence of 'thisness,' then we cannot say the 'this' is a true 'this'; and if we know that the 'thatness' is not in a 'that,' i.e., the 'that' does not have an essence of 'thatness,' then we cannot say the 'that' is a true 'that.'" Seeing from this rephrasing, Gongsun Long believes that language represents the essence of things. He was not just "the David Hume of one-name-one-thing-ism" (Hansen, 1983: 148), but would have been happier to join Plato in saying that a name is used to express the nature because the essence of a thing is in its name.

This position of his is also witnessed in *On Reference*, which is justifiably known as the most challenging of the pre-Qin essays. What makes it so difficult to interpret that has led to the diversity of explanations is the key word of "指, *zhǐ*", which has occurred 48 times in the essay that has only 268 Chinese characters. The *zhǐ* denotes "*finger*" in everyday speech, which is extended to mean "point (*things*) out" or "point to (*things*)," but in an abstract sense, it comes to mean "*refer to*" or "*reference*." Even in modern Chinese, the word "*reference*" is "*zhi-cheng*." With this made clear, we can go back to see what that statement is saying: it expresses Gongsun Long's idea of language and thought, quite compatible with modern cognitive linguistics theory. It says: "All the 'things' are nothing but what we refer to (*zhǐ*) (by language), and 'reference' (*zhǐ*) here does not merely mean to point things out (*zhǐ*)." We cannot obtain our knowledge by knowing one by one all the things in the world and therefore we have to use names to categorize the things and grasp their essence through linguistic conceptualization.

Clearly, Gongsun Long realized the necessity of clarification of concepts and ideas in philosophical debates, and exerted his efforts in such a clarification via the speculative analysis of language meaning (the meaning of names in the perspective of Chinese). In this respect, he was unmistakably doing philosophy of language. It is true that the Chinese language does not have the characteristics of the western languages that may facilitate the metaphysical speculations on being as being in western philosophy, but the Chinese language has its own characteristics that draw the attention of philosophers to the direct speculation on the meanings of names.

Such speculations on the Chinese language itself might have just as well given rise to metaphysical speculations. Only that the Chinese philosophers might have gone the other way around: from analytical speculation on language meaning issues towards ontology and epistemology.

3. Reinterpretation of the "sophistic" fragments of *Ming Jia* debaters

With the foregoing understanding of the basic philosophical spirit of *Ming Jia*, I now try to re-examine the so-called "sophistic" paradoxes of *Ming Jia*'s. These paradoxes are what Zhuangzi recorded in his book (*Zhuangzi* Ch.17), including 10 propositions of Hui Shi's, and 21 propositions of some other *Ming Jia* debaters. Limited by space, however, I can only select the ones that prove to be the most difficult to explain, which are popularly regarded as nonsensical sophism. There are those such as the first paradox of Hui Shi that goes: "The greatest has nothing beyond itself, and is called the Great; the smallest has nothing within itself, and is called the Small." Some regard it as a revelation of Hui Shi's relativistic position, while others consider it as agnostic proposition. As to such propositions, let's leave to future discussion.

Let me begin with the "inexplicable" paradox: "Mountain out of mouth (山出口)", which many researchers find impossible to explain and simply brush it aside (e.g. Hu Shi, 2000: 171; Zhang Xin, 1998: 189). Feng (1994: 200) rephrased this proposition into: "Mountains produce mouths," which simply does not make sense, reinforcing the impression that *Ming Jia* were talking nonsense. This paradox is difficult to explain partly because of the characteristics of the classical Chinese written language, which not only lacked structural forms such as inflexions, but did not even have punctuations. This makes it hard to tell whether the paradox is concerned with name and actuality or just a speculation on name and its nature of meaning. But if we confuse the actuality-involving language use with the meta-language use, it is likely that we shall interpret such propositions in an incorrect way. Here, the distinction between "use" and "mention" in modern philosophy may be of great importance, as it gives us a head-start. When we "use" a word, that word may have its referent and we can predicate of the object that the word refers to, but when we "mention" a word, putting it within quotation marks, we are not talking about any object the word refers to but about the word itself.

This is common sense in philosophy of language. But let me give a new understanding of the technique: the mentioning of a word can be an indication that we are performing metaphysical speculations on language meaning itself without connecting the meaning to the actuality. After all, in addition to the sound and form, a word has its meaning. If we can speculate on the form and the sound, why can't we also speculate on the meaning itself? In my following discussion, I shall apply quotation marks to the paradoxes to show that *Ming Jia* were performing speculations on the word meaning itself metaphysically, which I think is more compatible with what we have discussed above.

The proposition of "Mountain out of mouth," to me, should be rewritten as " 'Mountain' out of mouth." I explain this as a declaration of *Ming Jia* that their argument was concerned not with actuality but the meaning of name *per se*. The paradox actually says: "mountain" as a name is uttered from human mouth. I am not the first to explain it in this way. Far back to the Tang Dynasty (618—907AD), Cheng Xuanying, a Daoist scholar, already did (quoted in Chen, 1983: explanatory note by Cheng X. Y.), but his interpretation has been either neglected or regarded as unreasonable. Cheng, however, is right. Without punctuations or other linguistic means to rely on at the time, *Ming Jia* might have to resort to such statements as a means to demonstrate their meta-language speculation intention, i.e., confining their arguments to language meaning without an involvement of actuality.

Ming Jia had already realized that things did exist and that the knowledge about the things was not equal to the things-in-themselves (Cf. what we have discussed about "Reference does not reach actualities, because the actualities cannot be exhausted"). Because of this, there is always a question of right or wrong, true or false in what we claim to know about the actualities, though things in actuality do not invite such judgments at all. What is the nature of this knowledge? What is this "mountain" which is not any mountain that exists out there? These are the questions that *Ming Jia* had in mind, and this understanding is consistent with their theoretical program which we discussed in the previous section.

With this framework, let us now reexamine the "nonsensical" paradoxes. First, we shall examine Hui Shi. Of his 10 propositions, the following 3 are said to be most nonsensical:

(1) *The sky is as low as the earth; mountains are as high as lakes;*
(2) *Leaving for the Yue State today and arrived there yesterday;*
(3) *I know the center of the world is located to the north of Yen and to the south of Yue.*

Propositions (1) and (2) are said to be expressing a relativist viewpoint (Cf. Zhang, 1998: 125; Feng, 1994: 198), because (1) claims that the height of things is just relative to the perspective of the observer; and (2) states that the past and the present are relative to the time one mentions them in speaking. Proposition (3) is simply dismissed as "nonsensical," because Yen was a State in the north, while Yue a state in the south; how can the center of the world be in the north and the south at the same time? Many researchers explain (3) with the theory that the Earth is a spherical body, and therefore any point could be the center (Cf. Mou, 1979: 23; Liu, 2002: 77). Again this is explained as a relativistic nonsense.

The problem with such interpretation is that Hui Shi, one of the major masters of *Ming Jia*, was not relativistic in his thought, but was quite enthusiastic about rational speculation, seeking after certainty of knowledge, one example of which we have seen earlier in this article. There is a further problem with Proposition (3): over 2,500 years ago, the Chinese believed that the Earth was flat, and Historian's research (Hou, 1957: 439) has found that it was some 700 years later that the spherical view of the Earth began to occur in historical record and it was around 1,600AD that the spherical theory began to gain the upper hand. There was no ground, linguistic or not, on which Hui Shi could have developed this theory.

My interpretation of these propositions is different: these are Hui Shi's metaphysical speculations on important philosophical issues. Proposition (1) inquires into the ontological status of the meaning of names. Let me add quotation marks to make this clear:

The "sky" is as "low" as the "earth"; "mountains" are as "high" as "lakes."

This is a question raised of the Chinese language, which has no morphological features and the parts of speech of the names (in Chinese characters) cannot be distinguished by the form. In (1), for instance, the adjectives have the same form as the nouns. They are all names! Hui Shi has noticed this feature of the Chinese language and has set about to inquire into the nature of the meaning of names: If we use names to refer to things, what do adjectives refer to? It is acceptable to say "*sky*" refers to sky and "*earth*" refers to earth, and so on; we can empirically establish at least the ontological status of the referent of these names. But when we use "*low*" to refer to lowness or "*high*" highness, what are the referents of these names, and if they do have referents, what is the ontological essence of them? These are undoubtedly important philosophical questions because ontology question exactly is "What is there."

Proposition (2) asks a different question, that of the meaning of existence itself. This question is raised because of the syntactic features of the Chinese language, in which there is no declension of tenses and aspects of verbs. All statements about events and states, no matter past, present or future, are represented linguistically by the same unchanging verb form. When we say "what is" in Chinese, we might well be talking about "what was" or "what will be," unless we add other complementary names of time, such as "*yesterday*," "*today*" or "*tomorrow*." This feature might have pushed Hui Shi to the metaphysical speculation on the question of being, because he might have noticed the discrepancy between the timeless form of the verb in the statements about things and the empirical experiences of time about things in actuality.

Thus, (2) is not a proposition about what happens in actuality, but a reflection on the true meaning of existence itself. By "*leaving for the State of Yue today and arrived yesterday,*" Hui Shi was simply protruding the issue of time. His reasoning might have been this: a person has to be the same person and his being must not be time-relative, but an event is always a time sequence. Suppose a person left for Yue. At the time when we say "*he leave*" (past in Chinese), the event of his leaving already happened and should be a past event, though it just happened a brief moment ago. Then the person we talk about should be a "THAT person" in THAT past event and no longer be "THIS person" that our statement of "the person" refers to currently. There appears to be a discrepancy of the person in what actually happened and what we talk about currently. Our statement of "*he leave*" (past in Chinese) actually means that he left and not that he leaves. It seems that when we say a person is, we actually may mean he was instead of he is. What then is the true meaning of "is," because, in actuality, there is continuity in a person's identity. If we are focusing on the person's being, then, the time sequence should not be relevant. The person is the person, no more no less, and his identity of being should be unaffected by time.

In the eyes of non-Chinese speakers, there are problems with this claim, of course, because personal identity is established in virtue of continuity through time, so time cannot be irrelevant. But the peculiar syntax feature of the Chinese verb forced Hui Shi to raise a metaphysical question: "how can we prove that the person that was is the same as the person that is?" The person should always be a "this," whether he was at the time of leaving, or will be at the time of arriving. There is no historical record of how this puzzle is resolved, but if we understand (2) in this way, it does make some sense, though it appears to be logically problematic. I believe that what Hui Shi had in mind is that existence as such, the ontological being of things should be time transcendent. Because Chinese verbs have no tenses or aspects, Hui Shi had to use "leave today" and "arrive yesterday" in order to highlight the issue of time in relation to existence. This paradox therefore should not be comprehended in the framework of name-actuality relationship, but of a meta-linguistic reflection on the meaning of existence in relation to time, whose value it is to draw the attention to potential metaphysical issues involved in language use.

Proposition (3) is different from every other proposition of Hui Shi's, because there is a phrase of "*I know*" before the main clause of the sentence. If we put this statement as a proposition about certain fact in the world, it is certainly wrong. The key to the explanation lies with "*I know.*" I think Hui Shi was speculating on the question of the veracity of our knowledge claims. "*The center of the world is at …*" is different from "*I know the center of the world is at …*" We can say the former is false on the basis of whatever empirical or logical evidence we have. Its truth value is "false." But can we do the same with the latter statement? Certainly, with the same empirical or logical evidence, we can say that the speaker is wrong. But the problem is, a wrong belief is that speaker's belief, and it is always the speaker that is the subject of knowing. To generalize to our knowledge, it is always us who are saying we know and we regard what we say we know as true knowledge. As this proposition shows, what we say we know could be incorrect. Then what is the nature of knowledge and how can we have correct knowledge. "*Does 'I know' always give true statement?*" This might well be the question Hui Shi was concerned with.

In a word, Hui Shi was not proposing nonsense. But as a rational thinker, he was speculating on serious issues of what is and what is it that we know, through his critical examination of our use of language. This interpretation, I think, is more consistent with his other sayings and with the general ideological tendency of *Ming Jia*. As the two masters of *Ming Jia*, both Hui Shi and Gongsun Long were indeed engaged in the analysis of language meaning, and in doing so they raised metaphysical questions in and of language itself.

Next, let us look at some selected "sophistic" sayings of *Ming Jia* debaters and as with Hui Shi, I leave out the ones that are interpreted with our modern understanding of science and philosophy. I shall group these sophistic sayings into the following topics:

Group Ⅰ: the nature of names:
   1. *Dog may be sheep.*   2. *Puppy is not dog.*
   3. *Tortoise is longer than snake.*   4. *White dog is black.*

Group Ⅱ: "Have" and existence
   1. *Orphan colt has never had a mother.*   2. *Egg has hair.*
   3. *Horse has egg.*   4. *Ying State has the whole world.*

Group Ⅲ: metaphysical entities
   1. *Chicken has three feet.*   2. *Fire is not hot.*   3. *Eyes cannot see.*
   4. *T-square cannot make square; compass cannot make round-circle.*

Throughout history, these propositions have been taken as statements about what actually is in the world, assuming that the names in them refer to objective realities, which is the reason why they have been labeled "sophistic nonsense." With the understanding of *Ming Jia* ideas so far, however, I think we can now have a glimpse at what these "sophistic" sayings are really saying.

Group I : What is the nature of the meaning of names?

Group I aims at the speculation on the nature of names. If we add quotation marks to them, we can easily find that *Ming Jia* debaters hold the conventionalist view concerning names and things that they name. For instance: "*Dog*" *may be* "*sheep*"

63

or "*Puppy*" *is not* "*dog.*"

Conventionalist view is quite well-known in linguistics, that there is no natural connection between words and the things out there, and that we use a word to denote a thing completely on the basis of convention. To put it simply, a sound does not necessarily denote an object. The syllable [mæn] denotes man in English, but the same sound means "*slow*" or "*slow down*" in Chinese, for instance. It is quite right for *Ming Jia* to say, the sound of "*dog*" does not necessarily denote dog, and it could denote sheep, if our ancestors had agreed upon using "*dog*" to call the thing that we now call "*sheep.*" A puppy is certainly a dog, only that it is young. If we had agreed to call sheep "*dog,*" why is "*puppy*" necessarily the name of a young dog?

But their speculation does not seem to stop here. They continue to ponder over the nature of these names. By convention, we use such and such names to refer to such and such things, but since we have to set up our conventions, there must be something that we need to fall back on in making the names. That something must be the product of our cognition or thought about what defines the thing we give a name to. Since we have to use names to talk about things, hence obtaining knowledge from it, then there should be no confusion or contradiction in our giving the name, i.e. in our thought about the essence of thing we name. However, as our ordinary language use shows, such confusions do occur, which is an indication that something must be problematic in need of clarification.

Take I.3 for example. Some scholars have pointed out that this simply says that a tortoise lives longer than a snake does, while a snake is longer in form than a tortoise (Chen, 1983). But if this is a good interpretation, then the proposition is not nonsense at all, but just common sense. There would have been no reason why it should be denounced as sophistic nonsense. To me, this interpretation is right, but only preliminarily. It has actually pointed out the two different "*longs*" without, unfortunately, pressing further for why is it that enables us to have the same name for these two different "*longs.*" It is this that *Ming Jia* was probably trying to invite attention to. That a tortoise lives long refers to temporal length, while that a snake is long refers to spatial length. They are totally different categories of length, named by the same term. What is the nature of the length of time and of the length in space? Is there a "*long*" being the long-in-itself (remember that in Chinese, adjectives are also names, no different in form from the names as nouns or verbs)? What is the essence of the long-in-itself? These questions do appear to be strange, but they are profound in thinking. They are concerned with existence of time and space and the essence of such existence. Even today, I do not think we can turn up with a satisfactory answer to these questions. It is not surprising for *Ming Jia* to raise these apparently strange and practically useless questions, because they are reflecting on issues of philosophy through analyzing the meaning of names.

Issues of similar kind can also be found in I.4. To understand it, let me cite Gongsun Long's argument for his proposition of *"white-horse not horse"* (*On White-Horse*). To adhere to his principle for establishing the true meaning of names, namely "the 'thisness' in 'this' and 'thatness' in 'that,' " Gongsun Long argued that *"white"* is a name that names a color, while *"horse"* is one that names a shape; one cannot confuse their categories; and since a thing can have only one essence, he could not accept that *"white-horse"* has two different categories of essence, one of color and the other shape, in the same name, though this name is a compound. This is why Gongsun Long suggested that *"white-horse"* is an independent category which has its essence different from either whiteness or horseness.

Speculating in similar fashion, the *Ming Jia* debaters argued that *"dog"* is the name that names shape or form, while *"white"* and *"black"* are the names that name color. The name that names shape certainly cannot name color, nor vice versa; but a name that names color certainly names color. Since there is no formal distinction between adjectives and nouns in Chinese, then as names, they both appear to name things of the same nature, i.e., things that exist out there. If *"dog"* is a name that names the shape of a dog or dogs, then *"white, black"* should be names that name color. Problems arise, because dogs do have features in common but colors can be totally different, such as the sharp contrast of black and white. If we say *"white is color"* and *"black is color,"* can we logically say *"White dog is black?"* This has actually raised an important question: what is the color of color itself? Or does *"color"* have a color? It is quite dismay for us to find that in natural world, there is no color at all. What we see are only red, white, black etc, but we can never see color. Such inquiries, if continued, will inevitably lead to metaphysical speculation on ontological issues concerning terms such as *"color."*

Group II: *"Have" or "not-have" is a question of to be or not to be.*

Group II propositions are structurally different from the other propositions of *Ming Jia*'s; they all have the verb *"have"* (III.1 has this form in English, but in original Chinese, it is actually: "chicken three foot"). Again they are nonsensical if one reads them in the framework of everyday language, and this is what many scholars have done in interpreting them, resulting in their keeping the label of "sophistic nonsense." However, they are serious speculations on the question of "being." The Chinese language does not have the copula *to be* at the time of *Ming Jia*, but it had the word *"have* [有, *yǒu*]" and this word is still used in modern Chinese to mean "in possession of" and more importantly "exist." The near equivalents to the concepts of *"being"* in the sense of *"existence"* and *"not being"* in the sense of *"non-existence, nothingness"* in European languages, are the antonym pair of *"have* [有, *yǒu*]" and *"not-have* [无, *wú*]" in the Chinese language. The Chinese sentence structure of *"X has Y"* may have two propositional meanings: 1) "X possesses

Y", and 2) "Y exists in X." The second propositional meaning of the structure is obviously of greater philosophical significance.

That the antonym pair of *yǒu* and *wú* has been used in Chinese philosophy for reflections on existence has been noted by quite a few philosophers. Wang H. Y. (1997: 222) says, "In the Chinese language, there is no purely formalized expressions like *be*, *to be* and *being*. ... Gongsun Long [*Ming Jia*] had to use the concepts available in Chinese, expressions like '*yǒu*,' '*wú*' and '*fei* [negative adverb]' to think over the question of existence, giving them top priority among all philosophical questions." Jiang Y. (2006) stated clearly: "The concept of '*yǒu*' in the theory of Chinese philosophy originates from '*wú*': whether in the thought of Confucianism or of Daoism, the concept of '*wú*' has been looked upon as the source from which everything is generated. ... All the '*yǒu*' have their origin in the '*wú*,' and the '*wú*' is the destination of '*yǒu*.' The concepts of '*yǒu*' and '*wú*' are the core categories in the traditional Chinese philosophy of ontology."

With this background, we can understand these propositions of *Ming Jia*'s more fruitfully. Proposition II.1, for instance, was interpreted as nonsense, because "*an orphan colt*" as a universal does mean a colt without a mother, yet in fact for any one particular colt, there must be a time when it had a mother; and therefore, we simply cannot say an orphan colt has never had a mother (Feng, 1994: 219). If *Ming Jia* were rationalist thinkers, it is unlikely that they would fail to see the point of logic that any orphan must have had a mother once. The problem with this interpretation is that it fails to see that *Ming Jia* were really reflecting on the verb "*to have*" rather than on nouns. Common sense has it that a colt cannot be called "*orphan colt*," when it has a mother and once it is called "*orphan*," surely it has no mother any more. But *Ming Jia* had detected a problem with the Chinese verb (tenseless in Chinese). Given the property of the verb "*have*," our ordinary sentences can be quite imprecise and even semantically contradictory. With no inflexions, the Chinese sentences for propositions of "*An orphan colt has a mother*" and "*An orphan colt had a mother*" can be identical in form, unless one adds adverbials to mark the past or the present; the same is true with "*An orphan colt has no mother*" and "*An orphan colt had no mother*." In both cases, the Chinese sentences may be "孤驹有母 (literally: Orphan colt have mother)" and "孤驹无母 (literally: Orphan colt not-have mother)," with the sole difference of "have [有]" and "not-have [无]." Given this language feature, whatever we say, using Chinese sentences like these, we may land ourselves in contradictions: when we say "*Orphan colt have mother*," we contradict ourselves, because we cannot call a colt "*orphan*" since it has a mother; yet when we agree then that "*Orphan colt not-have mother*," we face another trouble, because a colt must have a mother, or else it simply could not have been.

Given the Chinese language condition, it was not easy for *Ming Jia* to drive home to their audience their point of speculation by just using the above forms of sentences. They had to add some more elements of grammar in order to sharpen the question. And their use of the phrase "未尝有 (literally: 'never taste have'; meaning: 'have never had')" in II.1 presented their point of speculation clearly before the audience: does the name of "*orphan colt*" denote a univocal identity? The orphan colt, envisaged with a mother, refers to its past state of existence, while the orphan colt without a mother denotes a present state of existence. Is the colt in the present state the same as the colt in the past state? Does the name "*orphan colt*" refer to an eternal idea of its existence that transcends time, or to the existence of it as a process of becoming? If the Chinese language had the same verb inflexions as those in European languages, *Ming Jia* might as well be speculating on the question of "that which is *is*, and if it is *becoming*, it *is* not," befriending Parmenides. This is undoubtedly a question of ontological importance, a question, however, posed on the basis of the characters of the Chinese language. This interpretation makes the idea of II.1 consistent with Hui Shi's proposition, "*Leaving for the Yue State and arrived there yesterday.*" They are all questions concerning being as being, the being itself that transcends time.

The other 3 propositions in Group II have the same structure, but they ask somewhat different questions through another angle. Of course, it is common sense that eggs don't have hair; horses don't have (lay) eggs; and the *Ying* State doesn't contain the whole world. In terms of commonsense language, they are nonsensical. But these are propositions concerning the verb "*have*" that *Ming Jia* debaters used to think about questions of knowledge. If the meaning is what we categorize of the essence of things in actuality, then we do have ways to verify whether what we know and what we say are true or not; i.e. we can engage in verification of knowledge by empirical observations, because names stand for things and some of the things we name actually do exist. But when we use "无[*wú*, not-have; nothing]" to say of something, how are we go about verifying it, since the thing that we talk about simply does not exist? What then is the essence of *wú*, or nothing / non-existence? There is nothing, and we should have a name to name that nothingness! We can empirically and correctly master the meaning of "[*yǒu*]", how can we as correctly master the meaning of "[*wú*]"? Can what does not exist be known, thought about and talked about? These are also undoubtedly metaphysical questions, with an eye on the issue of what is. *Ming Jia* put forward those "strange" propositions in order to make their audience aware of the questions of the essence of existence or of non-existence.

Group III: the construction of Platonic universals.

Group III propositions are further confirmation that *Ming Jia* were not sophists at all, or at least not in the pejorative sense the term has been used, contradicting common sense for the sake of contradicting it, but they were serious philosophers. To *Ming Jia*, our true knowledge is the universal, rational abstraction of the essence of things.

Proposition III.1 is not only one of the *Ming Jia* debaters propositions, but also discussed by Gongsun Long in his *On Explaining Change*, which is convincing evidence that *Ming Jia* debaters were not talking nonsense. Again, remember the fact that the Chinese language does not have formal distinction of singular and plural and that there is no morphological inflexion of the noun to show whether a noun is concrete or abstract. The original goes:

谓鸡足一，数足二，故三。(Say chicken-foot one, count foot two, therefore three.)

Coming to the topic of "*A chicken has three feet*," Gongsun Long said: "We say a chicken has '*foot*,' and we count two feet of a chicken; this is why [I say] a chicken has three feet." In another place in the same essay, Gongsun Long reiterated the same idea: "A brown horse and a black ox make cattle; they count three."

Obviously, Gongsun Long and the *Ming Jia* debaters were saying that in addition to the two real feet that a chicken actually has, there is another "*foot*," which is the meaning of our name. In European languages, similar ideas can be expressed by forms such as "foot" and "footness,"[1] which is not the case in Chinese. As said before, both a concrete concept and an abstract concept about something are expressed by the same name form. This is the reason why *Ming Jia* debaters should have come up with such a counter-intuitive proposition: they had to make their sayings in this way in order to draw attention to what human language understanding of things really is. Concrete chicken feet cannot be permanent object of knowledge. The true knowledge that we have about "*chicken-foot*" is the rational abstraction of the universal property, or the essence, of chicken foot. This essence is what every chicken foot must have and what only chicken feet have. A thing without this essence cannot be named "*chicken-foot*." With this proposition, *Ming Jia* conveyed to others their philosophical idea that the meaning of the name of a thing is not the same as the thing in actuality. The true meaning of a name is the correct conceptualization of the essence of the things. Such conceptualization constitutes what we know about the things in the world. This point of theirs is important because it is concerned with what the nature of knowledge is.

---

[1] This language feature might have been conducive to Plato's construction of two worlds in his *Republic*, one of the Thing world and the other of the Form world, and to Aristotle's criticism on the "Third Man Argument" in his *Metaphysics*. Limited by space, I shall not talk about this issue here. The footnote is added to highlight the point I am making, that the Chinese philosophers had to come to the speculation on similar problems on the basis of their own language features.

The same metaphysical speculation is also what Ⅲ.2, Ⅲ.3 and Ⅲ.4 have in common. The concepts of *"fire"* and *"eye"* are not the fire and eye in the natural world. We use fire to cook and to get warmth and use eyes to see, but we cannot use *"fire"* to cook and to get warmth nor can we use *"eyes"* to see. As language meanings, they are what fire and eye in the natural world have in common, which we pin down with names. What we pin down must be the universal property of these things that exist out there. Once we pin them down, these universals are linguistic entities themselves, which differ in nature from the real entities out there. This is why we can say, *"fire"* is not hot, or *"eyes"* do not see. Similarly, we can use a T-square to draw a square figure, or compass to draw a round figure. This is common sense knowledge, whose truth can be verified with empirical rigidity. It has experiential necessity. Therefore, there is only one reasonable explanation as to why *Ming Jia* debaters ran counter to this common sense and proposed *"T-square cannot make square; compass cannot make round-circle"*: They were not talking about what we could or could not do with these drawing tools. Rather, they were concerned with conceptualized universals of *"square"* and *"roundness."* The speculation of *Ming Jia* should have been very clear: we can use a T-square to draw a specific figure of square or a compass to draw a specific round figure, yet we cannot use these tools to draw the definition of square or of roundness. The true Square should be the essence that all square shapes have and only square shapes have, and the true roundness should be the essence that all round circles have and only round circles have. Such essence constitutes the knowledge that we have and the true meaning of names of *"square"* and *"round."*

The explanation I have presented here about Group III propositions is not entirely my innovation, of course. Philosophers in modern China have already pointed out that with these propositions, *Ming Jia* philosophers were discussing conceptual universals, metaphysical entities that were idealistic in nature (Cf. Hou et al, 1957: 419). But my presentation is new in two senses. First, philosophers have not given an internally consistent explanation of the *Ming Jia* sayings to decode their philosophical ideas. This is why they admit that *Ming Jia* did have some philosophical inspirations on the one hand, but dismiss on the other hand many of their other sayings as nonsensical, or at best inexplicable. Second, philosophers have not tried to interpret *Ming Jia* propositions from the dimension of philosophy of language, from which we probably can better understand why *Ming Jia* were saying things as they did, hence their failure as endeavors to disclose the rationalist nature of *Ming Jia* philosophy. There does have one latest publication that lauds *Ming Jia* as rationalist philosophers of language, which is the main point made by Zhou C. Z. (2005) in his book, entitled *The Pre-Qin Inquiry into Names and Its Scientific Thoughts*. In this book, Zhou has attributed the title of "cognitive philosophy of language" to

Gongsun Long and addressed some of the "21 Paradoxes" of *Ming Jia* debaters in the light of scientific cognition, but he dismisses Hui Shi, a major *Ming Jia* master of thought, simply as the "nonessential" of the thought of philosophy of name and actuality. Thus Zhou's comment on *Ming Jia* is threatened by incompleteness and self-contradiction, which makes this article necessary.

4. Concluding Remarks

On the basis of the foregoing discussions, I have confidence to say that metaphysical speculation on ontology and epistemology as a mode of abstract philosophical thinking, is not language-specific. European languages, with their emphasis on syntax form, are conducive to such a philosophical rationalism, but it is equally possible for this rationalism to bud and grow on the soil of the classical Chinese language, a language that is meaning-centered.

The ideas of *Ming Jia* might have started the traditional Chinese philosophy on to the path of metaphysical speculation oriented towards truth seeking. An analytical speculation on the concepts of "*Dao*" and "*Ren*" in Chinese philosophy, pressing for what a "*Dao*" is and how can man know the truth of "*Dao*," might have given rise to a philosophical "what-ology," an ontology without the word "being," with the Chinese language characteristics. The classical language is no obstacle for the Chinese to speculate on what exists and what is true or false, in a manner no less speculative and rational than what western philosophers have done, only that the starting points might differ. The love of wisdom is universal.

References

Chan, W. T. 1973. *A Source Book in Chinese Philosophy*. New Jersey: Princeton University Press.

Chen, G. Y. 1983. *Interpretation and Modern Chinese Translation of Zhuangzi*. Beijing: China Books Press.

Feng, Y. L. 1994. *A History of Chinese Philosophy*. New Delhi: Motilal Banarsidass Publishers Limited.

Hansen, C. 1983. *Language and Logic in Ancient China*. Ann Arbor: The University of Michigan Press.

Hou, W. L., et al. 1957. *A General History of Chinese Thoughts*. Beijing: People's Press House.

Hu, Shi. 2000. *Outline of History of Chinese Philosophy*. Shanghai: Shanghai Classics Press House.

Li, D. 1998. *A Survey of the pre-Qin School of Names*. Changsha: Hunan University Press.

Liu, C. 2003. *Ming-Jia* (the Logicians) and Zeno: a comparative study. In B. Mou (ed.), *Comparative Approaches to Chinese Philosophy*. Burlington, VT: Ashgate Publishing Company.

Liu, Y. J. 1995. "A chicken has three feet" and pre-Qin School of Names. *Journal of Shanxi Normal University*, 7: 41-47.

Liu, Y. J. 2002. *A Preliminary Study on Ming Jia*. Taipei: Taiwan Chengyi Press.

Mou, Z. S. 1979. *Ming Jia and Xunzi*. Taipei: Taiwan Student Books Press.

Qian, G. L. 2002. *Pragmatics in Chinese Culture: Speechology in Humanistic Networks*. Beijing: Tsinghua University Press.

Song, J. 2002. *Being and the Tradition of Western Philosophy*. Baoding: Hebei University Press.

Sun, Z. Y. 1987. *History of Logic Thoughts in China*. Beijing: Renmin University Press.

Wang, H. Y. 1997. *Interpretation of Gongsun Long*. Xi'an: Sanqin Press House.

Wang, L. 2000. *Collection of Linguistics Essays of Wang Li*. Beijing: The Commercial Press.

Zhang, D. S. 1995. *Rationlity and Conscience*. Shanghai: Far-East Press.

Zhang, X. 1998. *Ming Jia of Ancient China*. Beijing: Religious Culture Press.

Zhou, C. Z. 2005. *The Pre-Qin Inquiry into Names and Its Scientific Thoughts*. Beijing: Science Press House.

通讯地址：610064 四川大学外国语学院英文系 <llmcc@scu.edu.cn>

先秦名家"诡辩"命题：通往理性主义的语言之途

刘利民

提　要：本文从语言哲学的角度对先秦名家的"诡辩"命题进行解读，认为这些命题并非传统上被指责的那样是诡辩，而是从语言分析的角度对于语言意义的本质进行的形而上学思辨。这些命题之所以被误解，很大程度上是由于古汉语的孤立语特征。而名家正是由这些特征所促动，而对语义问题、知识的确定性问题进行哲学反思的。

关键词：先秦名家　语言哲学　理性主义

解析语言逻辑哲学难题

重庆大学　黄斌

提　要：语言中含有三个层次，它们之间存在着重合、透明、转换等复杂的关系和机制。混淆这三个层次是西方语言逻辑哲学中产生许多难题和困惑的根源。只要我们懂得了语言层次之间的关系和机制，这些难题和困惑就不难分析和解决。

关键词：语言层次；重合；透明；转换

语言逻辑哲学，亦称语言哲学或分析哲学，是现代西方哲学的主要流派。但是中国在这方面的研究还比较薄弱，这严重地影响了中国哲学整体研究水平的提高。

另一方面，我们也不必妄自菲薄。西方哲学界固然率先认识到了语言逻辑分析对于哲学研究的重要性，但是由于受"拒绝形而上学"观念的影响，排斥逻辑和哲学研究的本体论立场，使得其理论和逻辑缺少正确的理论前提和根基，从而出现了许多难以解决的难题。而我们在正确的世界观和方法论指导下，完全可以后来居上。笔者运用辩证唯物论的基本观点，研究西方分析哲学多年，发现他们提出的一些难题其实都不难解决。以下就对这些问题进行一些简明的分析。

1. 语言分析的基础——语言层次理论

分析语言逻辑问题，关键是要有正确的方法。这个方法就是语言层次理论。辩证唯物论是形成正确的语言层次理论的方法论前提。根据唯物论的基本观点，我们可以发现语言中包含三个层次（或层面，layer），即语言的符号形式、语言的意义（或内涵）、语言的所指（或外延）。在这三个层次之间存在着重合、透明、转换等关系和机制，这又体现了辩证法的精神。

考虑以下语句：

（1）晨星在天空中闪烁。
（2）〈晨星〉的意思在英语中是"Morning Star"。
（3）《晨星》是两个汉字。
（传统的办法是用引号来区别语词的不同用法和层次，这里我改用尖括号来区别，以避免与引号的通常用法相混淆。）

在这三个语句中，"晨星"一词具有不同的用法和含义：在（1）中，它代表一个物质天体；在（2）中，它表达一种思想观念；在（3）中，它就显示自身的语言形式。

词的第一种用法称为外延用法或指称用法，一个词在这里是指示或代表它的外延或所指；

词的第二种用法称为内涵用法或观念用法，即一个词表达它的内涵或意义；

词的第三种用法称为形式用法或反身用法，即一个词在这里只表示它自身的语言符号形式。

把上面三个句子的顺序倒过来看，这三种用法显示出语词包含着三个层次：第一个层次是由一定的语言符号所组成的语言形式；第二个层次是由一定的语言形式所表达的意义；第三个层次是由一定的语言形式及其所表达的意义所指示的对象。

这三种用法体现了语言三个层次的重合与透明关系：

（1）中的"晨星"是外延用法，它重合了形式（符号）、内涵（观念）和外延（所指）三个层次，只不过前两个层次是透明的。晨星这个天体本身不可能出现在语言中，而只能用语词来代表。但是我们在这里使用"晨星"这个词的时候并不反省它，它的语词形式和观念形式对于我们是透明的，我们不注意它们，而透过它们去意谓或领悟到那个天体本身。词的外延用法通过它所处的语境显示出来，在天空闪烁的只能是天体本身，而不能是"晨星"的语词形式或它所表达的观念。

（2）中的"晨星"是内涵用法，它重合了意义和形式两个层次，其中形式层次是透明的。只有观念或概念，即一个词的意义才能够被翻译。意义或观念就是人们在不同的语言形式中所把握到的共同的东西。向外国人解释"晨星"这个汉语词的意义，只需指出相对应的外语词就行，而无需指出天上的晨星本身。

（3）中的"晨星"是形式用法，此时只剩下语言形式一个层次，它是不透明的，即只表示其语言形式本身。我们不透过它去看它的意义和所指。不知道《晨星》这个词的意义和所指，不妨碍我们了解其符号形式是汉字。

语言层次之所以能够重合，是因为这些层次在语言中具有相同的形式，即外延和内涵都通过同样的语言形式来表达，其层次区别是通过思维的反省才区分出来的。语言和观念具有透明性，我们才能透过一个层次去看到另一个层次。

上述例句是对西方分析哲学中常用例句的改造。弗雷格就是通过对类似例句的分析，得出语词的涵义和指称这两个层次的区别，他指出"暮星和晨星的指称虽然是同一个星辰，但这两个名称具有不同的涵义"（1998：2）。其他逻辑学家也曾区分了语言的形式和涵义。但是，他们都没有同时指出语言的这三个层次，更不懂得这三个层次之间重合、透明和转换的关系。

语词的层次在语句里得到显示和表达。语句又有其本身的层次，如以下三个语句：

（1）'雪是白的。
（2）'〈雪是白的〉是真的。
（3）'《雪是白的》是中文的。

（1）'中的"雪是白的"是外延语句，它代表客观事实，我们不怀疑它的真假，也不注意它的语言形式。（2）'中的〈雪是白的〉是内涵语句，即语句所表达的意义或思想，通常称为命题。只有命题即思想才有真假。客观事实没有真假，语言形式也没有真假。断言"雪是白的"是真的，即表明我们已把"雪是白的"反省为有可能假，因而其真则是需要判断的思想。（3）'中的《雪是白的》是形式语句或语句形式，此时我们不注意它的意义，也不注意它代表什么客观事实，而只注意它的语言符号形式。

语句的三个层次同样也存在着迭合与透明的关系：语词的层次在语句里得到表达或显示，简单语句的层次在复合语句里得到表达或显示，复合语句的层次又在更复杂的复合语句里得到表达或显示。顺便指出，笔者提出的语言层次论与西方哲学家为解决语义悖论而提出的语言层次论或类型论有根本的不同，后者应当称为语言的阶，是指语言研究中工具语言（或所谓元语言）和对象语言的区分。语言层次和语言阶既有区别又有联系。西方哲学家们总是把这两个不同的范畴混淆在一起。

掌握了以上的基本观点，我们就可以分析西方哲学和逻辑研究中出现的许多难题。

2. 名称

什么是名称？名称是否具有意义？名称的意义是什么？这些问题使许多著名哲学家如罗素、弗雷格、克里普克等感到困惑。关于名称的争论可以归纳为两个主要问题：一个是什么样的表达式可以称为一个名称，即衡量一个表达式是否能成为名称的标准问题；另一个是名称有无意义的问题。

一派是以弗雷格、罗素和维特根斯坦等人为代表的传统的"摹状词论"（这里忽略他们之间意见的差别），认为所有的名字都既有内涵又有外延，它们等值于或同义于一个或一些描述其所指对象的特性的限定摹状词。比如"亚里士多德"这个名字就等值或同义于"柏拉图的学生"、"亚历山大大帝的老师"、"《形而上学》的作者"等等一簇限定摹状词，这些摹状词所描述的属性，既是这个名字的意义，又是确定它的指称的方式，确定"亚里士多德"的指称也就是寻找那个具有这些属性的人。罗素甚至认为名字的意义就是其指称。

另一派源自近代英国哲学家穆勒的观点，到了现代则以美国哲学家克里普克和普特兰等人为代表。穆勒认为通名既有外延又有内涵，但是专名只有外延，没有内涵。克里普克则不仅认为专名只有指称，没有意义，而且认为通名，至少自然事物的名称，也没有意义即内涵，只有指称即外延。他提出了历史的、因果的命名理论来解释名字与它们的指称之间的关系。

这两派观点都既有其合理因素，又都有其错误之处。他们的错误都是由于混淆了不同的语言逻辑层次。一般来说，一个名称是指称（指示、代表）一个对象的语言符号。语言是一种形式符号系统，不可能容纳客观物质对象本身，只能使用符号来代表其所指的对象。如说"雪是白的"，我不可能在这篇文章里放上一把真正的雪，只能用名称"雪"来代表。名称有两种：通名和专名。通名即通常所说的概念，它们具有内涵和外延两个方面。我们也可以说它们具有内涵意义和外延意义。内涵意义是这个名称对所指对象所描述的本质属性或特有属性的反映，外延意义是对这个名称的外延亦即所指对象**整体**的反映。注意，概念的外延本身并不是意义，而是概念所指的客观对象的集合，但是我们对于这个外延的反映或知识，则是概念的外延意义。例如，"金属"这个概念的内涵可以是"一类具有光泽、可延展性、导电性等属性的矿物质"，它的外延则包括金、银、铜、铁等等。这些金属本身当然不是概念的意义，而是客观世界中的事物。但是，只要我们知道它们属于"金属"这个概念的外延，这种知识就成为"金属"这个概念的外延意义了。

其实严格地说，概念的内涵意义也不是概念所指事物的属性本身，而是对属性的反映。事物的属性也是客观的，存在于客观事物之中的。但是属性不可能独立存在于客观世界，所以，当我们单独地说"光泽、可延展性、导电性"等属性时，已经是一种思维的抽象，所以被直接当作概念的内涵意义，而不至于与事物的客观属性相混淆。但是，概念的外延与外延意义却常常被混淆。例如，罗素就把名称的指称当作其意义，从而产生了他的所谓三大难题之一，成为他否认弗雷格的涵义和指称的区分的理由（1998：67）。

专名与通名有所不同。专名的语言形式不必具有内涵意义。即使一个专名的语言形式具有字面上的意义，但这个意义与它指称的对象可以没有任何关系。如一个弱智人可以取名"天才"，一个丑女可能取名"美丽"，等等。有些名字本来具有描述其所指对象的属性或特征的意义，但是随着时间的推移，这些名字本来的意义失去了与其所指对象的联系，却仍然可以用来指称这些对象。如日本人姓名中的"松下"、"山口"、"田中"等，最早是根据其居住地的特点而来，但后来都失去其意义了，不能作为确定其所指何人的根据。总之，名字的字面意义可以不影响其指称功能。在这个意义上，我们可以说专名只有所指而没有意义。

但确切地说，专名没有内涵意义而可有外延意义，因为专名可以从它的所指中获得意义。例如，在句子"亚里士多德是古代世界的黑格尔"中，名字"黑格尔"被作为谓语使用，它具有"伟大的哲学家"之类的涵义。否则，这个句子就没有意义了。事实上，我们不可能谈论一个名字的所指而没有对于该所指的**了解**或**认识**。当我们知道、**想到**和**谈论**一个名字的所指的时候，这个名字就具有了存在于我们心中的某种意义。这就是为什么通常只有外延或指称用法的专名可以被作为谓语使用的原因。

另一方面，描述事物属性的内涵性形容词、摹状词组等，也可以被外延性地使用为名称或指称词组而作为句子的主语，好像它们也在现实世界中具有所指一样，如"金山"、"飞马"等。这是产生所谓"柏拉图主义"，即把观念的创造物客观化，当成客观事物的原因。摹状词可以作为名字使用，它的意义可以帮助、指导我们去寻找它的所指，也可以误导我们去错误地选择其所指，它的内涵意义和指称功能可能相互冲突。所以，克里普克指出摹状词不能是"固定指称词"，这是对的。然而，他进一步认为，名称作为指称词不能有任何意义，这就有问题了。下面我们着重分析一下他的观点。

克里普克认为："弗雷格在两种意思上使用'内涵'一词，应对这种做法进行批评。因为他既把一个指示词的内涵看作就是它的意义；又把内涵看作确定其指称的方式。他把这两者相等同，以为它们都是由限定摹状词给出的。我坚决反对第二种假定；最终也反对第一种假定"（1998：60）。

这就是说，克里普克首先反对把内涵看作确定一个名字的指称的方式，最终也反对把内涵看作一个名字的意义。他认为：专名都是固定指称词，它们只有指称，没有意义。"亚里士多德"不能被理解为"柏拉图的学生"等摹状词，因为即使亚里士多德没有那些事迹或属性，我们仍然必须固定地用"亚里士多德"这个名字来称呼他。内涵不是一个名字的意义，因为内涵不过是一些偶然的属性，和所指对象没有固定的、必然的联系，因此不能作为确定名字的指称的根据。一个对象和它的名字的固定联系，只有历史的、因果的传递链条才能决定。亚里士多德的父母把他们的儿子命名为"亚里士多德"，那些认识亚里士多德的人就用这个名字来称呼他，并把这个名字逐步传播开去，"亚里士多德"这个名字就是通过这条看不见的链条与它的指称对象联系起来。所有名词的指称都是由这种历史、因果的传递链条决定的。

克里普克的观点中包含几点合理因素：首先，专名不描述其所指对象的属性或呈现方式。专名通常是没有意义结构的简单符号，它们的形式与其所指对象的结构或属性没有什么关系。如"亚里士多德"这个名字在中文里由五个没有意义联系的汉字组成，并不构成一个有意义的语言单位。其次，即使一个专名本来有描述对象属性的字面上的意义，这个意义也与它的指称对象没有必然的、固定的联系，不能作为确定其指称的根据。没有任何一个或有限的一簇摹状词能绝对地确定一个专名的指称。第三，就专名的命名和流传来说，历史的因果的传递链条的观点也是合理的。一个名字和它的指称对象的联系，确实是由一个客观的、不以我们的意志和认识为转移的命名和传递过程传给我们的。

然而，克里普克观点中的合理因素，却未必能否定专名可以具有意义。关键就在于他是仅仅从内容（对象的属性或呈现方式）而不是从形式上去理解"意义"这个范畴的，没有抓住"意义"作为观念的本质。他不懂得语言和思维的透明性，不懂得外延意义及其向内涵意义的转化。意义不等于就是对于对象的属性或呈现方式的反映，而也可以是对于名称的所指的整体**反映**。一个专名在它的所指不再存在的时候，也仍然可以具有意义。一个人死去了，他的名字仍然对那些知道其所指的人具有意义。我们可以说该名字的所指死去了，而不能说它的意义也死了。克里普克混淆了客观的指称对象本身和我们对于指称的反映，混淆了外延和外延意义。

意义和指称的区别本来是思维和存在、反映和被反映者的区别。但这种区别反映在思维和语言里，又只是思维和语言内部可以透明的层次区别。我们只有透过名字的形式和意义，才能看到它的所指。但是语言的透明性却常常使我们忘记这一点，以为我们不是通过思维和语言，而是直接涉及了客观对象。其实，那透过我们的思维和语言的客观事物，已不是那客观的对象本身，而只是对象的映象或影象，它是属于思维而不属于存在，因此它也不再是名字的所指而成为名字的意义了。

罗素主张一个表达式的意义就是其指称，这种迷误也有其天才之处，他隐约猜测到了意义对于指称的透明性。正是这种透明性使他产生了幻觉，以为意义和指称并没有区别。而正确的说法应该是，名字的意义不是其所指，而是对其所指的**反映**。克里普克表面看来和罗素正好相反，认为专名没有意义，只有所指，即认为意义和所指根本不同。其实他的错误和罗素是同出一源，都是没有弄清意义和指称之间的层次和透明关系，没有看到指称向意义的转化，即"指称"的二重化。他们都没有能区分开作为客观对象的真实指称和那已透过认识而成为思维内容即意义的"指称"，他们把两者混为一谈，而又各强调一个片面，罗素实际上讲的是思维对指称对象的反映是意义，而克里普克则强调客观的指称对象本身不是意义。

为了区分上述情况，有必要引入语言阶的概念。语言阶的区分即是西方语言哲学中所讲的对象语言和元语言的区分，它不同于我所讲的语言层次的区分，而是区分语言层次的工具基础。根据语言阶的观点：从一阶语言的立场看，名字的所指不是意义，而是客观对象；站在二阶语言的立场上看，名字的所指也被反省成了名字的意义。换言之，一阶语言把语言区别为符号、意义和在语言之外的指称，二阶语言则把它们又统一反省为语言中的三个层次。罗素不自觉地站在了二阶语言的高度，把指称反省成了意义，克里普克不自觉地坚持一阶语言的立场，认为指称不是意义。他们都混淆了不同的语言阶，从而也混淆了不同的语言层次。

3. 同一性陈述

维特根斯坦说："对于两个东西，说它们是同一的，乃是一个无意义的话；对于一个东西，说其是与自己是同一的，等于什么也没说。"所以，"同一性不是对象间的一种关系，这是显然的"（1998）。那么，同一到底是什么样的关系？同一性存在于什么东西之间？这个问题使许多西方哲学家感到困惑。理解同一性陈述是解决许多语言逻辑问题的关键。弗雷格从讨论这个问题出发，区分了语言表达式的意义和所指。罗素把这个问题列为他的三大难题之一。它也是分析哲学中遇到的最大难题之一即所谓"分析悖论"的根源。我们来分析一下这个"分析悖论"：

日本哲学家永井成男把这个悖论定式化为："如果表明被分析项的语言表达跟与表明分析项的语言表达具有相同意义（same meaning），那么由于这种分析只讲述了相同问题而乏味无聊；另外，如果两种语言表达不讲述相同意义，那么这个分析就不正确"（1992）。例如：

（3）"兄弟"的概念跟"男性同胞"的概念是同一的。
（4）"兄弟"的概念跟"兄弟"的概念是同一的。

这两个语句中，（3）是对"兄弟"这个概念进行分析的语句，（4）是乏味无聊的同语反复。但是如果（3）是真的，即"兄弟"和"男性同胞"的意义相同，它们能够相互置换而不改变语句的意义，那么（3）就变成（4）这样乏味的同语反复了。反之，如果"兄弟"和"男性同胞"的意义不同，（3）当然不会成为无意义的同语反复，但却成为假的、不正确的分析了（永井成男，1992: 163-164）。显而易见，这个所谓"分析悖论"实际上是同一性陈述问题的翻版。卡尔纳普以区分"内涵"和"内涵结构"来解决这个"悖论"，永井成男则以区分语义学悖论与哲学悖论，区分语义学、语形学与语用学来解决这个悖论，但都未得要领，解释不清这个"悖论"。

其实，懂得了关于语言层次的理论，同一性陈述问题就变得十分简单了。同一性陈述表达的是一种三项关系。两个东西不可能同一，一个东西毋须断定其同一。因此，那被断定为同一的东西既不是两个东西，也不是一个东西，或者说，既是两个东西，又是一个东西：它是两个东西关于一个东西的同一。要解决两个东西同时又是一个东西的矛盾，就要看到思维和语言的层次，认识到所谓的同一其实是说，那在思维和语言的某一个层次里是分开的东西，在思维和语言的另一个层次里又合在一起。同一就是在某一个思维和语言层次里的不同的东西，在另一个思维和语言层次里是同一个东西。简言之，同一是跨思维和语言层次的立体关系。平面的理解，把同一性陈述理解为例如：

晨星=暮星；或〈晨星〉=〈暮星〉；或《晨星》=《暮星》；

这些都是错误的。第一种等于是说两个事物又是同一个事物，这是荒谬的。第二种把同一理解为两个观念的同一，这也显然是错误的。"早晨的星"和"晚上的星"是两个不同的观念。第三种把同一理解为两个符号形式的同一，显而易见也是错误的。"晨"字和"暮"字是不同的汉字。这类平面的理解是引起哲学家们发生困惑的原因。只有从立体的语言层次的观点去看，同一性陈述才可得到全面、正确的解释。

语言有不同层次，所以有几种不同情况的同一性陈述：

a. 异形异义同指

即被断定为同一的语词的形式不同、意义（内涵）也不同，而所指（外延）相同，可图示如下（在文章中，我们只能用一些图形符号来代表外延或所指，而语词的意义和形式的区别则用单层尖括号和双层尖括号来区别）：

☆　　　　　　　（所指、外延）
〈晨星〉＝〈暮星〉　　（意义、内涵）
‖
《晨星》＝《暮星》　　（名称、形式）

"晨星"和"暮星"这两个词的形式不同，意义也不同，但它们指同一个天体，即金星。这是最常见的同一性陈述。弗雷格从分析这个例子得出了语词的意义和所指的区别。

但是西方分析哲学家通常只是指出两个词的所指相同而意义不同，忽略了它们形式上也不同。他们把两个词形式上的不同看作不言而喻的。这种分析既是不全面的，也隐藏着发生错误的危险。

可以看出,"晨星就是暮星"既可看成是名称关于所指的同一,也可看成是内涵关于外延的同一。所谓同一,就是在一个层次里是不同符号或不同概念的东西,在另一个层次里是同一个概念或同一个对象,或说在一个层次里不同的东西投影、透明在另一层次里的同一对象里。

b. 异形同义同指
即语词的形式不同而内涵、外延都相同。此即通常的同义词。可图示为:

```
    iiiiiiii              (外延)
       ‖
   〈单身男人〉           (意义、内涵)
       ‖
《单身汉》=《未结婚的男人》(名称、语言形式)
```

注意:同义词之间仍然有修辞色彩上的差别,其内涵相同只是大致的,并不是在任何语境中都可以互换使用的。

c. 异形同指
这种情况是说,不同形式的名称直接指示同样的对象,而缺少了内涵这个中间层次:

```
     ♀         (鲁迅本人,所指)
     ‖
    "♀"       (对鲁迅的印象,外延意义)
     ‖
《鲁迅》=《周树人》(名字,符号形式)
```

注意:在名称直接指称对象的情况下,我们不知道对象的属性,即名字不具有内涵意义。但是我们知道这个名字指称谁,这同样是一种意义,即外延意义。这时内涵意义只是暂时空缺,随着我们逐步认识到所指对象的特有属性或本质属性,我们可以把这些认识填入意义这个中间层次。这时,外延意义就转化为内涵意义。比较:

```
     ♀         (鲁迅本人,所指)
     ‖
"祝福"的作者 (对鲁迅的属性的反映,内涵意义)
     ‖
  《鲁迅》    (名字,符号形式)
```

总之,理解同一性陈述,要看到它是一种跨层次的、立体的关系。通常表现同一律的公式A = A,其实是引人误解的。因为它要么是毫无内容,要么是不合逻辑。这就是维特根斯坦说的,说一个东西与自身同一,等于什么也没有说。说鲁迅就是鲁迅,不能增加我们对鲁迅的知识。说两个东西同一,则是自相矛盾。即

79

使是双胞胎，也是两个不同的个体。A = A 不能理解为两边的A是同一个A，两个A至少占据不同位置，并不是同一个符号。A = A 其实说的是，形式相同的符号的**不同出现**总是代表同样的**对象**或**概念**，即也是一种跨层次的关系。

4. "存在"

"存在"这个词的功能是什么？它可以是一个谓词吗？如果它是一个谓词，它把什么样的属性归属给主词？通常的主谓语句的功能，是通过谓词把一定的属性归属给主词所代表的事物。如"雪是白的"，就把白色这个属性归属给雪这个事物。但是，"某物存在"，却没有把任何属性归属给主词。此外，在关于"某物"存在或不存在的判断中，被断定的主词又是什么？如果它是一个已经存在的事物，说"某物存在"岂非同语反复？说"某物不存在"岂不是自相矛盾？反之，如果某物并不存在，它又如何能作为判断的主词？这些问题如果从巴门尼德算起，困扰了哲学家们几千年，即使从康德算起，也困扰了哲学家们几百年。

有了语言层次理论，这些问题并不难解决。"存在"并不是普通的谓词，它并不把普通的属性归属给主词所指称的事物，而是改变主词的语言逻辑层次，它是概念或名称的层次转换联结词。当我们说"某物存在"时，我们把一个形式上的名称转变为一个真实的名称，它可以被外延性地使用来指称现实世界中的真实事物。当我们说"某物不存在时"，则是指出"某物"是一个假名称，它只可用来指称观念世界（神话、小说等）里的虚构事物，或者只是一个无意义的、不指称任何事物的符号。用公式来表示：

"X"存在，当且仅当，"X"指称现实世界中的事物。

或者：

"X"存在，当且仅当，在现实世界中有事物被"X"所指称。

例如：

"飞马"存在，当且仅当，在现实世界中有飞马。

假如"飞马"不存在，那么它只是人心中的观念，在现实世界中不存在可以被"飞马"指称的对象。

这里有两种不同的情况：一种是对通名即概念的断定，一种是对专名的断定。断定一个通名的所指不存在，则它只是人心中的观念，还可有一定的意义；断定一个专名的所指不存在，则它只是无意义的符号。

但是问题还不能这么简单地解决。美国哲学家奎因反驳说（1987：2），当人们否认"飞马"存在的时候，并不是在否认一个观念或精神对象的存在，亦即"存在"并不是断定观念或精神对象的谓词。

奎因的疑难并不难回答。"存在"并不是普通谓词，而是层次转换联结词。当我们断定"某物"存在或不存在的时候，我们当然并不是肯定或否定一个观念或精神对象在人们心中的"存在"，而只是断定这个观念或精神对象是否与现实世界中的真实对象相对应。"存在"或"不存在"具有双重功能：首先，它把主词反省为一个名称或概念，然后断定它在现实世界中是否有对应的所指对象。换句话说，是断定这个名称或观念是否对语言的外延层次透明，它是否可以有外延用法。如果断定了"飞马"存在，那么，说"我买了一匹飞马"，或"我骑过飞马"，都可以是真实的；而如果断定了"飞马"并不存在，那么我们可以断定上述语句都是假话，只有"我梦见了飞马"或"我在神话里读到过飞马"才有可能是真的。

类似地，我们可以断定一个语言或符号形式是否具有意义。我们可以说"'匹加索斯'的意思是飞马"或者说"'匹加索斯'没有意义"。此时"有意义"或"没有意义"的作用与"存在"或"不存在"的作用是相似的，是用来断定一个符号是否具有意义，是一个概念或只是无意义的符号组合。这是在形式层次和内涵层次之间的转换。

5. "真"与"假"

"真"或"假"的作用与"存在"和"不存在"的作用相似，也是语言层次的转换联结词，但不是用于语词，而是用于语句。当我们说"'雪是白的'是真的"，我们就是把内涵语句即命题"雪是白的"变成一个代表现实世界里的事实或事态的外延语句。"……是真的"起着双重作用：首先，它把"雪是白的"反省成一个内涵语句即命题，因为只有命题才有真假，事实或语句形式都没有真假；其次，它把这个内涵语句转换成一个外延语句，或者说，它使这个内涵语句与一个外延语句重合、透明。换句话说，如果一个内涵语句是真的，那么它就对外延世界或客观世界透明。

反之，当我们说"语句P是假的"，我们就是说语句P只是一个内涵语句，只能具有内涵用法，亦即只能表达我们的思想或观念，而不能用来描述客观世界中的事实或事态。

所以"真"是非常重要的逻辑谓词，不能被看作普通谓词，更不能被看作是"多余的"。

这里我们顺便评论一下著名波兰逻辑学家塔斯基关于"真"的定义的公式。塔斯基认为：

"雪是白的"是真的，当且仅当，雪是白的。

右边的"雪是白的"（不带引号）是语句，而在左边的带引号的同样的语句是这个语句的名称。这是一个明显的错误。其实，在右边不带引号的"雪是白的"应当是代表客观事实或事态。因为如果它是一个语句，那么它可以有真假，但是我们能够表达成"雪是白的是真的"吗？显然，这样的语句形式是错误的。塔斯基认为这是由于语言的"被使用"和"被提及"的区别所致。但是他没有懂得这种区分的实质。语句的"被使用"其实是它的外延用法——语句被透明地用来代表客观事实，所以没有真假，不能被反省为语句。语句的"被提及"才是它被反省为语句或命题，才有真假之分。

当然，当我说"雪是白的"的时候，我不可能从我的嘴里吐出一个事实来，语言作为形式系统不可能容纳客观事物或事实。"雪是白的"在这里只能具有语句的形式，但是这个语句在这里是外延性地、透明地使用的，不能反省为语句。

这样，在左边带引号的"雪是白的"就不是什么语句的名称，而是内涵语句亦即命题。当然我们也可以用一个名称来代表一个语句，但这不是必要的。在语言中我们必须用名称来代表或指称客观事物，但是我们没有必要用一个名称来代表语句或命题，因为它们本身就在语言中，或已经通过语言表达出来。使得塔斯基发生错误的原因是，他已经把右边的"雪是白的"反省为语句，所以他必须把左边带引号的同样语句反省为语句的名称。但是他忽略了，名称和语句具有不同的性质。语句必须具有意义，所以必然具有内容结构。但是名称只是代表一个对象的符号，不必具有意义和结构。所以，塔斯基的（T）公式

X是真的，当且仅当P。

其形式是明显错误的。

"雪是白的"是真的，当且仅当，雪是白的。

其形式应当是

"P"是真的，当且仅当P。

两边的语句 P 具有相同的语句结构形式，它们之间的区别只是层次的区别：加引号的"P"是内涵语句，即表达命题（思想、观念），而不加引号的 P 则是外延语句，表达客观事实。但是它们的观念内容是完全相同的，在同一种语言中具有相同的表达形式。"是真的"起着转换层次的作用，使得不同层次的语句能够通约。两边语句的等值实际上表示的是不同层次语句的重合、透明。塔斯基（T）公式误解了语句等值的性质，用不同的符号来代表内容相同而只是层次不同的语句，消除了它们之间的形式相似性。而为了定义语句的真值条件，他又不得不通过构造所谓"结构摹状名称"来恢复两个语句的形式相似，这完全是不必要的弯路。"结构摹状名称"是一个错误的观念。名称只是指称或代表一个对象的符号，它不需要具有描述其所指对象结构的功能。塔斯基在构造语句真值条件的形式化定义上做出了重要的贡献，但是如果他能正确地理解语句等值的性质，可以在研究中减少许多麻烦和弯路。

这里对西方关于"真"的理解中的所谓"紧缩主义"（deflationism）作点评论。紧缩主义是对"真"的概念的理解中的一种倾向，而不是一种单一的观点，包括"多余论"（Redundancy thesis）、"去引号论"（Disquotational thesis）、"赞同论"（Endorsement thesis）、"概括论"（Generalization thesis）等几种观点，他们认为"真"作为谓词的作用无非或者是去引号，或者是表示赞同，或者是进行概括，总之是无足轻重，是"多余"的，所以要"紧缩"，减少其使用（参见 Anil Gupta, 2000）。

这类观点的肤浅显而易见，其共同特点是否定"真"作为谓词的实质意义，认为"真"不过是一种无足轻重的形式工具。"真"作为谓词，其作用当然会有各种形式上的表现，但是这些形式上的表现都没有说明"真"作为谓词的实质意义。从哲学上说，"真"是表现了从表达主观思想的命题向表达客观事实的命题

的转换；从逻辑上说，则是表现了语言逻辑层次的转换。普通语法都假定了不加引号的语句是表示客观事实，而加上引号进行真值断定，则表现我们已经把它反省为思维中的命题（客观事实没有真假，命题才有真假）。所以断定"'雪是白的'是真的"，必须把"雪是白的"加上引号，以与通常的外延用法相区别。"真"作为谓词具有加引号和去引号的双重作用：加引号表示把外延语句反省为内涵语句；去引号则（由于它是真的）把它还原为外延语句。"真"所以具有去引号的作用，是因为我们的日常语法假定了不加引号的语句都是表达客观事实，真语句都对客观事实透明。

""'雪是白的'是真的"是真的"是真的……

都可以还原到第一个"'雪是白的'是真的"。在这个意义上，后面的"是真的"都是"多余"的，可以被"紧缩"掉。这是因为第一个"是真的"已经把"雪是白的"反省为内涵语句即命题了，后面的"是真的"不过是重复这种反省。但是第一个"是真的"却不是多余的，如果去掉它，不带引号的"雪是白的"就是一个代表客观事实的外延语句，而不是一个其真值需要断定的内涵语句（命题）了。

6. 语义悖论

综合运用前述的观点，我们可以找到分析长期困扰人类思维的语义悖论的思路。以"贝利悖论"为例，这个"悖论"是说，我们可以为每一个数都取一个名称，用一定数量的字（或字母）构成的名称数量是有限的，而数目是无限的，因此必然存在用少于一定数量的字构成的名字不能指称的数。"用少于100个汉字构成的名字不能指称的最小数"这个名称少于 100 个汉字（只有23个汉字），但是它却似乎指称了那个数，这就构成一个"悖论"。

这显然是混淆了名字和摹状词，混淆了"指称"和"描述"这两种不同的功能，混淆了不同的语言层次。"用少于100个汉字构成的名字不能指称的最小数"并不是名字而是一个摹状词，它不是直接指称（代表）一个数而是描述其指称形式。我们可以把它当作一个名称去指称那个数，此时其作为摹状词所包含的意义就完全丧失，不与其指称功能发生冲突，不形成什么悖论。

这个悖论严格一点的形式是："具有用少于100个符号构成的专有名称的数"，其数量必然不大于用100个符号构成的名称的数量。换句话说，用少于100个符号的排列组合构成的专有名称的数量是有限的，而数目是无限多的，所以必然存在不能用这有限数量的名称来指称的数。现在考虑词组"不能用少于100个符号构成的专有名称来指称的最小数"，它只用了25个符号（汉字），而且假定这25个汉字属于我们选取的100个基本符号的范围，但它似乎指称那个数！这岂不是悖论？

这还是混淆了"指称"和"描述"这两种不同的功能，混淆了不同的语言层次。"不能用少于100个符号构成的专有名称来指称的最小数"是摹状词即描述性词组，具有内涵意义，而名称应当是起指称作用的简单符号，代表其指称对象，不具有内涵意义。所以，如果它是一个名称，因为它属于"用少于100个符号构成的专有名称"的数量范围，因此已经被使用来指称能被这个数量范围的名称指称的某个数目，而不再能指称超出这个范围的数目（即"不能用少于100个符号构成的专有名称来指称的数"），但是它的意义仍然可以描述超出那个范围的数目，这个意义与它的实际指称作用无关。这根本不是什么悖论。

我们可以把这个"悖论"简化成，"一个不能用任何名称来指称的对象"，它是否可以作为一个名称来指称某个对象？可以。这是否构成悖论？并不。因为作为名称，原词组的内涵意义完全无关紧要，完全可以被忽略掉。北京大学有个"未名湖"，"未名"就成了它的名，我们用这名称去指称那个湖，并不会产生歧义，也不认为有什么矛盾。关键就在于，指称和描述两者属于不同的语言层次，前者代表客观事物，后者表达观念意义。如果我们用"无人"来命名一个人，则可以说"'无人'在房间里，所以房间里有人"。这并不是什么悖论。

还可以把这个悖论改变成例如"用少于100个字不能描述的最小数"这样的形式，它只有16个字，但它却似乎描述了那个数！而且这里没有讲"指称"而是讲"描述"。这仍然不能改变问题的实质。因为这个语句并不是对数本身属性的描述，而是对那个数的描述形式的描述。这两种描述属于不同的语言阶和语言层次。我们有时说，某处风景美得"不能用语言来描述（或形容）"。可是"不能用语言来描述"，难道不正是一种语言的描述？然而，"不能用语言描述"的对象是那客观的风景本身，而把"不能用语言描述"这句话看成一种语言描述，则是对描述的语言形式本身的反省。"不能用语言描述"本身还得通过语言来表达。这两种"描述"不是属于同一的语言阶和语言层次。

困扰人类思维几千年的"说谎者悖论"要复杂一些，不能像上面那样简单地解决。但是分析它的基本方法与上述方法是一致的。说谎者悖论常表示为这样的形式：

P：P是假的。（即冒号左面的P是"P是假的"的名称）

这样就会产生

P是真的，当且仅当，P是假的。

这样的悖论。

其实，前一个P作为语句"P是假的"的名称，代表该语句的整体，而与作为该语句一部分的P不同，两者是处在不同的语言层次上。我们用符号把不同的P标示出来，如写成

P′：P是假的。

这样，悖论语句"P是真的，当且仅当，P是假的"也就变成

P′是真的，当且仅当，P是假的。

这并不是悖论。

换句话说：如果P′是语句"P是假的"的名称，那么这个名称本身没有自己的意义和真值，它只是代表语句"P是假的"。"P′是真的"的意思就是"'P是假的'是真的"。根据塔斯基的真理定义，有

"P是假的"是真的，当且仅当，P是假的。

这当然不是悖论。

简言之，产生悖论的原因是由于混淆了语言层次。只要把层次区别开，悖论就不存在了。但是，问题在于，混淆层次的自我否定会产生悖论，而混淆层次的自我肯定为什么不会产生悖论呢？罗素为了避免悖论，曾提出"恶性循环原则"，禁止一个语句自我指称。这被人们指出是禁止得太多，因为肯定性的自我指称并不造成悖论，反而是数学和逻辑中不可缺少并经常使用的论证方式。如

P：P是真的。

则有

P是真的，当且仅当，P是真的。

它具有 A = A 的形式，这是表达形式逻辑的同一律的公式，是逻辑和数学论证的基础，当然不是悖论。相反，如果我们用符号把两个P区别开，成为

P′：P是真的。

从而有

P′是真的，当且仅当，P是真的。（即P′ = P）

这倒反而不能表达逻辑规律和"真"的定义了。可是，在"P：P是真的"中，两个P也应当是在不同的语言层次上，为什么不会产生悖论呢？

运用我们上面所讲的语言层次的转换和透明的观点来分析，这个问题很容易解决。语言层次相互区别，但又可以而且必须能够相互通约、转换，这是逻辑推理的基础。真值断定实际上起着转换或区别（等同或分离）语言层次的作用。断定一个内涵语句（命题）是真的，就是把它转换为（或等值、透明于）一个外延语句（事实）；断定一个内涵语句是假的，就是断定它仅仅是一个反映观念的内涵语句，不对客观事实透明，不能转换或等同于一个外延语句。

根据塔斯基关于"真"的定义，可有

"P"是真的，当且仅当，P。

用我们前面约定的符号来表示，即

〈P〉是真的，当且仅当，P。

注意名称没有真假，只有命题才有真假。因此，如果P代表反映客观事实的外延语句，〈P〉则代表表达观念的内涵语句，它们实际上有相同的意义和形式，只是所处的语言层次不同。简言之，不能把〈P〉简单地看作是一般的名称（那样它就可以与它所代表的语句形式不同），而应当理解为代表内涵语句，必须保持〈P〉和P在形式上的相似。断定〈P〉为真，就使它等同于P，从而仿佛是P在自我断定一样。

形式逻辑没有理解语言层次转换这个实质，但它抓住了不同层次但意义相同的语句在形式上的相同，用同样的符号形式来代表层次不同但意义相同的语句，以使不同层次的语句能够相互通约。"真"作为语句的层次转换联结词，具有转换语言层次，亦即去引号（括号）的力量：如果一个内涵语句是真的，它就等值或透明于一个外延语句，即

"雪是白的"是真的 = 雪是白的

亦即

雪是白的 = 雪是白的

形式逻辑允许A = A，所以允许"P：P真"（或P = P真）。两个语句在层次上相通、透明，在形式上相同，可以看作是同一个语句。这就是为什么自我肯定虽然也混淆层次，却不导致悖论的原因。

但是自我否定却不同。如果P是假的，那么P不能是一个反映客观事实的外延语句，而仅仅是表达错误观念的一个内涵语句，相应的外延语句的形式就不是P，而是~P，语言层次的区别就在形式上凸现出来。

"雪是白的"是假的，当且仅当，雪不是白的。

亦即

"雪是白的"是假的 = 雪不是白的。

显然"雪是白的"与"雪不是白的"不同构，即

雪是白的 ≠ 雪不是白的。

"P是假的"不能还原为P，只能表现为~P。~P与P在形式上不同，不能相通。形式逻辑不允许A = ~A，亦即不允许P = "P是假的"。换言之，说谎者悖论的前提"P：P是假的"是不成立的。

总之，语言层次理论可以成为我们分析许多语言逻辑难题的有力工具。而这种理论完全是建立在唯物主义本体论立场上、以承认外部客观世界的存在为基础的，同时又看到思维反映存在时的辩证特性和机制。而西方分析哲学家们的错误，则源于他们既"拒斥形而上学"，也不懂辩证法，缺少了正确的本体论和方法论前提。西方分析哲学家们的贡献，是主张用精密的语言逻辑方法去分析哲学问题，这对于克服传统思辨哲学笼统、模糊的思维方法的缺陷，是有巨大的积极意义的。我们把正确的方法论立场和精密的逻辑分析方法结合起来，不仅可以大大促进哲学的发展，也可以促进各种科学理论的发展。因为任何理论，都必须通过观念和语言来表达。弄清语言的逻辑结构，是进行正确的理论研究和表达的重要前提。

参考文献

Gupta, A. 2000. A critique of deflationlism. In S. Blackburn & K. Simmons (eds.), *Truth*. London: Oxford University Press.

弗雷格，1998，论涵义和指称，载《语言哲学名著选辑》，涂纪亮主编。上海：三联书店。

罗　素，1998，论指谓，载《语言哲学名著选辑》，涂纪亮主编。上海：三联书店。

克里普克，1998，《命名与必然性》。上海：上海译文出版社。

维特根斯坦，1988，《名理论（逻辑哲学论）》。北京：北京大学出版社。

永井成男，1992，《分析哲学》。北京：中国社会科学出版社。

奎　因，1987，《从逻辑的观点看》。上海：上海译文出版社。

通讯地址：400030 重庆大学贸易与行政学院哲学系 <hhbb1599@sina.com.cn>

Analyze the Puzzles in Philosophy of Language and Logic
Huang Bin

Abstract: There are three layers for a linguistic expression: its symbolic form, meaning (connotation), and extension (reference or denotation). The three layers are related in a complex way, such as overlapping, transparency and transition. Confusing these three layers is the source of the problems and puzzles about names, identity, existence, truth, paradoxes, etc., in the Western philosophy of language and logic. These problems and puzzles can be analyzed and resolved easily if we understand the relations and mechanism among the three layers of a linguistic expression.

Keywords: layers of language; overlapping; transparency; transition

语言思维、语言模块与语言进化

东北师范大学、辽宁师范大学 成晓光

提　要：关于语言与思维关系的研究有两个两极分化的观点，一是语言的认知观，一是语言的交际观。语言认知观认为，人的思维离不开自然语言，所以语言即认知。而语言交际观则把语言看作是一个交际工具，是思维的附属物和外壳。在两极之间有一些调和的观点，如Paivio的双重代码理论、Bickerton对线上思维和线下思维的区分以及Clark的语言超交际观等。Carruthers从进化论的视角出发，提出了模块框架下的语言认知观。本文认为，所有这些假说虽然没有解决语言与思维的关系问题，且本身都有局限性，却拓宽了我们的认识。

关键词：语言思维；语言模块；语言进化；语言认知观；语言交际观

1. 引言

对语言与思维的关系的研究可以说经历了两个发展阶段。第一个阶段从苏格拉底开始，历经两千多年，其特点是哲学思辨，用的是内省的方法。在这一阶段，哲学家们主要根据自身的体验来进行逻辑推理，从而推导出语言和思维的关系。第二阶段开始于20世纪50年代。随着现代心理学、现代脑科学和认知科学的发展，特别是关于人类大脑的模块说推出以来，对语言和思维关系的研究，就进入了一个实验科学的时期。各种实验和临床证据被用来证明两者的联系。在整个发展过程中形成了两个两极分化的观点，一是语言的认知观，一是语言的交际观。这两种观点各持己说，互不妥协。目前的发展特点是，认知观已逐渐失去其主导地位，而交际观却得到了越来越多的认可。然而，极端的交际观也遭到了许多质疑。于是，有人（Carruthers, 1998, 2006）就企图在两个观点中搞调和，走第三条路子，提出了模块主义框架下的温和的语言认知观。

2. 语言的认知观

语言认知观的基本观点可以概括为：人的思维离不开自然语言。换言之，人是用自然语言来思维和认知的，所以语言即认知。自然，持语言认知观的学者们不认为语言只用来思维。语言还有诸多其他功能，如交际、储存信息、范畴化即认知世界等。

关于语言怎样作用于思维，认知观里也有两种说法，一是条件说（requirement-thesis），一是构成说（constitution-thesis）（Carruthers,

1998）。条件说认为思维需要语言才能进行，因此语言是思维的必要条件（这种说法实际上和语言的交际观有相似之处）。而构成说则认为只有语言才能构成思维，因此思维就是语言活动。关于条件说，不言而喻，人们的思维需要语言，如小孩子就是通过语言来学习有关世界的知识和概念。但人们的思维是否都是语言的思维？除去抽象思维外人们还有形象思维。形象思维也借助语言吗？构成说的回答是肯定的。Wittgenstein（1953）和Bickerton（1995）都持有这种观点。

构成说的理论依据是，人类思维的广度和复杂程度是任何其他动物都不能比拟的。同时，语言也是只有人类才具有的特征。这两个特征人类同时共有。对此，唯一合理的解释就是，只有语言才能使人的思维成为可能。所以，希腊人早就把人定义为"会说话的动物"。苏格拉底在和其弟子的对话中就指出，语言结构的复杂性决定了语言的根本作用不是表达情感和协调活动，而是认识存在与非存在、揭示和表达事物的本质。

构成说的理论听起来很有道理，但是，它既无法证实人类所有的思维都要依靠语言，也无法证明构成说优于条件说。所以，一些哲学家（主要是Wittgenstein、Davidson等）就从普遍性和范畴化的角度来为语言的认知观辩护。他们认为，人类范畴化的思维只有使用语言才能进行，这是一个普遍的现象。思维就是语言，语言就是思维。因此，其他动物和人类婴儿不可能有思维，因为他们没有语言。Wittgenstein（1953）甚至说，思维是一个被误解了的词汇，因为根本不存在思维这个东西。思维原本是人们的一个错觉。思维其实就是自己对自己说话。思维就是语言使用。我们之所以提出思维的问题，是因为当我在问我自己这个问题的时候，我是在和自己说话。要想知道思维是什么，只需要看自己正在做什么就足够了。由于和自己说话用的一定是某一特定语言，因此思维一定是某一特定语言的思维。Wittgenstein反问，不用某一特定语言可以思维吗？不用任何语言可以思维吗？然后再用英语或法语来思维，词序会一样吗？结果会一样吗？

语言认知观的构成说坚持语言的本质是认知的观点。Davidson（2001）举例说，在"金星落下了"和"启明星落下了"这两个句子里，尽管"金星"和"启明星"的所指都是同一物体，但这两个命题在内容上是有区别的。只有使用语言才能在肯定"金星落下了"这个命题的同时，否定"启明星落下了"的命题。

Davidson的论点不是没有漏洞的。如果不以他的假设为前提，那么在逻辑上，不知道其他生物在想什么就等于它们没有思维的判断是不成立的。另外，如果承认思维的基础是现实，那么没有语言的动物也极有可能对现实有思维活动。只是我们不知道它们的思维是什么。所以，Davidson的观点是一种反现实的观点。儿童的发展也提供了相似的证据。儿童在习得语言之前对周围的世界应该是有思维的。说儿童在习得语言之前没有思维显然是令人无法接受的。

对此 Bickerton（1995）提出了一个解决方法。他把思维分为两种，线上思维（on-line thinking）和线下思维（off-line thinking）。线上思维是由于外界事物的存在与刺激引起了神经元反应的结果，是生物的本能，遵循的是此时此地（here and now）的原则。所有脊椎动物和众多无脊椎动物都具有这种能力。这也是思维（学习）的能力，如巴普洛夫的狗听到铃声就知道食物到了。线上思维是人与其他动物所共有的，Bickerton称之为PRS（第一表征系统）。除此之外，人还有另外一种思维方式，就是线下思维。线下思维是抽象的语言思维，完全在人脑中用语言来进行。它不一定需要外界的刺激，也不必产生即时的运动反应。线下思维是对外部世界的间接表现，所以叫SRS（第二表征系统）。它是人类独有的思维方式。它可以使人们产生意识并由此控制自己的行为。而线上思维及后果则是无法控制的。线下思维可以使人类有意去学习某些和生存无关的特殊技能，并使人的行为产生变化。而行为的变化又能使人类迅速地适应自然环境，甚至改造自然环境使之适应于人类。相比之下，其他动物只能通过慢慢改变自身的基因去适应自然环境，因为它们不具备线下（也就是语言）思维的能力。

Bickerton比较令人信服地解决了人与动物及婴儿的思维的差别。按照这个观点，其他动物和婴儿也有思维，只不过它们的思维是线上思维。而有了语言的成年人不但有线上思维，还能进行线下思维。不过，Bickerton认为，成年人所谓的形象思维，其实也是语言思维的结果，而不是像普遍认为的那样，形象思维在前，抽象思维在后。形象思维是因，抽象思维是果。Bickerton举例说，对"The cat sat on the mat"这个句子，你以为你是"看"到了那只猫坐在席子上，但这里面有两点是人们忽视了的。第一，意象是具体的。你"看"到的一定是一只具体的猫和一张具体的席子，而不可能是抽象的猫和抽象的席子。语言不能提供具体的形象，它表征的只是抽象的语言概念。所以，当被问及你怎么"看"到了你"看"的那只猫和那张席子，而别人"看"到的和你"看"到的不一样的时候，你的回答应该是，"这是我想象的猫和席子"。Bickerton说，这已经是语言思维了（1995: 23）。

第二，"The cat sat on the mat"这个句子表征的是已经发生过的事，猫现在已经不在席子上了。既然如此，你怎么还能"看"到这个画面呢？意象怎么能够表征"The cat sat on the mat,""The cat will sit on the mat,"和"The cat is sitting on the mat"呢？还有，"The cat is sitting on the mat"和"The mat is lying underneath the cat,"又怎样用意象来区分呢？在这里，意象是不变的，而命题则是不同的。所以，Bickerton断言说，我们不是先生成一幅图画，然后再用语言来表征图画。恰恰相反，是语言生成了我们用来思维和交流的图画（1995: 23）。

除了哲学家外，持语言认知观的心理学家也不在少数。特别是一些前苏联的心理学家，围绕着"内部言语"（inner speech）的假设做了许多实验。Sokolov（1972）通过实验证明，许多思维活动都涉及内部言语，这些活动包括非言语能力的标准测试和重现图画材料等。Luria（1959）把内部言语称为"第二信号系统"，并证明除了比较高级的智力活动之外，对运动行为的有意控制也需要内部言语。在Luria和他的同事做过的另一项研究中（1956），有一对双胞胎儿童，他们由于特殊的家庭原因直到五岁还不会说话。Luria和他的同事把两个孩子分开，其中一个给予语言训练。三个月后，这个孩子的认知能力有明显的提高。

内部言语的提出者 Vygotsky 在其名著 *Thought and Language*（1934）里讨论

了语言在儿童的科学概念发展过程中的作用。Vygotsky 认为，概念有两种，一种是自然概念，一种是科学概念。自然概念是儿童自然而然得来的，而科学概念是由语言抽象、概括、定义而来的，它的实质就是词语意义。这两种概念的发展相辅相成、互相影响，但科学概念对儿童来说要难得多，这是因为科学概念的形成依赖于语言。只有抽象的语言才能把感性经验从具体的现象中分离出来，这就是概念化。所以，儿童智力的发展就是科学概念的发展，就是抽象的语言思维能力的发展。实际上，儿童在习得了语言之后，思维就变成语言的了。

值得注意的是，这些心理学家虽然也同意语言认知观的构成说，但他们却并不像前面提到的哲学家们那样，坚持认为所有的思维都需要语言。如 Vygotsky虽然坚持思维借助语言的观点，但他同时也认为语言和思维并非同源，两者在儿童习得语言之前以不同的方式运作。因此这是一种较为温和的语言认知观。

最强硬的语言认知观不是心理学或哲学理论，而是语言学理论。其中最为著名的就是萨皮尔—沃尔夫假说。Whorf（1956）提出的语言决定论和语言相对论，把人们思维的差异、对世界的概念的差异和文化间的差异，统统归结于自然语言的结构的差异，认为所有这些差异都是后天语言习得和语言使用的结果。Pinker（1994）把这个假说讥讽为"标准社会科学模式"（SSSM）。Pinker认为不能把人的生物性和文化性、遗传和环境因素对立起来。语言作为人类的本能之一，具有普遍性特征。不同的自然语言之间的差异是表象，而语言内部的运算设计结构只有一个，即普遍语法。

20世纪后期兴起的认知语言学研究也支持语言的认知观。认知语言学和Chomsky的以语言模块说为基础的生成语法是针锋相对的。顾名思义，认知语言学研究认知与语言的关系，它把语言看成是人类思维的媒体，体现在人的认知能力之中。认知语言学的一个根本哲学假设就是，语言能力是人的认知能力的一部分。人的感性经验、概念知识以及话语功能都和语言结构有关。人的思维认知机制是建立在语言基础之上的，只有通过语言才能运作。

3. 语言的交际观

与语言的认知观相反，语言的交际观把语言看作是一个交际工具，是思维的附属物和外壳。语言的功能和目的只是交流思想，思想则是独立于传递手段之外而存在的。语言交际观是当前众多认知科学领域里的主流理论，包括认知心理学、人工智能以及以经验主义为基础的哲学和语言学等。

同语言认知观一样，语言交际观的支持者也包括了哲学家、心理学家和语言学家。哲学家里主要有Russell（1921）、Grice（1957, 1969）、Fodor（1978）、Searle（1983）等。在他们看来，语言的功能只是社会或人际交流，而不是个人的认知与思维。诚然，当个体进行认知活动的时候，仍然需要使用和处理语言。但是，这种处理活动仅仅是为了保障语言的社会交际功能。语言并不具体执行个体的思维及推理。

语言交际观也有两个基本理论支持，一个是传统的意象说，还有一个就是大脑功能的模块说。

　　意象说最初采用的是简单推理的方法。既然语言是用来交际的，可以用视觉意象来思维，那么所有的思维都可以不用语言。这个推理看起来似乎不值得一驳，但在上一节讨论 Bickerton 的观点的时候，我们讲到，在常识上许多人都会认为意象思维产生于语言思维之前。如果真是这个顺序，那么语言就不仅仅是意象的表现手段，而且意象思维也不一定非要付诸语言表现。所以，思维在本质上就一定是意象的了。这就是简单推理法的逻辑所在。

　　支持意象说的还有一个意义论。最早的意义论来自Locke（1690）和 Russell（1921）。他们认为，从意义论的角度来说，我们必须解释某个东西（无论是语言、思想，或是其他什么东西）为什么能够并且怎样赋予其他东西以某种意义，或叫再现。对意象（包括视觉和其他意象）来说，这种意义或再现是通过相似性来完成的，这是再明显不过的了。一个心的意象意味着爱，不会有别的解释。然而，语言不具有相似性，所以它怎么能担负起再现的任务呢？所以，语言即使具有再现力，那这种再现力也只能来自心理意象的再现力。语言即使有意义，那它的意义也只能来自于心理意象的意义。换言之，意义的本源是意象，而不是语言。所以语言的功能就只能是传达了。

　　这个传统的意象说显然过于幼稚。虽然有些思维似乎可以借助于意象（在上一节说过Bickerton是不同意这个观点的），但不是所有的思维都可以用意象来进行，特别是抽象的命题思维用意象是绝对办不到的。Bickerton给了一个例子，"My trust in you has been shattered forever by your unfaithfulness"（1995：22）。这个命题能够用意象来思维吗？Bickerton断言说，要有这个思想，就必须用词语过一遍。否则脑子里只能是一片空白。

　　意象说的现代版是 Grice（1957，1969）和 Searle（1983）的意向说。他们仍然认为可以用思想的语义特征来解释语言的语义特征。例如，说话者的意图若要使某具体话语的意义为 P，那么他就必须努力使听话者理解并相信 P，同时使听话者接受说话者传达 P 的意图。意向说的假设是，思想内容（意图）比语言意义更原始、更具有本质性，所以，自然语言的表达远不能传达说话者的真实意图。

　　大脑功能的模块说是当前语言交际观的主流理论，它的代表人物是 Chomsky 和 Fodor。

　　作为哲学家，Fodor 深受 Chomsky 的影响。他在1983年推出并推广了模块的概念。他认为，大脑的结构是输入和输出系统外加中央处理器。大脑的输入和输出系统是由边缘模块组成的。这些模块各自独立、各司其职，负责不同的感知和语言活动。它们的作用是因果的、功能的。换言之，它们保持着与外部世界的因果关系，并对这些关系的结果进行处理。正因为如此，大脑的各种状态才有了关于外部世界的内容。大脑的中枢系统则不是模块。作为一个中央处理器，这个中枢系统只进行综合的、非属于某一具体领域的活动。它只负责各种不同的内容以及输入和输出之间的逻辑关系。

模块说把语言的地位从思维的主导降低为一个边缘模块。语言不是用来思维，而是把思维的内容具体化。例如，我们的脑子里存有关于世界的知识，但这些知识是以一个个具体的命题并通过语言符号来表达的。语言符号可能是英语，也可能是汉语，但这并不重要。因为自然语言的符号只是实现大脑里的知识，只是被交际者用来交流这些知识。这些符号在使用时可以省略掉任何可以省掉信息，从而达到最大的简洁。而交际者可以根据语境并通过自己的想象补充上那些省略掉的信息。相反，"思维的语言"则不可以把任何信息留给想象。它包含所有的信息，因为它本身就是所有的想象。所以，"思维的语言"远比自然语言要丰富得多。

自然语言不能用来思维的第二个原因是它的模糊性。自然语言的话语经常会产生理解上的歧义。英语的句子可以在大脑里有两个意义，但大脑里的知识却不可能是英语的句子。第三，自然语言的话语充满了功能词如介词、冠词和其他标记，这是因为信息从一个大脑传递到另一个大脑时借助的是口和耳朵，这是一个线性的、缓慢的传递方式，所以必须依靠这些标记来保证信息传递的完整性。而信息在同一个大脑里进行传递时靠的是神经元的连接，所以，大脑里的知识就不可能是某一个自然语言，而必须是一种更丰富、更微妙的语言——思维语。美国的英语遗产大辞典将"思维语"定义为，一种在大脑里不用词语来表征概念和命题的假想的语言。

Fodor的思维语得到了许多学者的支持。Pinker作为一个认知心理学家，既承认语言的天赋论，又接受大脑的模块说和思维语的观点。他在《语言本能》（1994）一书里，专门用了一章来论证思维语。他的基本观点是，语言是人的天生的生物本能，所以，语言的共项不受自然语言的限制。"人们思维时用的不是英语、汉语或阿帕契语，而是一种思维语"（1994: 81）。"会一种语言其实就是会把思维语和成串的词语进行互译。没有语言的人也有思维语"（1994: 82）。

Pinker代表的无疑是一种极端的语言交际观。这种观点在理论上还得到了心理理论（Theory of Mind）的支持。根据心理理论的说法，人的社会认知能力的基础是一个社会认知模块，即心理理论机制。这种特殊的认知能力使得人可以理解他人的意图如信念、愿望等等。人类智商之所以能够进化，完全是出于对这种社会交往的需求。所以，语言的基本功能，甚至是唯一的功能，就只能是传达（交际）人的意图。

更多的心理学理论支持温和的语言交际观。实际上，早在19世纪就开始了机能心理学的研究。自19世纪中期在左脑发现语言的布罗卡区和韦尼克区以来，人们就开始认识到大脑的功能定位。这其实也是大脑模块说的先驱。迄今为止，许多临床案例和心理语言学的实验都证明，语言障碍和特异语言残缺往往是语言能力受到损伤，但认知能力却仍然正常。反之，如威廉综合症病人的临床症状表现的那样，语言能力正常，认知能力却出现了问题。这充分证明了语言的模块性质。Gardner（1983）提出了的多元智能理论，就把语言确立为一个独立的智能。这就意味着语言可以独立于其他智能而发展，而其他智能则不一定要借助于语言来工作。

温和语言交际观的另一个主要心理学家是Piaget（1923）。他的儿童智力发展四阶段理论早已为人们所知。他认为，儿童在两岁之前的感觉运动阶段，虽然还没有语言能力,但通过感觉运动方式,已经开始了智力的发展。到第二个阶段——前运算阶段,儿童开始习得语言。在这个过程中,儿童逐渐学会使用语言的象征功能。但同时他们还会用其他的象征手段来思维,如象征性游戏。这表明思维先于语言,但语言的发展反过来又作用于思维。直到第三阶段——具体运算阶段和第四阶段——形式运算阶段都完成之后,他们才具有了用语言进行抽象思维的能力。所以语言和思维互相依存,但智力来自于生活经验,而且独立于语言之外。

语言交际观最主要的理论不是来自哲学,也不是来自心理学,而是来自 Chomsky 的语言学研究。Chomsky 在他早期的生成语法里,就发展了一整套怎样把深层结构的概念转换成表层结构的语言表达的理论和规则。Chomsky 最终放弃了生成语法,但他始终坚持他的语言观,那就是,语言作为一个模块,是大脑里一个相对独立的组成部分,由人的遗传基因决定。人类的语言在本质上是一样的。各种自然语言都是在普遍语法的原则和程式的基础上派生出来的产物。所以,外化语言(E-language)只是内化语言(I-language)的外部实现。研究外化语言是不可能了解语言的本质的,只有内化语言才能揭示语言的现实。Chomsky 在2002年为外研社出版的《当代国外语言学与应用语言学文库》写的序言里就说道,"研究语言使用就是要研究内部语言的资源怎样被用来表达思想、谈论世界、交流信息、和建立社会联系等等。"

4. 两种观点的中和

综上所述,对语言和思维关系的研究呈现出两极分化的趋势。在两种不同的观点里,都有人坚持极端的立场。原因是多方面的,例如,交际观的坚持者们把认知观和沃尔夫的语言决定论混为一谈,错以为接受了认知观就等于接受了语言决定论,从而背离他们模块说和天赋论的理论基础。另一方面,由于 Wittgenstein 和 Davidson 等人的权威性,认知观的支持者宁愿相信,语言是人类和其他动物的唯一区别,因为只有语言才能使人进行理性思维,而这一点是其他动物做不到的。

从以上的讨论中,我们已经看到了一些对这两种极端论的反驳和批判。诚然,许多思维离开了语言是无法进行的,如推测别人的想法,对因果关系进行推理等,但是这并不意味着所有的思维都需要语言。动物和婴儿也具有某些思维能力,这是人所共知的事实。某些推理活动,如空间推理,就可以不用语言来进行。还有,语言障碍和特异语言残缺的研究也证明,语言发生了障碍,不等于其他的认知能力也发生了障碍。所以,在两极之间,也有学者采取的是温和或折中的态度,例如,在认知观里有 Vygotsky,在交际观里有 Piaget,而且目前已有越来越多的说法对两种极端的观点进行中和。

Paivio 在1971年提出了一个双重代码理论,可以看作是对认知观和交际观的调和。双重代码理论以认知理论为基础,提出人们在处理信息时使用两套系统,一套是语言系统,另一套是非语言系统。语言系统处理的是线形的、序列的、按层次排列的语言代码并加以储存,而第二套非语言系统则处理意象。这些意象是直观的,人们可以在脑海里"看见"的某种东西。除此之外,意象还有其他感觉方式——听觉的、嗅觉的、味觉的、触觉的、动觉的,如许多人会有听音乐的意象,能在回忆中闻到大海的味道或茶的芳香。和语言信息不同的是,非语言系统表现的是整体的、嵌入式的信息,所以,一张面孔的意象一定是整体,包含着眼睛、眉毛、鼻子和嘴,而嘴的意象则包含唇与牙齿。但语言符号的离散性使得语言系统在处理这些信息时必须把它们拆开来对待。双重代码理论认为,这两种符号系统可以分别工作。而且这两个过程之间还可以互相转换。输入到一个系统里的信息,也可以被另一个系统所储存并表现,如我们在阅读描述长城的文章时(语言处理)可以用意象来进行储存(非语言表现)。同样,我们还可以用语言向别人来描述我们的这个意象。更多的时候,两个系统是以综合的方式同时工作。比如,我们可以看无声电影,也可以阅读电影脚本,但更有效的方式是让电影有声并加上字幕。计算机时代的多媒体信息处理就是这个原理。从这个意义上,双重代码理论可以说是迄今为止对认知观和交际观最全面的中和。

Bickerton(1995)对线上思维和线下思维的区分,如果抛开他极端的语言认知观,也可以说解决语言和思维关系的另一种尝试。动物和婴儿具有线上思维能力,这是一种本能。当看到豹子猎取食物的时候,我们不能不惊叹它那精确的计算能力。思维其实就是一种计算。但是当猎物不在视线以内的时候,动物是不会去进行这种计算的。人则不同。人的思维(计算)不受外部世界的限制。人的思维(计算)可以超越现实。这就是语言的作用。这样看来,如Wittgenstein所建议的那样,问题出在了词语上。不是思维是否用语言来进行的问题,而是思维采用什么方式的问题。关键在于要怎样定义思维。思维可以借助语言,也可以不借助语言,但这是两种本质不同的活动。因此,任何有关思维的说法都不能坚持普遍性的原则。具体情况要具体分析。如果要划两条线来区别语言的思维和非语言的思维的话,那么一条是平行线,区分不同类型的思维内容;一条是垂直线,区分表达这些内容的不同方式。

Clark(1998)也提出了一个交际观和认知观的调和说法,叫做语言的超交际观(the supra-communicative conception)。Clark认为,语言应被看作一个认知工具,因为语言不仅是用来交际的,而且也是用来提高认知能力的。这就是超交际观和交际观的主要区别。超交际观认为,人类的许多问题都有计算(思维)空间。语言将这些空间重新组合,从而使这些问题更容易处理。例如,阿拉伯数字的十进位制使得加减乘除的运算非常便捷,而用罗马数字或汉字数字则困难得多。所以,语言具有提高认知能力的作用。

超交际观也有别于认知观。诚然,超交际观认为语句标符(sentence token)只是促进、但不构成思维,而极端的认知观则坚持语句标符本身就是思维。实际上,很少有人认为自然语言的语句标符本身就是思维,或者足以构成思维。例如,只会汉语的人鹦鹉学舌地说了一句英语,这能构成思维吗?标符语句的内容一定包含了多种更为基本的连接和更为隐秘的个体活动。应该说,语句只是思维的必要成分,某些推理活动一定要使用语句而已。所以,超交际观和认知观的真正区别是，对认知观来说，一个内在语句的特定标符一定是其心理活动的不可分割的组成部分。它承载着这个标符思维的内容。除了这个语句之外，不可能再有其他独立的神经或心理活动。因此，语言构成认知。而对超交际观来说，我们只有在进行长时间的扩展性思维或推理时才需要语言。例如，在构思这篇文章时，我们必须用语句写下自己的想法，以便减少记忆的压力。在这一点上，超交际观认同交际观，即神经活动承载着思维的内容。这种活动可以不依靠自然语言的语句来进行，同时也可以产生出自然语言的表述。

同许多连接主义的心理学家一样，Clark 也认为大脑的认知结构是以连接方式来工作的，在信息处理时采用并行式。但是，和他们不同的是，Clark 不同意一旦习得了语言，就从根本上把大脑重新编程为一个序列的、处理语句的计算机的说法。他认为，语言可以提高或改善现存系统的计算能力，但不能从根本上改变它的结构。所以，我们不是因为有了语言才有心理活动，而是如果没有语言，许多扩展的思维活动则不可能进行。这就是语言的超交际观的基本内涵。

前面谈到的连接主义可以说是近年来对语言交际观和模块论的最大挑战。在连接主义的框架里，人类的学习和行为被解释为并行分布式处理。用计算机模拟人的行为和大脑的功能，使我们更加了解人的信息处理方式。研究证明，人脑不像天赋论所坚持的那样，先天具有那么多的天赋才能。实际上，人脑里蕴藏着极大的学习潜力。这意味着把人脑按功能分为预先设置的、各自独立的模块的说法是不可靠的。语言和思维之间不一定有一个严格的界限。当进行信息处理时，整个网络系统都在激活的状态下进行互动。因此，语言和思维的活动互相包含是完全可能的。这样，连接主义就从理论上为两种语言观的中和清除了障碍。

5. 进化论的解释

在所有两种语言观的中和版本中，Carruthers 是独树一帜的。他自从1996年提出了模块框架下的语言认知观以来，1998年进行了详细的阐述，一直到最近的2006年仍然在为之辩护。他的假说中最鲜明的特点就是进化论的视角。他认为，从进化论的角度来看，语言既是大脑的一个边缘模块，又在中枢认知活动里起着重要的作用。这样，他就调和了认知观和以模块论为核心的交际观，为语言和思维的关系找到了另一种说法。

Carruthers 的基本观点可以概括为，虽然中枢认知在语言进化之前就已存在，但语言的进化促进了中枢认知的进化。在人类创造性思维的发展过程中，语言起到了至关重要的作用。语言不仅为"内部言语"的有意识的主题思维提供了工具，而且也为显性的概念性思维提供了媒介。在有着众多的、具有特殊功能、准模块性质的中枢认知系统里（包括心理理论、大众生物学、常识物理学等），语言扮演了"通用语"的角色。

Carruthers 首先要解决的是大脑结构的本质问题。他认为，接受语言认知观不等于就一定要放弃模块论。大脑在本质上是模块的，但是，传统的模块论

（Fodor, 1983）把模块说成是固化的则未免有些夸张。实际上，所有的生物系统，尤其是在发展的初期，都有相当程度的可塑性。尽管感觉和运动子系统的发展在很大程度上取决于其正常环境里的生物性而不取决于学习，但一旦学习发生，涉及的很可能是特殊领域，而不是普遍的学习原则。所以，有理由相信，模块系统的发展一方面是生物内部的天生因素，另一方面也有与环境的互动。另外，模块同中枢认知之间也不是绝对封闭的。所有的信息输入和输出系统都应该依靠一个丰富的网络。这个网络由在后部投射的神经通道所组成。输入和输出系统通过这个网络，来引导感觉信息的搜索和识别，并帮助监控和调校运动输出。

至于为什么语言作为一个边缘输入输出模块却能参与中枢认知活动的问题，Carruthers 建议比较一下视觉想象。众所周知，视觉系统作为一个独立的输入模块，专门接受视觉信息。但是，视觉模块的资源也可以被用来产生心象。人们在想象时和在观看时一样，视觉神经也在活动。这就说明，中枢认知在工作时可以利用边缘模块的资源，激活它们的表现内容，从而来实现思维和推理的中枢认知功能。同理，中枢认知也可以利用语言模块的资源，来产生自然语言语句的表现内容。这种表征的方式叫"内部言语"，它被用来进行不同的概念推理活动。

Carruthers 认知观的核心就是这个"内部言语"。内部言语需要一个执行系统才能工作。换言之，只有在某个特殊用途的执行系统作用于内部言语时才生成内部言语的细相。一旦内部言语生成，我们就可以直达我们自己的概念表征，将其知觉化，并对其进行评论和反省。所以，如果说无知觉的概念表征不一定要借助于自然语言的话，那么知觉化的概念思维（与视觉空间的思维相反）就一定要依靠自然语言的语句才能进行。实际上，建立一个这样的执行系统，不需要给中枢认知增加任何内容，只需要语言、想象和心理理论就足够了。有了这几个机能，就可以在想象中生成内部言语的语句，这些语句会由语言系统用正常的方式加以解释，其内容就会被元表征思维所利用。

在 Carruthers 的理论里，无知觉和知觉化的概念表征之间有着重大的区别。知觉化的概念表征形式是语音，而无知觉的概念表征则是"逻辑形式"（Logical Form 或 LF）。可以假设，中枢思维活动经常是通过借助和操控语言机能的表征来进行。如果表征的形式仅仅是 LF，那思维就是无知觉的。而一旦 LF 表征被用来生成完整的语音表现形式（听觉想象的语句，或内部言语的段落），于是就产生了知觉化的思维。Fodor（1983）和 Pinker（1994）认为无知觉的概念表征采用的是思维语。而 Carruthers 则认为，LF 不是纯粹的中枢表征活动。它依赖的是语言机能的资源，是来自某一自然语言。所以，它对不同的思维者来说不具有普遍性。另外，LF不像思维语那样被认作是所有中枢活动的语言。LF不构成中枢活动的语言，这是因为，一，许多中枢认知活动用的是直观等意象形式或其他认知模式。二，更为重要的是，LF只作为准模块中枢系统的媒介。这些系统的内部操作则至少部分地采取其他的表征方式。从根本上来说，各种中枢系统的构成使得它们能够把LF的自然语言表征作为输入来接受，然后又生成同样形式的输出。这样，某一准模块（如心理理论）的输出就可以被另一准模块（如欺骗侦查系统）当作输入来接受。这就形成了准模块系统之间的合作，在互动中构成思维链，以达到解决问题的目的。

那么，为什么是 LF，而不是思维语，承担了大脑内准模块之间沟通的媒介角色呢？关于这个问题，Carruthers 同意 Mithen（1996）的观点，认为原始人（如直立人和尼安德鲁人等）的大脑里已有不同的、相对封闭的中枢模块来负责不同的活动，如心理理论模块处理社会交往、解释和预测不同的行为，自然历史模块处理有关动植物生活方式的信息，物理模块负责石器的生产等。当语言模块出现的时候，一个中枢模块的输出很自然地就转化成另一中枢模块的输入，所以原始人就可以开始谈论社会交往、生物世界和物质世界。同时，这些模块也随之变化，不但接受感觉输入，也开始接受语言输入。于是，只要被告知某一事件，就足以引起相应的专门化处理系统的活动。一旦中枢模块开始接受语言输入并生成语言输出，语言就成为大脑内模块系统之间的交流媒介。人类只需要不断地进行想象，就可以生成内部言语的语句，这些语句随之也就被不同的准模块系统当作输入来加以处理。这个过程经过不断地学习演练（亦可能经过神经连接的进化），逐渐演变成半自动化的活动。于是，即便没有知觉化的思维，LF 的语句照样可以生成，担负起中枢认知系统间的媒介角色。

Carruthers 一再声称他的语言认知观是建立在模块论的基础之上的，所以和 Bickerton（1995）的网络论的语言认知观有区别。Carruthers 认为，人类思维的进化经历了三个阶段——前语言阶段、原始语言阶段和句法语言阶段。在第一阶段，即语言尚未进化的阶段，人类的祖先有着和现代人相同的感觉和运动模块，只不过现代人的这些模块在语言的作用下已经经历了一些改变。除此之外，更为重要的是，人类的祖先已经有了一些具有特殊用途的、准模块性质的中枢计算系统。这些系统各司其职，如辨别欺骗行为、对自然事物进行分类、对因果关系进行推理等。这些系统的工作原理可能是思维语，也可能是它们之间组成的一个个联合网络。各种不同的感觉（输入）模块的输出成了这些系统的输入。可以推测，由于这些信息输入，我们的祖先已具有相关领域的知识，只不过这些知识仍是隐性的，无法外显化。换言之，这些系统给我们的祖先提供了一种敏感和能力，使他们能对周围的社会和自然环境中隐秘的事物作出不同的反应。不过，这种能力受制于具体的环境和程序，因此，我们祖先的思维无法脱离具体的环境。

第二个阶段——原始语言阶段发生在大约两百万到一百六十万年前。这时直立人开始进化，大脑容量开始增加。原始语是一种简单的交流和表征系统。它只有有限的词汇，基本上没有句法结构。按照 Bickerton（1995）的说法，原始语虽具有一些实义词汇，但由于缺乏句法关系，真正意义上的思维是不可能的。但 Carruthers 指出，原始语言虽然抽象程度低，却能改变原有的具有特殊用途的推理系统，使其能够在不依赖感觉输入的前提下工作。这时，这些系统处理的是由原始语表征的输入，生成的是原始语表征的输出。这就是"内部话语"。我们可以用心理理论这个准模块来举例。随着原始语的出现，人们只需要通过话语行为，就可以来推测和解释他人的意图和动机。其他的准模块也是如此。只要被告知最近发生的事，就足以使因果推理准模块开始工作，从而推导出最合理的因果关系的解释。到这个阶段，元表征思维的、知觉化的中枢执行系统已经初具规模、概念表征的条件已经开始形成。当然，在句法语言到来之前，原始语还不足以让人们进行真正创造性的思维。

大约十万年前，现代人类首先出现在南非。同时，有着完整句法的自然语言机能也开始进化。这使得人类思维的范围和精密程度进一步扩大。例如，外化的条件式和虚拟推理开始出现。而在这之前，这种推理只限于隐性的、具体领域的活动。当然，自然语言的表征仍然是为具有特殊用途的推理系统所用，但这些系统现在处理的是具有句法规则的自然语言的语句。这时，一个具有自反意识的中枢执行系统所必需的全部条件都已就位，人类创造性思维在五万至四万年前开始了爆发。

有人会问，原始语不是模块，那为什么句法语言进化成自然语言模块了呢？对此，Carruthers的猜测是，原始人在使用原始语的时候主要是进行言语诠释。由于原始语具有极大的模糊性，所以它的语句的解释要高度依赖具体的语境和对说话者意图的猜测。句法语言的进化给话语赋予了高度的结构性，使得言语诠释在结构的基础上就能进行。这样，句法机能的到来就使得言语诠释成为半自动化。所以，自然语言就进化成模块了。

句法语言出现在约十万年前，而创造性思维在五万至四万年前才开始进化。如果语言给了人类条件式思维和虚拟推理能力，如果早期现代人已具有了我们现在的智商，那么为什么在这段时间内没有任何创造性发明的痕迹？在这漫长的五万年中，尽管木制品有了改变，人们开始使用骨制工具，但早期现代人仍然使用着直立人使用过的石器。迄今没有发现任何人体饰物，没有任何艺术创作（Mithen, 1996）。对此，Carruthers认为，这完全是因为在语言的基础上，我们还需要一个简单的认知机制，这就是假想游戏（pretend play）。假想应该是现代人创造力的核心。这是一种假设猜想的推理能力。虽然原始人也具有视觉或其他方式的想象力，但在语言出现之前和在出现以后的一段时间里，这种能力并没有加以利用。句法语言第一次成就了条件式的虚拟思维能力。它充分应用在儿童的假想游戏中。虽然所有哺乳动物的幼子都会游戏，但人类儿童不光是游戏，更重要的是，他们在进行假想。所以，有理由相信，假想和推测应是儿童的一种固化的内在心理机制。

至此，Carruthers的语言认知观的进化论解释可以概括如下。随着现代人的进化，出现了语法模块。语言提供的表征资源使得自由、显性的假设思维成为可能。这给早期现代人的生活带来了相当的影响，使他们可以进行计划活动、从事社会协作、创造某些工具等。但在这个时期，他们的假设思维主要还是实用性质的，还被限制在具体的活动范围里，如狩猎、社会交流、制造工具等。随着进化压力的需求，一个简单的假想游戏机制于五万至四万年前出现，使得人类儿童在这个特定的人类行为方式上起跑。从此，创造性思维像雪球一样开始滚动，而且至今没有停止。现代人开始有了其他物种所没有的、独一无二的大脑和思维（1998, 2006）。

6. 结束语

思维和语言的关系是每一个哲学家、心理学家和语言学家必须要面对和研究的问题。毫无疑问，在写这篇文章时，作者是用语言来思维的。但是，是不是所有的思维都是语言的思维？人还可不可以以其他方式思维的？语言对人的思维有什么影响？人究竟有几种思维？说到底，思维究竟是什么？诚然，思维可以从不同的角度、在不同的学科里研究，比如语言的、心理的，还有生物神经的。Bickerton（1995）就曾不无讽刺地建议，思维充其量不过是大脑皮层里神经元的活动，因为在大脑里既没有图像，也没有词语。所以，研究思维也不过就是搞清大脑神经的活动而已。当然，这并不意味着 Bickerton 一定要强加给我们一个庸俗唯物论的观点。这恰恰说明在面对思维这个人人都在从事的现象时，人类是多么的无奈。我们解释不了思维，但我们知道我们在思维。人是思维的动物。人的行为都有目的性（Deacon, 1997; Dennet, 1991）。有了思维，我们就必然要问为什么。所以，研究思维还是离不开语言。尽管没有哪一个理论能够给我们一个完美的答案，但每一次认真的尝试都使我们向真理跨近了一步。

　　Carruthers 的模块框架下的进化论的语言认知观是一种比较全面的解释。当然，这个假说中还是有些问题。第一，Carruthers 宣称原始语不是模块。那么为什么句法语言进化成了模块了呢？又是怎样进化成模块的呢？对此 Carruthers 并没有给出正面回答。第二，Carruthers 的假想游戏机制也过于含糊。在约五万年的时间里，有句法语言却没有创造性思维。这怎么能说得通？在这一点上，也许 Bickerton 的线上思维和线下思维理论更为合理。Carruthers 仅仅用一个简单的假想游戏机制就一带而过。假设真有这个机制，那它是怎样出现的呢？它是独立的还是附着于语言模块上，作为后者的组成部分呢？如果是独立的，那它是不是一个模块呢？还有，Carruthers 的这个机制好像是专门为小孩子设计的。那么成年人呢？成年人也得经历儿童时期吧？"机制"是一个太含糊的词语。这也可能是 Carruthers 假说中最不令人信服的部分。第三，Carruthers 自己也承认，所有他的假说都有待于进一步的实证研究。假说毕竟是假说。再合理的假说也是假说，更何况是有逻辑上漏洞的假说。不过，Carruthers 给了我们一个全新的视角，拓宽了我们对语言和思维关系的认识。他的贡献是显而易见的。

参考文献

Bickerton, D. 1995. *Language and Human Behavior*. Seattle: University of Washington Press.

Carruthers, P. 1998. Thinking in language? Evolution and a modularist possibility. In P. Carruthers & J. Boucher. (eds.), *Language and Thought*. Cambridge: Cambridge University Press.

Carruthers, 2006. *The Architecture of the Mind: Massive Modularity and the Flexibility of Thought*. Oxford: Oxford University Press.

Chomsky, N. 1995. Language and nature. *Mind*, 104, 1-61.

Clark, A. 1998. Majic words: how language augments human computation. In P. Carruthers & J. Boucher. (eds.), *Language and Thought*. Cambridge: Cambridge University Press. 184-200.

Davidson, D. 2001. *Subjective, Intersubjective, Objective*. Oxford: Blackwell.

Deacon, T. W. 1997. *The Symbolic Species*. New York: W. W. Norton.

Dennet, D. C. 1991. *Consciousness Explained.* New York: Little Brown and Co.

Fodor, J. 1978. Propositional attitudes. Reprinted in Fordor, J, 1981, *RePresentations*. Hassocks: Harvester Press.

Fodor, J. 1983. *The Modularity of Mind: An Eassy on Faculty Psychology.* Cambridge: MIT Press.

Gardner, H. 1983. *Frames of Mind: The Theory of Multiple Intelligences.* London: Heinemann.

Grice, H. P. 1957. Meaning. *Philosophical Review*, 66, 377-88.

Grice, H. P. 1969. Utterer's meaning and intenions. *Philosophical Review*, 78, 147-77.

Locke, J. 1690. An essay concerning human understanding. In Nidditch, P. H. (ed). Oxford: Clarendon.

Luria, A. R. 1956. *Problems of Higher Neural Activity of the Normal and Abnormal Child.* Moscow: Academy Pedagog Science Press.

Luria, A. 1959. The directive function of speech in development and dissolution. *Word*, 15, 341-52.

Mithen, S. 1996. *The Prehistory of Mind.* London: Thames and Hudson.

Paivio, A. 1971. *Imagery and Verbal Processes.* New York: Holt, Rinehart and Winston.

Piaget, J. 1923. *The Language and Thought of the Child.* London: Routledge and Kegan Paul.

Pinker, S. 1994. *The Language Instinct.* London: Penguin Books.

Russell, B. 1921. *The Analysis of Mind.* London: Allen and Unwin.

Searle, J. 1983. *Intentionality.* Cambridge: Cambridge University Press.

Sokolov, A. 1972. *Inner Speech and Thought.* New York: Plenum Press.

Vygotsky, L. 1934. *Thought and Language.* Trans. By Kozulin. Cambridge, Mass.: MIT Press.

Wittgenstein, L. 1953. *Philosophical Investigations.* Oxford: Blackwell.

Whorf, B. L. 1956. *Language, Thought and Reality.* Cambridge, mass.: MIT Press.

通讯地址：130024 东北师范大学外语学院；116029 辽宁师范大学外语学院
　　　　　<xiaoguangcheng@hotmail.com>

Language Thinking, Language Module and Language Evolution
Cheng Xiaoguang

Abstract: There are two polarized views on the relationship between language and thinking, one of which being the cognitive conception of language and the other being the communicative conception of language. The former believes that natural language constitutes human thinking, while the latter argues for a communicative nature of language. In between the poles are found various views of moderation. Carruthers' modularist cognitive conception from an evolutionary perspective is one of the best examples.

Keywords: language thinking; language module; language evolution; cognitive conception; communicative conception

Chomsky on the "Ordinary Language" View of Language

Lin Yunqing   Bei Hang University

Abstract: There is a commonsense view of language, which is held by Wittgenstein, Strawson, Dummett, Searle, Putnam, Lewis, Wiggins, and others. According to this view a language consists of conventions, it is rule-governed, rules are conventionalized, a language is learnt, there are general learning mechanisms in the brain, and so on. I shall call this view the "ordinary language" view of language. Chomsky's attitude towards this view of language has been rather negative, and his rejection of it is a major motivation for the development of his own theory. In this paper I shall review Chomsky's long-standing criticisms. I shall show that (1) Chomsky's argument does not constitute a dismissal of the "ordinary language" view of language, (2) Chomsky's conclusions about language do not follow from his argument, and (3) the "ordinary language" view actually points to a promising way for us to understand the true nature of language and mind.

Keywords: "ordinary language" view of language; Chomsky; conventions; rules

1. INTRODUCTION

There is a common-sense view of language, which is held by a host of scholars such as Wittgenstein, Strawson, Dummett, Searle, Putnam, Lewis, Wiggins, and others. According to this view, a language consists of conventions, it is rule-governed, rules are conventionalized, a language is learnt, there are general learning mechanisms in the brain, and so on. I shall call this view the "ordinary language" view of language.[1]

Chomsky's conception of language, by contrast, is starkly different. For many

---

[1] In its narrowest sense 'ordinary language' philosophy refers to the philosophy exercised by J. L. Austin. In a broad sense it covers philosophical works in which ordinary language is taken to be in order and the goal of philosophy is believed to be to describe and understand the workings of ordinary language. It is this broad sense of the term that is used in this paper.

years Chomsky has been intrigued by Plato's problem. Plato's problem is 'the problem of explaining how we can know so much given that we have such limited evidence' (Chomsky, 1986: xxv). The study of human language presents a version of Plato's problem. It is perplexing that the child is able to master a language, which is very complicated as everybody would agree, in a relatively short time span. This becomes more puzzling when we notice (A) that the linguistic data presented to the child is very limited, and (B) that the child can learn not just one, but any human language. The answer proposed by Plato to his problem is that knowledge is remembered from an earlier existence and is reawakened in the mind in experience. Chomsky's solution to the language problem, a version of Plato's problem, is rather similar to Plato's solution. Fact (B) noticed above leads Chomsky to think that there is a universal grammar (UG) in a person's mind, and fact (A) makes him believe that UG is "innate, part of our biological endowment, genetically determined, on a par with elements of our common nature that cause us to grow arms and legs rather than wings" (Chomsky, 1988: 4). Thus, according to Chomsky, there is a distinct language faculty in the brain, much of linguistic knowledge is innate, linguistic knowledge consists of abstract and unconscious principles, and a language is not learnt but rather "acquired," etc. I shall call this view the "innate" view of language.

The debate between the two sides has occupied the centre stage in linguistics, philosophy and cognitive science, and will certainly continue to do so for a long time. The importance of this debate cannot be overstated: it concerns the nature of language, the nature of mind, and the nature of human beings. The debate is also important in deciding how to direct our research energy fruitfully in linguistics, philosophy and cognitive science, because one line of inquiry may be more likely than the other to lead us to the true answers.

Chomsky's attitude towards the "ordinary language" view of language has been rather negative, and his development of the "innate" view is closely related to his rejection of the "ordinary language" view. In this paper I shall review Chomsky's long-standing criticisms. While admitting that some of Chomsky's remarks are important and they point out places where the "ordinary language" view needs to be improved on, I shall show that the majority of his criticisms are not well-founded. This has three important implications, as I shall argue. One is that Chomsky's argument does not constitute a dismissal of the "ordinary language" view of language. Secondly, Chomsky's conclusions about language do not actually follow from his argument. And thirdly, the "ordinary language" view of language is not wrong, as Chomsky believes; rather, it points to a promising way for us to understand the true nature of language and mind.

2. CHOMSKY'S CRITICISMS OF THE "ORDINARY LANGUAGE" VIEW

2.1 *Practical Abilities*

In his paper *What is a theory of meaning (II)* Dummett asks the question: What is it a speaker knows when he knows a language? His answer is "Of course, what he has when he knows the language is practical knowledge, knowledge how to speak the language" (Dummett, 1975: 36). Where does this knowledge come from? Dummett says that it is learnt: "when someone learns a language, what he learns is a practice; he learns to respond, verbally and non-verbally, to utterances and to make utterances of his own" (Dummett, 1975: 47). In a subsequent paper *What do I know when I know a Language*? Dummett tries to clarify the notion of practical knowledge. According to him, when a speaker masters a language, he possesses a practical ability to engage in language activities; in other words, he is able to perform certain kinds of "skilled operations" (Dummett, 1978: 95). The speaker, who can perform all sorts of skilled language operations, may not be able to tell exactly according to what he performs such operations, so his practical knowledge is in a sense *implicit*. But, as Dummett notes, this is not the same as saying that the speaker is unconscious of such practical knowledge at all: the speaker "may nevertheless be capable of acknowledging, and willing to acknowledge, the correctness of a statement of those principles [explaining the practical knowledge] when it is offered to him" (Dummett, 1978: 96). Thus, practical knowledge of a language must be on the one hand manifested in the practical ability of engaging in language activities, and on the other hand accessible to consciousness (Dummett, 1978: 96).

Chomsky attacks the notion of "practical ability" from two angles. He first argues that knowledge of a language cannot be explained in terms of practical abilities or skills at all. Skills are things obtained through training and experience, like the skills of riding a bicycle. He gives the following examples and arguments. First, he invites us to consider the following sentences (Chomsky, 1986: 8):

(1) John ate an apple.
(2) John ate.
(3) John is too stubborn to talk to Bill.
(4) John is too stubborn to talk to.

In (1) an apple was the thing that John ate. The object of "ate" in (2) is missing, and the sentence means that John ate something. We may generalize from sentences like (2) that:

(5) Whenever the object is missing, an arbitrary object is meant.[1]

Now, (3) means that John is so stubborn that he will not talk to Bill. Let us now look at (4), and we find that object of "talk to" is missing. If we apply (5), we should regard (4) as meaning that John is so stubborn that he will not talk to an arbitrary person. But (4) actually means that John is so stubborn that an arbitrary person will not talk to him.[2]

Chomsky points out that children are capable of knowing the correct meaning of all the sentences in (1)-(4). He asks: are children trained to do such things? The answer is, he suggests, no. He says that it is not the case that children interpret (4) on the analogy of (2) and then hear from their parents or teachers that the derived interpretation is incorrect, and he adds that "it is doubtful that anyone has undergone this experience and it is certain that not everyone who knows the facts has done so" (cf. Chomsky, 1988: 21, 24). He further points out that the differences shown in (1)-(4) are not noted in "even the most compendious traditional or teaching grammar" (Chomsky, 1986: 9). Children simply know how to derive the correct meaning of (1)-(4), and this is "knowledge without training or relevant experience" (Chomsky, 1986: 8). Children's knowledge of a language, Chomsky concludes, "is certainly not identifiable with some kind of ability or skill;" for example, children do not fail to interpret (4) by analogy to (2) "because of some lack of the skill or ability, which they could overcome by more training or practice" (Chomsky, 1988: 21).

Consider another example Chomsky (1986: 8) offers:

(6) I wonder who [the men expected to see them].
(7) [The men expected to see them].

---

[1] This generalisation is not entirely correct. When an object of a verb is missing, it is often the case that a specific type of object, not just any arbitrary object is meant. For example, in "Have you eaten yet?" the missing object is "the meal appropriate to the given time of day," and not an arbitrary object. But such qualifications are not central to the point under discussion.

[2] The above is Chomsky's argument. One may say that there is a fault in this argument. The fault is that the argument fails to distinguish between the case where the object of a verb is missing and the case where the object of a "verb + preposition" is missing. Generalization (5) applies in the former case but not in the latter case: it is not true that "John talks to" means that John talks to an arbitrary person. So one may say that (4) cannot be interpreted in the same way as (2), and therefore that Chomsky's argument does not hold for this reason. But I think that Chomsky can easily side-step this attack by replacing "talk to" in (3) and (4) with a word such as "persuade." In that case, the missing object will be the object of the verb (e.g., "persuade"), and (5) will be able to apply. So I shall not pursue the just mentioned criticism of Chomsky's argument.

The problem posed by this example is that, though the bracketed phrase in (6) and (7) are the same, the pronoun "them" receives different interpretations. In (6) the pronoun refers to either the men or some other persons, but in (7) it can only refer to some other persons but not the men. How are children able to know the difference? Have they been explicitly taught about this? Again, Chomsky's answer is no. Again, such knowledge is without instruction or experience, he argues.

The above two examples illustrate Plato's problem. They contain only simple and short sentences. But 'the problem, already difficult enough, rapidly becomes far more serious as we consider less simple cases' (Chomsky, 1988: 24). Examples of this nature are abundant. Chomsky tries to show this in many of his writings (e.g., Chomsky, 1980b, 1986, 1988). He argues that speakers "have a rich system of knowledge, with complex and curious consequences, a system that extends far beyond any specific instruction of experience more generally" (Chomsky, 1988: 24). Knowledge is not ability or skill, he concludes. The above examples and many similar ones reveal "the hopelessness of an attempt to account for knowledge in terms of ability or to account for the use of language in terms of analogy" (Chomsky, 1988: 20). The solution to such problems "must be based on ascribing the fixed principles of the language faculty to the human organism as part of its biological endowment" (Chomsky, 1988: 27). Two examples of such abstract principles are *Specified Subject Condition and Binding Principle B*, which are used to explain the phenomenon illustrated in (3)-(4) and (6)-(7) (see Chomsky 1986, 106ff) [1].

So far we have seen how Chomsky attacks the idea of regarding knowledge of a language as a practical ability on the practical grounds by charging that it is "hopeless" and "useless" for solving Plato's problem. Chomsky also attacks the idea on conceptual grounds, by arguing that it is "entirely untenable" (Chomsky, 1988: 9). He points out that knowledge simply cannot be identified with ability. Two speakers of a language may have the same knowledge of the language, but differ markedly in their ability to use the language. Furthermore, suppose that

---

[1] *Specified Subject Condition* states that a pronoun (e.g., "him," "them") must be free in the domain of the nearest subject. This condition gives rise to *Binding Principle B*, which says that a pronoun must be free in its governing category. The governing category of a pronoun is the minimal domain containing the pronoun, its governor and an accessible subject. X governs Y if and only if (I) X is a governor and (II) X c-commands Y and Y c-commands X. The notion of c-command is defined in terms of the abstract X-bar syntax: X c-commands Y if and only if (I) X does not dominate Y and Y doesn't dominate X, and (II) the first branching node dominating X also dominates Y. A node X dominates a node Y if X is higher up in the tree than Y and there is a line from X to Y only downwards. See Haegeman (1994) for these definitions. It is apparent that Specified Subject Conditions and Binding Principle B are abstract: they are not known to ordinary speakers and can only be assumed to be innate (or derived from some innate principles).

Peter suffers a head injury and loses all ability to speak and understand English, and that when he recovers from the injury he is able to speak and understand English again. We would not say that Peter lost his knowledge of English while obviously losing his ability to speak or understand it. One way of getting out of this difficulty is to see "practical ability" as being made up of two parts, and we might call them "potential ability" and "actual ability" (to speak and understand a language) respectively. "Potential ability" means something like this: if everything is normal, e.g., if a person is not physically or mentally impaired, then the person will be able to speak the language. And "actual ability" means roughly the ability to actually use "potential ability" to speak and understand a language. So we might say, in the case of mentally impaired Peter, that he retains the "potential ability" though he lost the "actual ability' to exercise it. And we may now identify knowledge of a language with "potential ability." To this reformulation Chomsky remarks that "Plainly nothing is achieved by these verbal manoeuvres" (Chomsky, 1988: 11), and that "the problems remain, exactly as before, now embedded in terminological confusion. The task of determining the nature of our knowledge ([=potential ability]), and accounting for its origins and use, remains exactly as challenging as before, despite the terminological innovations" (Chomsky, 1986: 11). Therefore, Chomsky concludes, "the attempt to account for knowledge in terms of ability (disposition, skill, etc.) is misconceived from that start" (Chomsky, 1988: 12).

2.2 *Analogy and General Learning Mechanisms*

The "ordinary language" view of language holds that a language is learnt, through training, conditioning, or practice (Quine, 1960; Strawson, 1970; Dummett, 1978). On this view there are general learning mechanisms, and analogy plays an important part in the innovative aspects of language behavior. In the previous section we have mentioned these notions in connection with the concept of practical ability/skill, and in this section we shall discuss them further.

Putnam submits that language understanding and acquisition can be explained by assuming that "our cognitive repertoire ... must include multipurpose learning strategies, heuristics, and so forth" (Putnam, 1980a: 295). He states moreover, that 'Once it is granted that such multipurpose learning strategies exist, the claim that they cannot account for language becomes highly dubious" (Putnam, 1980a: 296).

Chomsky provides two reasons for rejecting the notions of analogy and general learning mechanisms. One is that they are vague and have no substance. To the notion of analogy, Chomsky states that "There is no general notion of 'analogy' that applies to these and other cases. Rather, the term is being used, in an extremely misleading way, to refer to properties of particular subsystems of our knowledge, entirely different properties in different cases" (Chomsky, 1988: 26-7). To the notion of general learning mechanisms, Chomsky says:

All that Putnam has so far assumed is that S_0^L [the genetically determined initial state for language learning], whatever it may be, contains only the general mechanisms for learning. Recall that he gives no hint as to what these are. To invoke an unspecified "general intelligence" or unspecified "multipurpose learning strategies" is no more illuminating than his reference, at one point, to divine intervention. We have no way of knowing what, if anything, Putnam has assumed. The point is worth stressing, since it illustrates a common fallacy in discussions of this sort. The use of words such as "general intelligence" does not constitute an empirical assumption unless these notions are somehow clarified (Chomsky, 1980a: 320).

The second reason Chomsky has for dismissing the employment of the terms "analogy" and "general learning mechanisms" is that such notions are "useless," as he says, in answering Plato's problem, e.g., in accounting for the facts shown in (1)-(4) and (6)-(7). We have seen Chomsky's dismissive remark about analogy in the preceding section. To the idea of general learning mechanisms he remarks that:

all this is wrong, dramatically so, as we can see even from simple cases such as [the two shown in Section 2.1]. Evidently, the language faculty incorporates quite specific principles that lie well beyond any "general learning mechanisms," and there is good reason to suppose that it is only one of a number of such special faculties of mind. It is, in fact, doubtful that "general learning mechanisms," if they exist, play a major part in the growth of our systems of knowledge and belief about the world in which we live-our cognitive systems. (Chomsky, 1988: 47-8)

He therefore concludes that "these ideas are not simply in error but entirely beyond any hope of repair. They must be abandoned, as essentially worthless" (Chomsky, 1988: 137).

If a language is not learnt, then how does it come about that the child can master a language? Chomsky's answer is that the child is born with a language faculty-part of his brain-which consists of "fixed and invariant principles ... and the parameters of variation associated with them" (Chomsky, 1988: 133). Language learning is "the process of determining the values of the parameters left unspecified by universal grammar" (Chomsky, 1988: 134). So "Language learning is not really something that the child does; it is something that happens to the child placed in an appropriate environment, much as the child's body grows and matures in a predetermined way when provided with appropriate nutrition and environmental simulation" (Chomsky, 1988: 134). A language is thus not learnt, but "acquired."

2.3 Conventions and Communication

2.3.1 *Conventions*

The "ordinary language" view holds that a language consists of conventions. According to Lewis, conventions are "regularities in action, or in action and belief, which are arbitrary but perpetuate themselves because they serve some sort of common interest" (Lewis, 1975: 4). Conventions in a population *P* have several characteristics, e.g., they are known by everyone in *P*, everyone in *P* conforms to them and everyone in *P* believes that others in *P* also conform to them, believing that other people in *P* conform to them is a good reason for everyone in *P* to conform to them too, and so on (cf. Lewis, 1975: 5-6).

Lewis states that "It is a platitude-something only a philosopher would dream of denying-that there are conventions of language" (Lewis, 1975: 7). But he does not "find it easy to say what those conventions are" (Lewis, 1975: 7).[1] He offers one example of conventions, namely, the convention of *truthfulness* and *trust*, which he argues satisfies the above criteria. To be truthful in a language L is to avoid uttering any sentence of L unless one believes it to be true in L. To be trusting in L is to believe that other members of *P* are also truthful. With these conventions in hand Lewis is able to define what it means to say that a language L is used by a population *P* : "a language L is used by a population *P* if and only if there prevails in *P* a convention of truthfulness and trust in L, sustained by an interest in communication" (Lewis, 1975: 10).

It seems reasonably clear that if a population *P* uses L to communicate, then there must be a convention of truthfulness and trust, or something of a similar sort. But how can the members of *P* share the same language L in the first place? Conventions in L are finite, but L is infinite. So "A person can neither follow conventions for an infinite language nor have expectations with regard to observance of conventions by others, without some finite characterization of the language that is somehow under his control" (Chomsky, 1980b: 84). So it seems that there must be a grammar, which is finite and which determines L, shared by members of P and internalized in their brains, in order for them to use L (Chomsky, 1980b: 84). Lewis is of course aware of the need of having a grammar, as he admits that he is "ready enough to believe in internally represented grammars" (Lewis, 1975: 22). But a language

---

[1] I think that Lewis is not talking about the conventions which *constitute* a language. Rather, he is talking about the conventions of *using* a language. But if we want to see some conventions which constitute a language, then we will find the task very easy. See Section 3.2.1 below.

may be characterized by many grammars, and he knows "no promising way to make objective sense of the assertion that a grammar γ is used by a population P whereas another grammar γ which generates the same language as γ, is not" (Lewis, 1975: 20). So he decides to proceed to discuss language and meaning in a way that is "independent of our evaluation of grammars" (Lewis, 1975: 20).[1]

Chomsky thinks that Lewis "is wrong on all counts" (Chomsky, 1980b: 83). He rejects Lewis's belief that it is easier to make sense of the notion "Language L is used by population P" than of the notion "Language L is determined by internally represented grammar G" as "quite wrong" and "fundamentally flawed" (Chomsky, 1980b: 85), stating that:

he presents no way to make sense of his notion, and I can imagine no way except derivatively, in terms of shared internal representation. His problem is to explain how a person can use an infinite language, or have an infinite set of expectations about sound-meaning pairings and much else, without any internal representation of that infinite object, and further, how that infinite object-a language-can be "shared" by a population without any internal representations in the minds of members of this population.

In contrast, UG proposed by Chomsky does seem to offer an explanation as to why the members of a population can use a language, because they share the same internalized grammar, according to Chomsky.

2.3.2 *Communication*

It is a common belief that the essential purpose of language is communication. We have seen in Section 2.3.1 that Lewis speaks of the

---

[1] It is not the case that Lewis rejects internal representations. What he is questioning is the notion of "an internal representation of a grammar for a language L" as talked about by Chomsky. Lewis has two problems with this notion. One is that L can be generated by different grammars, and it is difficult to ascertain which grammar is the grammar of L. Lewis is thus echoing Quine's (1972) "indeterminacy thesis." The other problem with the notion is that the sort of internal representation of a grammar in Chomsky's theory is unconscious (cf. Lewis, 1975: 22). And the idea of unconscious internal representations of grammars obviously runs foul of the idea of conventions, which Lewis advocates. I think that these two problems explain why Lewis says that he is 'much less certain that there are internally represented grammars' which are indeterminate and unconscious (Lewis, 1975: 22). The point of the above discussion is this. I think that the two problems just stated can be resolved. Firstly, though a language L can be generated by many grammars, as the existence of many grammatical theories shows, I believe that there is only one grammar that the speakers of L know. I am suggesting then that explicit knowledge is a key to Quine's "indeterminacy problem." In Section 3, I shall argue that grammar consists largely of "sentence frames," which are conventions and are known to the speakers. Secondly, I shall argue that the sentence frames the speakers know are internally represented in their brains. Such representations are conscious. I shall return to this point in Sections 3.2 and 4.

convention of truthfulness and trust in a language as sustained by an interest in communication. Searle makes the idea more explicit, when he says that "The purpose of language is communication in much the same sense that the purpose of the heart is to pump blood. In both cases it is possible to study the structure independently of function but pointless and perverse to do so, since structure and function so obviously interact. We communicate primarily with other people, but also with ourselves, as when we talk or think in words to ourselves" (Searle, 1972).[1]

The way Chomsky tackles the contention that the function of language is communication is the same as his way of attacking the notions of practical ability and conventions, which we have seen in previous text. It consists of two parts: claiming that the idea is simply wrong, and arguing that it is useless in explaining language phenomena related to Plato's problem (see below).

To show that it is wrong to say that the essential purpose of language is communication, Chomsky asks us to consider the following cases: "Suppose that in the quiet of my study I think about a problem using language, and even write down what I think. Suppose that someone speaks honestly, merely out of a sense of integrity, fully aware that his audience will refuse to comprehend or even consider what he is saying. Consider informal conversation conducted for the sole purpose of maintaining casual friendly relations with no particular concern as to its content"(Chomsky, 1980b: 230). He then questions: "Are these examples of 'communication'?" If so, what do we mean by "communication" in the absence of an audience, or with an audience assumed to be completely unresponsive, or with no intention to convey information or modify belief or attitude? (Chomsky, 1980b: 230). Given these questions and observations, Chomsky comes to the conclusion that "either we must deprive the notion 'communication' of all significance, or else we must reject the view that the purpose of language is communication" (Chomsky, 1980b: 230). He further remarks that "It is difficult to say what 'the purpose' of language is, except, perhaps, the expression of thought, a rather empty formulation. The functions of language are various. It is unclear what might be meant by the statement that some of them are 'central' or 'essential' " (Chomsky, 1980b: 230).

On the other hand, Chomsky (1975: 57ff.) argues that there is no way in

---

[1] Searle's remark that *the* function of language is communication seems to be too strong, for language may be said to have other functions. I think that what Searle really wants to say is that the *essential* function of language is communication. Even this weaker claim is attacked by Chomsky (see below). But in Section 3.2.3 I shall defend this weaker claim.

which certain general properties-e.g., structure-dependence-of "an interesting class of linguistic rules," e.g., the *Specified Subject Condition* mentioned in Section 2.1, could be accounted for in terms of communicative purpose:

let us try to account for it [i.e., structure-dependence] in terms of communication. I see no way of doing so. Surely this principle enters into the function of language; we might well study the ways in which it does. But a language could function for communication (or otherwise) just as well with structure independent rules, so it would seem. For a mind differently constituted, structure-independent rules would be far superior, in that they require no abstract analysis of a sentence beyond words. I think that the example is typical. Where it can be shown that structures serve a particular function, that is a valuable discovery. To account for or somehow explain the structure of UG, or of particular grammar, on the basis of functional considerations is a pretty hopeless prospect. (Chomsky, 1975: 57).

2.4 *Defining Language*

In ordinary usage a language is a kind of social phenomenon, a shared property of a community; and many philosophers agree with this. For example, Dummett says that "A language in the everyday sense is something essentially social, a practice in which many people engage" (Dummett, 1975: 30). Wiggins (1997) regards a language as a social object. And Lewis contends that a language is "a form of rational, convention-governed human social activity" (Lewis, 1975: 7).

Chomsky finds this common-sense notion of languages to be of little use in understanding the nature of language. He points out that "We speak of Chinese as 'language' although the various 'Chinese dialects' are as diverse as the several Romance languages. We speak of Dutch and German as two separate languages, although some dialects are not mutually intelligible with others that we call 'German'" (Chomsky, 1986: 15). He therefore asserts that "That any coherent account can be given of 'language' in this sense is doubtful; and that none has been offered or even seriously attempted. Rather, all scientific approaches have simply abandoned these elements of what is called "language" in common usage" (Chomsky, 1986: 15).

Not only does Chomsky doubt the possibility of giving a coherent account to language in "socio-political" terms, he also thinks that the common-sense notion has also a "normative-teleological element" (Chomsky, 1986: 16), which is unfit for scientific studies of language: "Consider the way we describe a child or a foreigner learning English. We have no way of referring directly to what that person knows. It is not English. We do not for example say that the person has a perfect knowledge of some language L similar to English but still different from it. What we say is that the child or foreigner has a 'partial knowledge of English,' or is 'on his or her way' toward acquiring knowledge of English, and if they reach the goal they will then know English. Whether or not a coherent account can be given of this aspect of the common-sense terminology, it does not seem to be one that has any role in any eventual science of language" (Chomsky, 1986: 16).

To Chomsky talking about language in socio-political or normative-teleological terms is too "informal" (Chomsky, 1986: 16). He suggests that, as in other scientific inquiries, we must make some idealizations, e.g., assuming a homogeneous speech community "with no dialect diversity and no variation among speakers" (Chomsky, 1986: 16) and assuming that "the property of mind ... is a species characteristic, common to all humans" (Chomsky, 1986: 18). We "must refine, modify, or simply replace the concepts of ordinary usage, just as physics assigns a precise technical meaning to such terms as 'energy,' 'force,' and 'work,' departing from the imprecise and rather obscure concepts of ordinary usage" (Chomsky, 1988: 37). Only in this way can we "have some grasp of the properties and principles of language" (Chomsky, 1988: 37). It may be possible and worthwhile to undertake the study of language in its socio-political dimensions, but "it is difficult to imagine how such studies might fruitfully progress without taking into account the real properties of mind that enter into the acquisition of language, specifically, the properties of the initial state of the language faculty characterized by UG" (Chomsky, 1986: 18).

2.5 *Conscious vs. Unconscious Rules and Knowledge*

It is generally agreed that there are rules of grammar. What the rules are is no simple matter, and it is the subject of linguistic and philosophical research. One important question about rules of grammar concerns the question whether they are conscious or unconscious. On the "ordinary language" view, rules of grammar and/or knowledge of language must be accessible to consciousness. Searle writes that "It is in general characteristic of attribution of unconscious mental states that the attribution presupposes that the state can become conscious, and without this presupposition the attributions lose much of their explanatory power" (Searle, 1976). He explains this as follows:

> when I claim that there are unconscious rules for performing speech-acts I believe that if I have stated the rules correctly then the intelligent native speaker should be able to recognize the rules as rules he has been following all along... if the rules are indeed the rules of English then English-speakers ought to be capable of a sense of how they guide their speech behavior in so far as their speech behavior is a matter of following the rules of English... it would seem at least prima facie to be a condition of adequacy of any theory purporting to state

the rules that the speaker should be in principle capable of an awareness of how the rules enter into his behavior (Searle, 1976).

In his *Philosophical Investigations* Wittgenstein says that the rules of games are known to members of the community, that the members follow the rules and are guided by them (Wittgenstein, 1953; see also Baker & Hacker, 1985: 62-3). Quine (1972) states that we may legitimately speak of guiding only when rules are consciously applied to cause behavior. Dummett writes that knowledge of a language "shows itself partly by manifestation of the practical ability and partly by a readiness to acknowledge as correct a formulation of that which is known when it is presented" (Dummett, 1978: 90; see also Section 2.1). The basic idea shared by all these philosophers is that, when we talk about rules of a language or grammar "Additional evidence is required to show that they are rules that the agent is actually following and not mere hypotheses or generalizations that correctly describe his behavior. It is not enough to get rules that have the right predictive powers; there must be some independent reason for supposing that the rules are functioning causally" (Searle, 1980).

Chomsky defends his "innate" theory in two ways. First, he argues that these philosophers' requirement that rules of grammar must be accessible to consciousness is not justified. He writes: "Searle ... offers no argument at all. He merely stipulates that mental states must be accessible to consciousness, claiming without argument that otherwise attribution of mental states loses 'much of its explanatory power'... This [i.e., Searle's requirement that a person must be aware of the rules that guide his behavior] remains sheer dogmatism, supported by no hint of argument" (Chomsky, 1980b: 131). Chomsky also adds that "The doctrine of accessibility in any of its traditional or contemporary forms seems to me entirely without antecedent plausibility, and without empirical support" (Chomsky, 1980b: 133).

Secondly, Chomsky argues that the rules of UG do explain speakers' behavior and that speakers can indeed be said to follow the rules (I shall omit the detailed argument here, but see Chomsky, 1986: 249-56). The effect is that this makes Searle's charge that UG loses "much of its explanatory power" look apparently false.

3. ASSESSING CHOMSKY'S ARGUMENT

We can summarize the "ordinary language" view of language as follows. The view consists of three major parts, concerning the nature (i.e., what language is), the origin (i.e., where language comes from), and the acquisition (i.e., how children come to know a language). On the nature of language, it states that a language is a social phenomenon, a practice in which people are engaged, a convention (or rule)-governed activity. On the origin of language, it holds that the essential purpose of language is communication: it is out of need to communicate with others (and with oneself) that language arises. As for how children come to know a language, the proponents of the "ordinary language" view claim that a language is learnt. There are general learning mechanisms in the brain. Through training, conditioning, and practice children learn to speak a language, and develop a practical ability to engage in skilful language activities. Speakers of a language may not be able to state exactly what they know about the language, but they are able to acknowledge whether a formulation of this knowledge is true or not; in other words, knowledge of a language is accessible to consciousness.[1]

Chomsky attacks the "ordinary language" view of language mainly from two angles. One is to argue that the notions expressed in the "ordinary language" view are "untenable," "vacuous," or "imprecise," and so on, and the other is to try to show that they are 'useless' in accounting for Plato's problem. We have seen ample examples of Chomsky's tactics in the previous section. From such argument Chomsky comes to the conclusion that the "ordinary language" view is "fundamentally flawed," "wrong, and dramatically so," and must be "rejected." Such an argument also gives him a strong and decisive reason for developing his "innate" view of language.

Chomsky's argument is lucid and appears to be quite persuasive. But is his argument valid? Is it the case that the "ordinary language" view cannot give a coherent account for language and knowledge, as Chomsky strongly doubts? Is it the case that the "ordinary lauguage" view is hopeless in providing an answer to Plato's problem, as Chomsky confidently asserts? Is it the case that Chomsky's 'innate' view of language is definitely correct, as he fully believes? My goal in this section is to answer these intriguing questions, and I shall argue that the answer to all of them is no. But before I come to the notions employed in the "ordinary language" view and to Plato's problem, I would like to discuss first the basic elements of a language: words, and their use.

3.1 *Words and Their Use*

The basic ingredients of a language are words. Sentences (or utterances, whatever we might call them) are made up of words. Speakers know the words

---

[1] The "ordinary language" view of language claims that knowledge of language is not innate but is accessible to consciousness. According to Dummett (1975, 1978), knowledge of language may be implicit. But later he realises that implicit knowledge is problematic as well: because it is not explicitly known to the speaker, it cannot really guide his verbal behaviour. In this paper I actually claim that knowledge of language is explicit. In Section 4, I shall discuss some of the difficulties this position faces and offer some ways of resolving them.

in their language and know how they are used.[1] The meaning of "word use" is wide; it has several senses. One sense concerns how to put words together in an understandable way. Not every string of words is a sentence: certain combinations of words are grammatical while others are not. Speakers of a language know how to use words in this sense, and we may call this sense the *syntactic* sense of "word use." For example, while the string of words "The room is cold" is grammatical, the string "room cold the is," is not. Another sense of "word use" concerns the use of individual words. For example, we can investigate how the word "game" is used. As Wittgenstein points out, there are many kinds of games, there is no essence of games; games have a family of resemblance. We may call this sense the semantic sense of "word use." A third sense of "word use" concerns the use of sentences. The same sentence may be used to express different meanings in different contexts. For example, the sentence "The room is cold" <u>may</u> simply be a report of the condition of a room, but it may also be a hint that someone should go and close the window. This sense may be called the pragmatic sense of "word use."

I shall only talk about "word use" in its syntactic sense in this paper. In English, we say "John misses Mary," "John thinks about Mary," "John is in love with Mary," "It's kind of John to help Mary whenever she is in difficulty." But we do not say "*John misses about Mary," nor "*John thinks Mary," nor "*John is on love with Mary," nor "*It's kind with John to help Mary," nor "*It is kindness of John to help Mary." Why is this so: why are the first bunch of sentences grammatical English sentences while the second bunch are not? Well, most speakers of English, if not all of them, would say that in the first bunch of sentences words have been used correctly, while words in the second bunch have not. They would say, looking at the second bunch of sentences, "You just don't use the words in these ways!" It is clear, then, that there are ways in which words should be used in order to form grammatical sentences, which I shall refer to by the term *sentence frames*. The sentence frame(s) of a word specifies how this word should be used grammatically. If the words in a sentence conform to the relevant sentence frames, then we say that they are used grammatically correctly and that the sentence is grammatical; otherwise, if they do not conform to the relevant sentence frames we say that they are used grammatically incorrectly and that the sentence is ungrammatical.

---

[1] One might say that the basic ingredients of a language are sounds-after all spoken languages preceded written languages. But it still seems to me that we do recognise a level of words, and the speaker of a language certainly knows many words in that language. I claim in this paper that knowledge of grammar is largely knowledge about how words are used, and that this knowledge is explicit. I do not claim, however, that knowledge of phonology or phonetics is explicit.

What are the correct ways of using words like "miss," "think," "love," "kind," as involved in the example just given? To put it another way, what are the sentence frames which govern the grammatically correct use of these words? I think that most, if not all, English speakers would agree with me in listing the following:

(8) You miss somebody or something.
(9) You think about somebody or something.
(10) You think of somebody or something.
(11) It is <u>kind</u> of you to do something.

Let me point out two things that need to be noted. Firstly, in (8)-(11) words/expressions such as "you," "somebody," "something" and "do something" are general, and they can be substituted by many less general words/expressions. For example, by replacing "you" with "John" and "somebody" with "Mary" in (8), we get "John misses Mary" (I ignore the problem of subject-verb agreement here). Secondly, sentence frames have different degrees of generality. For example, in (8) we can substitute "you" with any expression which refers to a person (or even a thing without making the sentence ungrammatical), but in (11) not every adjective can fill the position occupied by "kind:" only a certain family of adjective such as "polite," "generous," "rude," "brave," but not "big," "red," "heavy," and the like.

We can say, without much controversy I hope, that in the previous example the first group of sentences are grammatical because they conform to the sentence frames expressed in (8)-(11) and the second group ungrammatical because they violate these sentence frames. We can also say without much controversy that this is known to the speakers of English.

It will be helpful if I briefly compare the idea of sentence frames discussed here and similar ideas in linguistics. Take the word "miss" for an example. According to the idea of sentence frames, the use of the word is specified in (8). In linguistics, what is captured in (8) is often expressed in terms of *valency*, *argument structure* and *subcategorization*: "miss" has a valency of 2, which equivalently says that "miss" takes two arguments; in addition to this, both of the arguments of "miss" must be a noun phrase (NP), in other words, the subcategorization frame of "miss" is [NP, NP]. It might seem that the idea of sentence frames is reducible to the ideas of valency, argument structure and subcategorization. Thus it might seem that I am simply repeating what has already been said in linguistics. But there are two differences between the two approaches. One is reflected in the treatment of certain sentences; for example, the sentence "John seems to be happy." In my approach, this sentence is simply an instance of the sentence frame "Somebody seems to be ADJ." In linguistics, the treatment is often this: "seem" has a valency of 1 and it subcategorizes an inflectional phrase (IP); thus the deep structure of the sentence is something like [seems [$_{IP}$John to be happy]]; the word "John" does not have case, so it has to move forward to the front of "seem" in order to have case; the resultant sentence is "John seems to be happy" and is grammatical because it satisfies *Case Filter*, which states that every overt NP must be assigned case (see Chomsky, 1986; Haegeman, 1994 for the details).

This first difference may be regarded as a difference in technicality. But the second difference between the two approaches is more fundamental and more important. According to the approach I take, sentence frames are conventionalized ways of describing experience (meaning, thought, etc.), and they are known to the speakers (this is a central theme of this paper). Most generalizations in linguistics, however, are not known to the speakers; so they have to be assumed to be either innate or implicit. I shall return to the issue of innate or implicit linguistic knowledge in Section 4.

It will also be helpful to consider the question, Are sentence frames surface structures, deep structures, or conceptual structures? I hold that sentence frames are known to the speakers. Some sentence frames can be derived from others, for example, we can derive "Do you miss somebody?" from "You miss somebody." But all this is explicitly known. So there is no need to talk about surface or deep structures, there is no need to create something mysterious. As for the question whether sentence frames are conceptual structures, I hold that sentence frames are conventionalized ways of describing experience (meaning, thought, etc.), I also believe that sentence frames are conceptual to a large extent. But the relationship between language and thought is a complicated issue, and I shall not discuss it in this paper.

3.2 *The Nature, Origin, and Acquisition of Language*

What do words and their use have to do with the "ordinary language" and the "innate" views of language? I shall want to submit that they are the key to assessing both views. In this section I shall show that the notions employed in the "ordinary language" view of language do make clear sense, and that a coherent account of language and knowledge of language can indeed be given based on this view.

3.2.1 *Conventions*

Let us start with the idea that a language is convention-governed activity. A language, no matter whether viewed as an external object (i.e., E-language) or as derived from an internalized language (i.e., I-language) (cf. Chomsky 1986, 24ff.), consists of all the sentences in the language, and sentences are made up of words and their grammaticality is determined by whether the words are used correctly or not. Now look at words themselves. Why do we call a table "a table" and not "a chair," a tree "a tree" and not "a rabbit," and so on? The answer that everyone would give is that this is pure convention: names are arbitrary and things could have been called otherwise. Next, look at the ways in which words should be used, i.e., sentence frames. Why do we have to say "You miss somebody" and not "*You miss about somebody?" Why must we say "You think about somebody" but not "*You think somebody," etc.? The answer is again that this is convention. Words could have been used in different ways, for example, in English it could have been the case that "John thinks Mary" and "John misses about Mary" are grammatical while "John thinks about Mary" and "John misses Mary" are not.

When Lewis remarks, having claimed that "It is a platitude-something only a philosopher would dream of denying-that there are conventions of language," that "we do not find it easy to say what those conventions are" (Lewis, 1975: 7), I believe that he is thinking about the conventions of using a language. But if we look at the basic elements of a language, words and their use, we should find that conventions are everywhere in the language.

3.2.2 *Conventions and Regularities*

One of the characteristics of conventions is that they are regularities in action, or in action and belief. Now look at words and their use, which are conventionalized as I have just shown. Aren't they regularities? Don't we regularly call tables "tables," trees "trees," and rabbits "rabbits" etc.? Don't we regularly say "You miss somebody" but not "*You miss about somebody," "You think about somebody" but not "*You thinks somebody," and the like? Regularities are essential to a language. As Wittgenstein points out, if "there is no regular connexion between what they [people in a community] say, the sounds they make, and their actions," then "There is not enough regularity for us to call it 'language' " (Wittgenstein, 1953 : 207).

Let us consider Chomsky's objection to the idea of regularities. He states that "there is little reason to suppose that aspects of language that are commonly called 'conventional' involve detectable regularities" (Chomsky, 1980b: 81). He would say, for example, that there is no "regularity" that relates to the fact that (3) is paired with roughly the same meaning as (12) but not with (13) (1) (cf. Chomsky, 1980b: 83) (I repeat (3) here for convenience):

(3) John is too stubborn to talk to Bill.

(12) John is so stubborn that he will not talk to Bill.

(13) John is so stubborn that he will talk to an arbitrary person.

What Chomsky seems to be saying is that it is simply not the case that (3) regularly means (12) while it regularly doesn't mean (13): (3) always mean something like (12) and it never means something like (13).

I think that Chomsky has missed the point of regularities. We know that (3) means (12), that is, we know (14). But how do we know this? We may have been explicitly taught about this, which is especially true if (3) is the first sentence of this particular construction we encounter. Or, we may have explicitly learnt that (15) means (16), that (17) means (18), etc.:

(14) "John is too stubborn to talk to Bill" means that John is so stubborn that he will not talk to Bill.

(15) Peter is too tired to walk.

(16) Peter is so tired that he will not walk.

(17) Sue is too excited to say anything.

(18) Sue is so excited that she will not say anything.

From such data, we noticed that there is a pattern, or sentence frame:

(19) Somebody is too ADJ to do something.

And we also noticed that (19) means something like (20):

(20) He is so ADJ that he will not do it.

Now we notice that (3) is of the pattern (19), so from (20) we deduce that (3) means something like (12).

Sentence frame (19) is a pattern that every normal English speaker knows, who also knows that (19) means roughly (20). Now the notion "pattern" itself implies regularity. If there are no regularities in English, how can we know the pattern of (19), and how can we know that (19) means something like (20)? Now consider sentence (4) (repeated here for convenience):

(4) John is too stubborn to talk to.

Sentence (4), though looking rather similar to (3), is in fact of a very different pattern: it falls under (21), and means something like (23) via (22):

(21) Somebody is too ADJ to do something to.

(22) He is so ADJ that an arbitrary person will not do it to him.

(23) John is so stubborn that an arbitrary person will not talk to him.

The reason why we are able to understand a sentence like (4) as meaning something like (23) is the same as in the case of (3) and (12): we have seen regularities in the relation between sentences like (4) on the one hand and sentences like (23) on the other, and we have got a generalization expressed in (21)-(22). Chomsky seems to have totally neglected the important role regularities play in language understanding. I will come back to the problems posed by (3) and (4) later in Section 3.3, when I discuss the notions of analogy and learning in relation to Plato's problem.

To summarize the above discussion, there are two sentence frames (19) and (21), and they mean (20) and (22) respectively. The reason why we can know this is that there are sufficient regularities in the use and meaning of sentence frames (19) and (21). This reason is similar to the reason why it is a rule of traffic that drivers must stop their cars when the traffic light turns red: there are sufficient regularities between the traffic light's turning red and the drivers stopping their cars. Sentence frames (19) and (21) are conventions in English, and they are rules of English grammar.

One might raise questions about sentence frames such as (19) and (21). For example one might say that "Somebody does something," which is part of (19), does not summarize sentences such as "John knows the answer" and "Peter is rich" because strictly speaking no actions are involved in these cases. But "Somebody does something" is not confined to action-sentences, action in the strict sense. "Somebody does something" is a "favourite sentence-form" in English (Bloomfield, 1935: 171-2). According to Bloomfield, "In English we have two favorite sentence-forms. One consists of *actor-action* phrases ... The other consists of a *command*-an infinitival verb with or without modifiers: *Come! Be good!*" (Bloomfield, 1935: 172). Though Bloomfield here uses the words "actor" and "action," he cannot mean actors and actions in the strict sense; otherwise he would have to recognize not just two but many more favorite sentence-forms in English in order to cover sentences like "John knows the answer," "John needs encouragement," "John is rich," etc. Actually, Bloomfield says explicitly that "I heard him" is of the *actor-action* type (Bloomfield, 1935: 174); and the word "hear" clearly does not refer to an action in the strict sense.

One might ask a related question: What do phrases "does something" and "does something to him" cover? The phrase "does something" practically covers all sorts of verb phrases, such as "comes," "laughs," "is rich," "drinks water," "gives food to the poor," "goes swimming every other day," etc. The phrase "does something to him" practically covers all sorts of verb phrases containing the word "him," such as "beat him," "laughs at him," "gives food to him," "buys presents for him," "discusses problems with him," "puts a snake hear him," etc.[1] There is a restriction though: "him" should be on the same level as the verb in question. This is to exclude verb phrases such as "drinks the water I brought for him," which I do not consider to be of the type "does something to him." Sentence frame (21) can be seen as if it were derived from "Somebody is too ADJ to do something to him" by deleting the last word "him." So sentences of the type (21) include "John is too strong to beat," "Peter is too difficult to get rid of ," "Bill is too stupid to discuss these questions with," and "That tiger is too dangerous to go near."

3.2.3 *Communication, Community, Rule–Following, etc.*

Why should there be regularities in conventions, and in language'? This question leads us to the notions of "communication," "community," "rule-following," "interest," "convention," "good reason," and so on, which I shall discuss in this subsection.

Why do we call a table "a table," not "a chair," not "a tree," not "a rabbit," not "an idea," and so on? Can we call a table anything we like? Yes. For instance, one can call a table "an elbat." But if he wants to be understood, or even to be understood by himself, he must use "elbat" consistently. If whenever he refers to a table he uses a random term and if he also uses "elbat" to refer to any random thing, then there are no regularities among his usage, and he cannot be understood by anyone, including himself.

It seems then that one can develop a vocabulary totally different from

---

[1] A speaker may not have the generalisation:

(i) 'Somebody *does something to him*'.

Instead what he may have is a list of more concrete patterns (frames), which includes:

(ii) Somebody V him, where V is a single verb, e.g., "beat," "hit," "love," etc.
(iii) Somebody VC him, where VC is complex verb, e.g., "get rid of," "laugh at," "look into," etc.
(iv) Somebody V NP P him, e.g., "discuss ... with him," "give ... to him," "put ...near him," etc.

It seems to me that even if a speaker does not have (i) he still has frames (ii)-(iv). I myself do know frame (i), but if I am asked to provide more details about it, I have to resort to frames (i)-(iv). To me then, frame (i) is simply a convenient way of referring to frames (ii)-(iv).

For convenience I shall only speak of frame (i) and not of frames (ii)-(iv). I claim that frame (i) is known to the speaker of English. If one disputes this, I shall say that the speaker knows frames (ii)-(iv), and that my talking about frame (i) is just a convenient way of talking about frames (ii)-(iv). No matter whether the speaker knows (i) or (ii)-(iv), my idea is the same: sentence frames are conventionalised, there are sufficient regularities in their use, and they are known to the speaker.

anyone else's, as long as there are regularities and consistency in one's usage. But why do speakers of a language use the same words (with possible but few exceptions) to refer to the same things? The reason must be that they want to communicate with one another. If everyone in the speech community had different words for the same things, then everyone would have to be able to understand everyone else's vocabulary. If the community is small, and each member has few words, then communication may be possible; otherwise, it would be very difficult and might even be impossible.

A language consists of not only words, but also sentences. Words are limited, but the possible combinations of words are infinite. In the case of sentences, the need for regularity is much stronger. If a speaker simply puts a random number of words in a random way when he utters something, how can it be possible for him to be understood by anyone (including himself)?[1]

Taking words and sentences together, it is apparent that if the members of a speech community want to communicate with one another, or even with themselves, then they must agree on what words to use to refer to certain things, they must also agree on how to express certain facts, desires, beliefs, and so on. It is highly reasonable to say that it is because of the need of communication that words and sentences come into existence, that there are regularities in words and their use, that language originates. Once the rules of using words are laid down in a speech community, the members follow them in order to communicate. Why do they have to follow such rules? If they do not, they will not be able to make themselves understood, and they will not be able to communicate.

Let us now consider Chomsky's counter examples to the idea that the essential purpose of language is communication, cases where language is used for thinking, for establishing interpersonal relations, for talking to an uninterested audience, etc. (see Section 2.3.2). Chomsky questions whether these cases can be called examples of communication. Whether the examples Chomsky enumerates are *proper* examples of communication or not, is not important. What is important is whether these cases, and cases where we think there is genuine communication, e.g., reporting and debating, are essentially the same. For example, as Dummett puts it, "The use of language for self-

---

[1] It is noted that, though serial word order is almost constitutive of the grammars of English and many other languages (e.g., French and Chinese), there are languages which make heavy use of inflections, such as Latin and Sanskrit. In the case of such languages, it is inappropriate to say that sentences are formed by putting words together. But this does not invalidate the claim that there must be sufficient regularities in these languages. One cannot inflect words in a random way to form utterances if one wants to be understood by others or even by oneself.

addressed utterances, whether silent or aloud, is an imitation of its use in linguistic interchange, and involves nothing essentially different" (Dummett 1989, 185). Vygotsky also points out that silent speech is evolved from social speech (Vygotsky, 1962: 19,138). All the cases we have considered involve words and their sentence frames, which are conventionalized, which contain sufficient regularity. The speaker of a language must intend himself to be understood, by another person or by himself. Even if the speaker knows that his audience will not listen to him, he is at least *offering* communication. If someone in the audience were to ask the speaker a question, the speaker would be obliged to respond.

One might just as well question whether what Wittgenstein calls language games, such as reporting, chatting, blaming, describing, and so on, are proper games or not. But that would miss the whole point of "language games"—all games, whether proper games, e.g., basketball and chess, or language games, are governed by rules. Rules are arbitrary, but once laid down they are followed.

Chomsky's attack on the idea of communication seems to be based on a misunderstanding of the nature of communication. His rejection of this idea on the basis of the proper or improper use of the notion 'communication' is in effect to throw out the baby with the bath water.

3.2.4 *The Definition of Language*

Chomsky is very critical of the "ordinary language" view that a language is a social phenomenon, a practice that many people are engaged in. As we have seen in Section 2.4, his major argument is that this notion of language has a normative element and a teleological element, which, according to him, prevent language being studied scientifically. He states that "That any coherent account can be given of language" in this [normative] sense is doubtful; surely, "none has been offered or even seriously attempted," and that "Whether or not a coherent account can be given of this [teleological] aspect of the common-sense terminology, it does not seem to be one that has any role in any eventual science of language." He therefore concludes that the "ordinary language" notion of language is "useless" and must be abandoned.

I would like to argue for the contrary, that is, that the "ordinary language" view of language is very useful for studying language scientifically and precisely. A language consists of words, and of sentences in which words are used grammatically. We have seen in the preceding text that words and their use are conventionalized, that this is so because people want to communicate. Thus, it is true to say that a language is a social phenomenon, a social practice. What about Chomsky's objections to the so called "normative" and "teleological" elements: can we give a coherent account for language in terms of them? I shall submit here that the answer is positive.

From one point of view, a language is "the totality of all the sentences in the language" (Bloomfield, 1928). From another point of view, sentences of a language are made up of the words in the language which are used grammatically; so a language is "generated" by the words in it and their use. Two dialects of a language are said to be dialects of the same language because they share almost the same vocabulary and the words are used in almost the same way; the differences between two dialects lie mainly in the pronunciation of the words. Two languages are said to be different languages because either they have different vocabularies and they use the words differently, or they use the same vocabulary in different ways (this is rare). The examples of Chinese, German and Dutch Chomsky gives (cf. Section 2.4 and Chomsky, 1986: 15) can be easily explained in this way.

The "teleological" element Chomsky talks about (see Section 2.4) is not actually teleological or mysterious. Recall that Chomsky says, "Consider the way we describe a child or a foreigner learning English. We have no way of referring directly to what that person knows. It is not English. We do not, for example, say that the person has a perfect knowledge of some language L, similar to English but still different from it. What we say is that the child or foreigner has a 'partial knowledge of English,' or is 'on his or her way' toward acquiring knowledge of English, and if they reach the goal, they will then know English" (see Section 2.4). When a person, be he a child or a foreigner, is learning English, he has not got a sufficient English vocabulary, for example, he may not know how to name a cow when it is pointed to him, and he may use a wrong word to refer to it. In addition to this, the person has not mastered how to use enough English words in a grammatically correct way, i.e., he does not know enough words and sentence frames and he makes mistakes in forming sentences. In either of these cases, we can say that the person has a partial knowledge of English or is on his way toward acquiring knowledge of English.

Chomsky is right, I think, in pointing out that in order for members of a speech community to share a language, which is infinite, there must be a finite internal representation in the minds of the members. I think that he is also right in drawing a distinction between E-language and I-language, as long as I-language is meant to be a finite representation in the brain. We have seen in Section 2.3.1 that Lewis is "ready enough to believe in internally represented grammars" (Lewis, 1975: 22). Putnam does not deny that there is some representation of the grammar in the brain either (cf. Putnam, 1980b: 336). What Lewis and Putnam are skeptical about is the abstract and innate picture which Chomsky casts on the internalized representation. I have been suggesting that this internal representation consists of words and sentence frames. It is words and sentence frames that are internalized in the minds of the speakers of a language, that enable them to share the same language. Thus, there is no contradiction in saying that there is a finite internalized representation of a grammar and in maintaining that a language is shared by the members of a society.

3.2.5 *Practical Ability*

When Dummett states that "what he [a speaker] has when he knows the language is practical knowledge, knowledge how to speak the language" (Dummett, 1975: 36; see also Section 2.1), he is saying that knowledge of a language is practical ability to speak the language. Chomsky is right, I think, to point out that there are cases where knowledge and ability are not easily identifiable, and that the notion of ability needs to be made clearer. As we have seen in Section 2.1, we can see the practical ability of understanding and speaking a language as consisting of two parts: potential ability and actual ability, and we can identify knowledge of a language with the potential ability to understand and speak the language.

It seems, then, that the distinction between potential ability and actual ability is the same as the one drawn by Chomsky between knowledge of language and the use of this knowledge (Chomsky, 1986: 8). It also seems that Chomsky is justified in claiming that "Plainly nothing is achieved by these verbal manoeuvres," and that "the problems remain, exactly as before, now embedded in terminological confusion. The task of determining the nature of our knowledge ([=potential ability]) and accounting for its origins and use, remains exactly as challenging as before, despite the terminological innovations' (Chomsky, 1986: 11; see also Section 2.1). But I think that something is gained in speaking of potential ability/skill and actual ability/skill, something that is in fact very important. This is that both are abilities/skills. It suggests that both are acquired through, say training, conditioning, and practicing. In the preceding text I have suggested that speakers of a language have in their brains the words and the relevant sentence frames, which are a finite internal representation of the language and which enable the speakers to share the language. Now we can think about whether knowing the words and the relevant sentence frames in a language is the potential ability to understand and speak the language. The answer I suggest is yes. It is also apparent that mastering words and sentence frames require certain training and/or conditioning and/or practicing: it is like mastering any other skills.

So far I have presented quite a coherent account of a variety of notions employed in the "ordinary language" view of language, such as "convention," "regularity," "communication," "ability/skill," "community," "rule-following," "conscious knowledge" etc., based on the concepts of words and word use. It shows that these notions are insightful, significant and quite correct, rather than being "entirely untenable," "vacuous," "wrong," as Chomsky claims. But Chomsky has another weapon which he employs to attack the "ordinary language" view, it being Plato's problem, as we have seen in Section 2. He may still say that, no matter what sense one can make out of the "ordinary view" of language, if it cannot provide an answer to Plato's problem then it will still be useless. He claims that the "ordinary language" view cannot solve Plato's problem, and therefore it is indeed "useless." I shall assess his relevant argument in the next section.

3.3 *Plato's Problem Reconsidered*

Recall that Plato's problem is "the problem of explaining how we can know so much given that we have such limited evidence" (Chomsky, 1986: xxv; see also Section 1 above). The version of Plato's problem in the study of human language is to explain how the child is capable of acquiring a complex human language in an environment characterized by "poverty of stimulus," and how the child is capable of acquiring any human language. According to the "ordinary language" view, the child has innate general learning mechanisms, which enable it to learnt, through training, conditioning, or practicing, how to understand and speak certain sentences; production and interpretation of new forms are done using analogy (see Section 2.2). Knowledge of a language is a kind of ability or skill, obtained in the process of learning the language (see Section 2.1).

But Chomsky asserts that the notion of analogy is "hopeless" and "useless" in accounting for how the child acquires a language. Over the years he has given a series of examples which he think prove his claim. Two such examples were shown in Section 2.1 above. Since these two examples are typical. I shall in this section concentrate on them only. Let us have a closer look at the first example, which is repeated here for convenience:

(1) John ate an apple.
(2) John ate.
(3) John is too stubborn to talk to Bill.

(4) John is too stubborn to talk to.
(5) Whenever the object is missing, an arbitrary object is meant.

Let me also repeat Chomsky's argument here. (1) means that John ate an apple. (2) is understood as meaning that John ate something or other, and on the basis of this we may arrive at generalization (5). (3) means that John is so stubborn that he will not talk to Bill. Now, the object of "talk to" is missing in (4), so (4) is analogous to (2). Thus by analogy, (4) should be interpreted relative to (3) just as (2) is interpreted relative to (1); (4) should mean something like that John is so stubborn that he will not talk to an arbitrary person. But (4) does not mean this, in fact it means that John is so stubborn that an arbitrary person will not talk to him. Since the child knows, unerringly, how to interpret (1)-(4), it does not employ analogy; and analogy cannot explain why the child can interpret these sentences without error.[1]

I think that Chomsky's argument is invalid, even though it is interesting. One weakness of his argument lies in his claim that the child knows, "unerringly," how to interpret (1)-(4). Chomsky does not offer any evidence to support this claim. Is it the case that any child, at any age, at any stage of its acquiring English, does not make any mistake in interpreting sentences such as (1)-(4)? It is quite conceivable that a child may make the mistake Chomsky mentions in interpreting a sentence like (4) (especially when the child encounters a sentence of this construction for the first time). If children do make mistakes in such cases, then there will be little ground for Chomsky's claim that children's knowledge of how to interpret (1)-(4) is "knowledge without experience." It will also mean that children do use analogy and generalization when interpreting sentences like (1)-(4).

It is also quite conceivable that children who have acquired enough English do not make mistakes in interpreting sentences like (1)-(4). There is a perfectly satisfactory explanation for this in terms of generalization and analogy. The word "stubborn" can be used in the following two ways, which are repeated here:

(19) Somebody is too ADJ to do something.
(21) Somebody is too ADJ to do something to.

Sentence (3) matches (19), and it means that John is so stubborn that he will not talk to Bill. Sentence (4) matches (21) easily, and it means that John is so stubborn that people do not want to talk to him. Sentence (4) does not match (19) easily. For them to match, "talk to" would have to be something that a person can do. But normally we do not say things like "John talks to" or "John talked to" (unlike "John kills" or "John ate"). If a child has learnt all this, it will think that (4) is an instance

---

[1] Cf. Note 2 above.

of (21) and not (19); it will interpret (4) accordingly, and correctly.[1] So even in the case when certain children do not make mistakes in interpreting (1)-(4), we do not really need to postulate "knowledge without experience."

I shall now turn to another example that Chomsky offers, which we have also seen in Section 2.1 and which is repeated here. Consider the following two sentences:

(6) I wonder who [the men expected to see them].
(7) [The men expected to see them].

Chomsky's argument is this. The two bracketed phrases are similar, analogous to each other. But they receive different interpretations: the pronoun "them" in (6) can mean either the men or some other people, but in (7) it can only mean some other people other than the men. If children understood a language using analogy, then they would understand (7) in the same way as they understand (6). But children do not do this, so the notion of analogy is not only useless but also wrong.

Again there is a weakness in Chomsky's argument. He does not offer evidence that children, whatever their age, do not make mistakes at all in interpreting (6)-(7). If children do make mistakes in such cases, then it will be against Chomsky's conclusions and it will be for the ideas of analogy and generalization. Even if children after a certain age, when they have acquired sufficient English, do not make any mistakes in such cases, there still exists a perfectly satisfactory explanation in terms of analogy and generalization. We only need to note that though the bracketed phrases in (6) and (7) are similar (in fact they are the same) in wording, the words are actually used very differently. To explicate what is involved, it is necessary here to digress a little. Let us start with a simple sentence:

(24) John shaved him.

(24) means that the man John shaved was someone other than John himself. How does the child know this? There are three explanations. One is that the child is explicitly taught about sentence (24) and the interpretation of 'him' in the sentence. This explanation is plausible especially when the sentence is the first one containing 'him' that the child encounters. We can also say that when the child explicitly learns the interpretation of "him" in (24), it also learns the interpretation "himself" in the sentence "John shaved himself:" "himself" here refers to "John."

---

[1] If the words "talk to" in (4) are replaced by the word "persuade," then (4) will match both (19) and (21), and will be ambiguous. (4) will mean either that John is so stubborn that he will not persuade anybody or that John is so stubborn that nobody can persuade him. This case actually supports the idea of generalization and analogy.

The child cannot have learnt the correct interpretation of "him" in "John shaved him" without having learnt the interpretation of "himself" in "John shaved himself." But I shall only concentrate on the use and interpretation of "him" here.

The second explanation is that the child has learnt sentences like (25):

(25) John hit him.

and it therefore interprets (24) on the analogy of (25). Now, this explanation seems to be circular. It seems that if the child is to understand (24) using analogy, it needs to have already understood (25). So it seems that if the child is to understand (25), it needs to have already understood another analogous sentence. The circularity thus seems to be obvious. But there is in fact no circularity in this second explanation. This second explanation assumes that (25) has been explicitly learnt by the child, through explicit teaching (see the first explanation discussed above). It does not assume that every sentence is learnt and understood on the analogy of another sentence. Analogy must end somewhere, and where it ends is explicit teaching and learning.

The third explanation is that the child has arrived at a generalization (26):

(26) Somebody does something to him.

where "him" and "somebody" do not refer to the same person,[1] after learning many sentences like (24) and (25) through explicit teaching or analogy. The child also knows that (24) is just an instance of (26), so interprets "him" in (24) accordingly and correctly. Again, there is no circularity in this explanation. The reason is that this explanation does not assume that every sentence is understood on the basis of a generalized sentence; an explanation assuming that would indeed be circular.

Now consider a slightly more complicated case:

(27) John wants to shave him.

I say that (27) is more complicated than (24) because while (24) has the sentence frame "X shaves Y," (27) has the frame "X wants to shave Y." The latter frame is more complicated than the former; a child who has learnt the former does

---

[1] There is actually an exception to this generalization: if "him" occurs after propositions describing space or time, then "him" and "somebody" can then co-refer. For example, in "John put the mug near him" "him" can refer to John. This exception seems to be also known to the speakers. For the meaning of the phrase "does something to him," see Note 1 above.

not necessarily know the latter. (27) is another way of using "him;" and "him" does not refer to "John." As in the previous example, there are three explanations about why the child knows this interpretation of "him." The child may simply have been taught that in this sentence "him" does not refer to "John." Or it may get this on the analogy of, say, (28):

(28) John wants to hit him.

which it has understood before. Or the child may interpret (27) correctly because it knows that (27) is an instance of (29):

(29) Somebody <u>wants</u> to do something to him.

It knows that in (29) "somebody" and "him" do not co-refer. Note that the child may also learn that other words can be used in the same way as "want" in (27)-(29), i.e., that it can also put other words such as "hope," "expect," "love," "would like," "hate," etc., in the place occupied by "want."

Let us now move on to a more complicated case:

(30) John <u>wants</u> Peter to shave him.

Now there is a difference between (27) and (30). In (27) "John" and "him" do not co-refer. But in (30) "him" may refer to John. Again the child may simply learn this, or it may get this on the analogy of (31) (assuming that the child has learnt (31)), or deduce it from a generalization (32):

(31) John <u>wants</u> Mary to kiss him, where "John" and "him" can co-refer.

(32) Somebody <u>wants</u> X to do something to him, where "somebody" and "him" can co-refer.

We are now in a position to explain the problem posed by (6)-(7). (7) is analogous to (27)-(28), and is an instance of (29). So in (7) 'them' has to mean some people other than the men. (6) is formed on the basis of (33):

(33) I wonder [the men expect who to see them].

And the bracketed phrase in (33) is analogous to (30)-(31) and is an instance of the generalisation (32). So in (6) "them" refers to either the men or some other people not mentioned in (6).

One might argue that "him" in (24), (27) and (30) is interpreted in the same way. According to this view, there is a generalization that in a clause a pronoun (such as "him") and the subject must not co-refer. This is in fact *Binding Principle B* (see Note 1; see also Chomsky, 1986 and Haegeman, 1994).

In (24) the subject is "John," so "him" does not refer to "John" according to this principle. (27) is analyzed as "John wants [PRO to shave him]," where PRO is a pronoun with no phonetic content and is "controlled" by "John" (i.e., PRO and "John" co-refer). According to Binding Principle B, in the clause [PRO to shave him] "him" and PRO must not co-refer; since PRO is controlled by "John," so "him" must not refer to "John." (30) is analyzed as "John wants [Peter to shave him]." In the clause [Peter to shave him], "Peter" is the subject. So according to Binding Principle B, "him" cannot refer to "Peter;" but this still leaves the possibility that "him" refers to "John." Thus, the principle also explains why "him" and "John" can co-refer in (30). See Chomsky (1986) and Haegeman (1994) for more details.

But I want to argue that it is not a logical necessity that in English "him" and "John" in (24) must not refer to the same person. If English had developed differently, it could have been the case that in (24) "him" can refer to "John." (If a language lacked reflexives, pronouns would have to be used to express reflexive ideas.) In fact, in Old English "him" was often used reflexively. I also want to argue that neither is it a logical necessity that if "him" and "John" do not co-refer in (24) then they must also not co-refer in (27). It could have been the case that the former is true while the latter is false (had English developed differently). It could have been the case that in (27) "him" refers either to John himself or to another man: the ambiguity could be resolved by contextual information.[1] Similarly, it could have been the case that in (30) "him" must not refer to "John," and that if the speaker wants the word at the position occupied by "him" to mean "John" then he must use "himself."

I argue, therefore, that not only are the sentence frames of (24), (27) and (30) conventionalized, the interpretations of "him" in the three sentences (and the three sentence frames) are also conventionalized. The sentence frames could have been different, and the interpretations could have been also different.

As a summary, the three conventionalized sentence frames concerning 'him' and the relevant interpretations of "him" are repeated here:

(26) Somebody does something to him, where "somebody" and "him" do not

---

[1] Just as "him" in "John found a snake near him" refers either John himself or to another man. The point is not whether it is the case in English that "him" and "John" in (27) co-refer or not. The point is whether it could have been the case in English had English developed differently. If this were indeed the case in English (or another language), that is, if it were the case that in (27) "him" could refer to "John," would this language not be a human language, would a human not be able to understand and use it? I believe that the answer is yes: the language would still be a human language, and a human would still be able to understand and use it.

co-refer.

(29) Somebody <u>wants</u> to do something to him, where "somebody" and "him" do not co-refer.

(32) Somebody <u>wants</u> X to do something to him, where "somebody" and "him" can co-refer.

From the community's point of view, sentence frames (26), (29) and (32) are conventionalized ways of describing certain experience (meaning, thought, etc.). From the child's point of view, after having learnt explicitly certain concrete exemplar sentences, such as (24), (27) and (30), its task is to apply these sentences to analogous sentences, or arrive at generalizations (26), (29) and (32) on the basis of the exemplar sentences. Thus, there is perfect harmony between the community's conventionalizing certain ways of describing meaning, thought and experience on the one hand, and the child's acquiring these conventionalized ways (rules) on the other.

The problem posed by (6)-(7), on which Chomsky focuses, can be explained quite easily in terms of conventionalized sentence frames and interpretations, analogy and generalization. The notions of analogy and generalization therefore, I argue, are very plausible and useful, contrary to Chomsky's claims. In my opinion Chomsky is wrong in rejecting the notions of analogy and generalization, solely on the basis that an explanation of certain problems, such as those posed by (3)-(4) and (6)-(7), in terms of these notions has not, according to him, been given. He has also jumped to the conclusion that knowledge of grammar is knowledge "without experience or instruction," and that it must be innate, and that it can only be characterized by UG principles, e.g., *Binding Principle B*.

It seems to me that we can seriously doubt the validity of Chomsky's innate syntactic principles, such as *Binding Principle B*. If the explanation I offered just now in terms of convention, analogy and generalization works well, then why should we need *Binding Principle B*? If my account of the conventional nature of (26), (29), and (32) is correct, then *Binding Principle B* will at best be a contingent and not a necessary syntactic generalization; so in what sense is the principle innate (for it could have been violated in English or another language easily) ? One might argue that even if *Binding Principle B* is a contingent generalization, it will be good enough in linguistics. But what good is a linguistic generalization if the speaker does not know it, if his verbal behavior is not guided by it? We have encountered the problem of whether linguistic knowledge is implicit or explicit in Section 3.1, and I shall return to it in Section 4.

I have been arguing for the idea of sentence frames, which are conventionalized ways of using words to describe certain experience (meaning, thought, etc.).

Chomsky might argue that the number of words and the number of sentence frames are finite, but a language is infinite, so a language can not be explained in terms of words and their use. For example, he might say that the explanation I offered to the problems posed in his two examples only "illustrate substitution of items in a fixed frame" (cf. Chomsky, 1980a: 315), and therefore it might only work for a small fragment of a language. I think that such a view reflects an under-estimation of the power of words and their use. It is true that the number of words and sentence frames is finite; it is also true that sentence frames are frames with slots. But sentence frames are general, each can cover a large, and even an infinite, number of sentences. For example, take:

(34) You believe that something is the case.

In (34) "something is the case" may be replaced by an arbitrary sentence. Sentence frames can be transformed, and combined, e.g.,

(35) Having done one thing, you start to do another, which combines (36) and (37):
(36) Having done something.
(37) Somebody starts to do something.

And (36) is transformed from (38):

(38) Somebody has done something.

So it is reasonable to expect that once the child learns a sufficient number of words and sentence frames of a language, and knows how to substitute, transform, and combine etc., it should be able, or at least has the potential ability, to speak the language; it should be able to create, in Jespersen's words, "free expressions" on the basis of the words and sentence frames it has acquired (Jespersen, 1924, 1937; see Lin, 1998 for a detailed discussion).

Plato's problem is a genuine problem. But the solution may not need to be found only in UG. In this section we have seen that problems of language, at least some of them, can be accounted for by using the notions of word use, convention, generalization, learning, and analogy. Chomsky's dismissal of these notions is, as I have argued, not well-founded. This section also suggests that Chomsky's own conception of language may not be grounded firmly either.

4. CONCLUSIONS AND DISCUSSIONS

We all have strong intuitions about language. Our intuitions may not be entirely correct, but they are very valuable to our study of language. Chomsky himself places great emphasis on the role of intuition, and he tries to develop a theory which can explain certain intuition of ours about language, e.g., why we think that some sentences are grammatical while some others are not, and why, among the latter, we think that some sentences are less acceptable than others. Our intuitions of language also tell us that a language is a social phenomenon, that it is used for communication, that it consists of conventions, that it is learnt, and so on. It is puzzling why Chomsky seems to adopt only the former kind of intuitions and try to explain them, while disregarding the second kind of intuitions altogether. Trying to explain only one kind of intuitions of ours about language is fine, but it would be better if both kinds could be accounted for. Since the "innate" view cannot accommodate the second kind of intuitions, it seems that the task of explaining both kinds can only be done in the "ordinary language" framework, given the current state of the study of language.

Chomsky himself is aware of the possibility of developing an account of knowledge of language based on the "ordinary language" view of language. But in his view no substantial research along this line has been made and he cannot see how the task can be achieved. For example he says of the belief that the purpose of language is communication that "there is no formulation of this belief, to my knowledge, from which any substantial proposals follow" (Chomsky, 1980b: 230), of the idea that a language has a socio-political dimension that "That any coherent account can be given of 'language' in this sense is doubtful" (Chomsky, 1986: 15), of the concept of a community language (i.e., a language shared by a community) that "there is virtually no attempt to explain what it might be" (Chomsky, 1993: 39; see also Chomsky, 1995a: 51), and of the notions of analogy, induction, etc., that "there is little hope in accounting for our knowledge in terms of such ideas" (Chomsky, 1986: 12). He therefore simply ignores the "ordinary language" view of language, and states explicitly that "As far as I can see, then, the only proper course is to take note of these attitudes, and then to disregard them, at least until some coherent argument or alternative is offered" (Chomsky, 1980b: 132).

In this paper I offered an account of both the grammatical aspect and the sociopolitical aspect of our intuitions about language, and the account does appear to be coherent. I started with words and word use, pointed out that they are conventions, stated that the use of words has sufficient regularity, which I argued is a must for the purposes of understanding and communication. I suggested that words and their use are learnt, through training, conditioning, or practice, and that they are internalized in the speaker's brain. I argued that once the child learns words and their use, it has the potential ability to engage in skilful language activities. I also illustrated that language understanding and production can be explained in terms of generalization, learning, and analogy, using some of Chomsky's own examples, which he designed to demolish these very notions.

The conclusion reached in this paper is this. Chomsky's dismissal of the "ordinary language" view lacks grounding, his argument against it is not valid. Since his rejection of the "ordinary language" view is a strong and decisive reason for developing his own "innate" view, it is questionable that the "innate" view is correct. The "ordinary language" view, by contrast, does seem to be a coherent and correct view of language.

Though Chomsky's argument against the "ordinary language" view of language does not constitute a dismissal of it, some of his criticisms and remarks are nonetheless reasonable and constructive. Firstly, Chomsky's criticisms make us realize that we should not be content with general and vague formulations of convention, ability, and so on. We must make such notions precise and provide details. Secondly, Chomsky points out that for it to make sense to say that a language is shared by a population there must be internal representations of the grammar in the minds of members of this population. We must try to find out what such internal representations are. Thirdly, Chomsky brings together language and the mind (cf. Chomsky, 1995a). His research reminds us that the study of language cannot be detached from how the mind works and how a language is learnt/acquired.

The present paper presents an outline of how to incorporate the above three ideas into the "ordinary language" framework. It shows that both the "ordinary language" view and the "innate" view have things constructive to offer. The paper is therefore an attempt to synthesize the discussions and debates in linguistics and philosophy in the past few decades. It also outlines a research paradigm in which the following three major questions needed to be addressed:

Firstly, how can we explain language data concerning grammar in terms of words and sentence frames? It will be useful if we can do this in a systematic way. Fortunately, Chomskyan linguistics has provided many principles, e.g., *Binding Theory*, *Case Theory*, *Control Theory*, etc., which are capable of accounting for a large variety of data. The best way for us to proceed is, in my view, to explain the grammatical problems which Chomskyan principles are designed to explain, using words and sentence frames. Some examples have already been provided in this paper (see Section 3.3). In doing this we can discover how the mind manipulates words and sentence frames to parse and generate sentences. The basic operations which the mind can perform on words and sentence frames include, I argue, generalization, substitution, and analogy (cf. Section 3.3). We still need to investigate the details of such operations.

Secondly, how does the child learn sentence frames and why is it able to learn them? It is hard to deny that words are learnt. Chomsky himself says that the lexicon is learnt, so are idioms, such as "X kicked the bucket" "X is as cool as a cucumber." I argue that sentence frames are learnt in the same way. The number of sentence frames is finite, but they are capable of generating an infinite number of sentences. But the learning of words, idioms and sentence frames requires some mental facilities. We must inquire into these mental facilities.

Thirdly, why is the child capable of learning not just one but any human language? Postulating a universal grammar is one way of answering this question. But I suggest a different answer. All human languages consist of words and sentence frames. The child has the mental capability to learn them (see the preceding paragraph). It also has the mental capability to do certain operations on words and sentence frames (see the paragraph before the last). Equipped with these mental capabilities, which are indeed innate, the child is able to master any human language.

Before ending this paper, let me make four brief discussions. The first topic is the acquisition of grammar. In this paper, I have been arguing that grammar consists of sentence frames and certain operations on them. The idea of sentence frames is philosophically plausible: it accords well with the 'ordinary language' view of language. This idea is also psychologically plausible. Researchers in child language acquisition have provided evidence that the child learns patterns similar to what I have here called sentence frames, and these patterns constitute early grammar (Braine, 1976; Schlesinger, 1977, 1982; Pine & Lieven, 1993).

The second discussion concerns the notion of rules. In this paper I argued that rules of grammar are conventionalized and known, rather than unconscious. It might be said that my criticisms of Chomsky's theory are off target because in Chomsky's recent works rules have been replaced by certain principles (Chomsky, 1986; Haegeman, 1994), which have in turn been replaced by certain even more abstract principles (Chomsky, 1995b). But in Chomsky's linguistics the nature of such principles is the same as that of rules: such principles are innate, unconscious. So my criticisms of Chomsky's "rules" also apply to his "principles."

The third issue I want to discuss concerns the nature of knowledge of grammar. There are three views on this. The first view says that grammatical knowledge is innate. The second says that it is accessible to consciousness but it is implicit. The third view states that it is explicit. This paper argues against the first view, i.e., the "innate view" of grammatical knowledge, and is sympathetic to the second view. But there is a problem with the second view. Recall that implicit knowledge is conscious, and that though a speaker "cannot himself formulate the content of the knowledge ... [he can] recognize as correct a formulation that is offered to him" (Dummett, 1993:

xi; see also Sections 2.1 and 2.5 above). Implicit knowledge is not explicitly known to the speaker, so how can such knowledge "operate to guide, prompt, or control the speaker's utterances?" -a problem that, Dummett now thinks, implicit knowledge and unconscious knowledge share (Dummett, 1993: xi). Dummett remarks: "Talking about unconscious knowledge does not solve this problem, nor does talking about implicit knowledge" (Dummett, 1993: xii).

In this paper, though I am sympathetic to the view that knowledge of grammar is conscious but implicit, I have in fact been arguing that this knowledge is explicit. This can be seen from my discussions about words and the frames in which they are used-both are, I have argued, explicitly known to the speaker (see Section 3 above). In other words, I have been advancing the third view mentioned just now. But there seems to be a difficulty with this third view. Note that in linguistics it is often the case that a speaker is not sure whether a particular sentence is grammatical or not, or that different speakers have different opinions about the grammaticality of a particular sentence, even if they are brought up in the same language community. For example:

? Which car don't you know how to fix?
? This is the book which reading would be fun.

So there is uncertainty in grammatical judgments. Now the difficulty with the third view is this: if speakers have explicit grammatical knowledge, then why should there be uncertainty in their grammatical judgments?

To answer this question, I shall try to provide an analogous case in everyday life. In the British traffic system, there is a rule which states that it is illegal to park a vehicle on the double yellow lines. This rule is explicit, and drivers and traffic wardens explicitly know this rule; this rule guides their relevant behavior. Now suppose that there is a vehicle carrying a long pole, and that though the vehicle is not parked on the double yellow lines, part of the pole is above them. Is the vehicle parked illegally? Different people may have different opinions on this: some may say yes, some may say no, and some may even say that they do not know. Why should there be uncertainty in judgments in this case since the rule just mentioned is so explicit? The reason is that when that rule was laid, not all the cases in which it would be applicable were specified. In Wittgenstein's words, the answer to the question, What is illegal parking?, was not "given once for all; and independently of any future experience" (Wittgenstein, 1953: 92). The legislators of the rule could not have imagined all its applicable cases. That particular parking rule has worked well in everyday life. Though there have been cases which generated problems for the application of the rule, people have often got away with them. But, should that parking rule prove to be seriously inadequate in the future, it will be amended.

Rules of grammar are, I suggest, of the same nature as the parking rule just discussed. Grammar rules are explicitly known. But there are always sentences which pose problems for the application of certain grammar rules, and this gives rise to uncertainty in grammatical judgments. Note that such sentences are usually queer and are not usually uttered by a speaker; they are in a sense "abnormal" sentences. Note also that usually there are ways of rephrasing such "abnormal" sentences, using other sentences whose grammaticality is not in doubt. As Wittgenstein (1953: 142) points out, "It is only in normal cases that the use of a word is clearly prescribed; we know, are in no doubt, what to say in this or that case. The more abnormal the case, the more doubtful it becomes what we are to say." So speakers can usually get away from such seemingly difficult situations. 'Abnormal' sentences do exist, but they rarely cause serious problems in everyday communication, and it is rarely the case that grammar rules have to be amended in order to eliminate "abnormal" sentences. The existence of "abnormal" sentences, which cause uncertainty in grammatical judgments, is a natural outcome of grammar rules. The existence of them does not invalidate the claim that knowledge of grammar is explicit, nor does it imply that ordinary language is imperfect. I believe that this issue is of the utmost importance in linguistics and philosophy, and I hope to discuss it further on another occasion.

The fourth and final issue I want to discuss briefly before ending this paper is the view that language is innate. There are in fact two such views, one is weak and the other is strong. The weak view says that there is an innate basis of language: there must be something innate in us humans which enables us to master a language, just as there is also an innate basis of mathematics, of chess-playing, of car-driving, etc. But just as there do not have to be innate principles which are *specific* to mathematics, chessplaying, or car-driving, there do not have to be innate principles which are *specific* to language. The strong view, by contrast, states that there are innate, *language-specific* principles. Chomsky's "innate view" of language discussed in this paper is a strong view.

Chomsky's "innate view" of language has generated a lot of discussions in linguistics, psychology, and evolution theory in recent years, see Piattelli-Palmarini (ed.) (1980), Lust (ed.) (1986), Pinker and Bloom (1990), Pinker (1994), to list a few. There are many arguments for the strong view of the innateness of language, and hence for Chomsky's theory of language. Elman et al. (1996) discuss twelve such arguments, namely: species specificity, genetically based language disorders, studies of lesioned brains, activation studies of grammar in the normal brain, structural eccentricity of language, poverty of the stimulus, linguistic universals, modularity of processing, dissociations, critical periods of language learning, and robustness under different learning conditions (see also Fromkin, 1997 for a survey). They examine these arguments carefully, and find that none of these arguments provides conclusive support to the proposition that there are innate, *language-specific* principles.

The "ordinary language" view of language defended in this paper is against the strong view of language innateness, but it is consistent with the weak view. It is an interesting research topic to investigate what the innate basis of language is, in the weak sense of the word "innate." I suggest that it consists of *notions* such as time, person, and number (Jespersen, 1924), and *notional abilities* such as those of individuating objects and processes (Strawson, 1959), of making the subject-predicate distinction (Jespersen, 1924; Strawson, 1974), of telling "major linkages" from "minor linkages" (Strawson, 1974), and so on. Such notions and notional abilities are, in Jespersen's words, "universal," "psychological," and "common to all mankind" (Jespersen, 1924).[1] I also suggest that such notions and notional abilities enable us to learn sentence frames and to create new sentences ("free expressions" in Jespersen's terminology). In other words, I suggest that such notions and notional abilities make human language possible. For a more detailed discussion, see Lin (1998).

ACKNOWLEDGEMENTS

I would like to thank Peter F. Strawson and Michael Dummett for stimulating discussions and encouraging comments. Thanks also to James Higginbotham, Gilbert Harman, Martin Davies, and Gordon P. Baker for comments and suggestions. Elinor Reynolds read an earlier version of this paper and provided me with many helpful suggestions.

REFERENCES

Baker, G. P. & P. M. S. Hacker. 1985. *Wittgenstein: Rules, Grammar and Necessity*. Oxford: Blackwell.

Bloomfield, L. 1928. A set of postulates for the science of language. *Language* 2. Reprinted

---

[1] Jespersen (1924) says that notions and the related principles constitute a "universal grammar." Jespersen's ideas have greatly influenced Chomsky, who claims that he is following the programme outlined by Jespersen (Chomsky, 1977: 59; 1995b: 3). But Lin (1998) shows that Chomsky has seriously misunderstood Jespersen's ideas, and that Jespersen's "universal grammar" is rather different from Chomsky's.

in M. Joos (ed.), *Readings in Linguistics*, American Council of Learned Sciences, Washington, 1957.

Bloomfield, L. 1935. *Language*. London: Allen and Unwin.

Braine, M. D. S. 1976. *Children's First Word Combinations*. Chicago: University of Chicago Press.

Chomsky N. 1975. *Reflections on Language*. New York: Pantheon Books.

Chomsky, N. 1977. *Essays on Form and Interpretation*. New York: North-Holland.

Chomsky, N. 1980a. Discussion of Putnam's comments. In M. Piattelli-Palmarini (ed.), 310-324.

Chomsky, N. 1980b. *Rules and Representation*. New York: Columbia University Press.

Chomsky, N. 1986. *Knowledge of Language: Its Nature, Origin, and Use*. New York: Praeger.

Chomsky, N. 1988. *Language and Problems of Knowledge: The Managua Lectures*. London: MIT Press.

Chomsky, N. 1993. Mental constructions and social reality. In E. Renland & W. Abraham (eds.), *Knowledge of Language*, Vol. 1. London: Kluwer.

Chomsky, N. 1995a. Language and Nature. *Mind* 104, 1-61.

Chomsky, N. 1995b. *The Minimalist Program*. London: MIT Press.

Dummett, M. 1975. What is a theory of meaning? (II). In G. Evans & J. McDowell (eds.), *Truth and Meaning*. London: Oxford University Press. Reprinted in Dummett 1993, 34-93.

Dummett, M. 1978. What do I know when I know a language? First published as a paper presented at the Centenary Celebrations, Stockholm University. Reprinted in Dummett 1993, 94-105.

Dummett, M. 1989. Language and communication. In A. George (ed.), *Reflections on Chomsky*. Oxford: Blackwell.

Dummett, M. 1993. *The Seas of Language*. Oxford: Clarendon Press.

Elman, J. L., E, A, Bates, M. H. Johnson, A. Karmiloff-Smith, D. Parisi, & K. Plunkett. 1996. *Rethinking Innateness: A Connectionist Perspective on Development*. London: MIT Press.

Fromkin, V. A. 1997. Some thoughts about the brain/mind/language interface. *Lingua* 100, 3-27.

Haegeman, L. 1994. *Introduction to Government and Binding Theory* (2nd edition). Oxford: Blackwell.

Jespersen, O. 1924. *The Philosophy of Grammar*. London: Allen and Unwin.

Jespersen, O. 1937. *Analytic Syntax*. London: Allen and Unwin. Reprinted in 1984 by University of Chicago Press, Chicago.

Lewis, D. 1975. Language and languages. In K. Gunderson (ed.), *Language, Mind, and Knowledge*. Minneapolis: University of Minnesota Press.

Lin, F. Y. 1998. *Jespersen, Skinner and Chomsky on Language*. Oxford: Somerville College.

Lust, B. (ed.). 1986. *Studies in the Acquisition of Anaphor*. Dordrecht: Reidel.

Piattelli-Palmarini, M. (ed.) 1980. *Language and Learning: The Debate between Jean Piaget and*

Noam Chomsky. London: Routlege and Kegan Paul.

Pine, J. M. & E. V. M. Lieven. 1993. Reanalyzing rote-learned phrases: individual differences in the transition to multi-word speech. *Journal of Child Language* 20, 551-71.

Pinker, S. & P. Bloom. 1990. Natural language and natural selection. *Behavioral and Brain Sciences* 13, 707-27.

Pinker, S. 1994. *The Language Instinct: The New Science of Language and Mind*. London: Allen Lane.

Putnam, H. 1980a. What is innate and why: comments on the debate. In Piattelli Palmarini (ed.), 287-309.

Putnam, H. 1980b. Comments on Chomsky's and Fodor's replies. In Piattelli-Palmarini (ed.), 335-40.

Quine, W. V. O. 1960. *Word and Object*. Cambridge, MA: MIT Press.

Quine, W. V. O. 1972. Methodological reflections on current linguistic theory. In G. Harman & D. Davidson (eds.), *Semantics of Natural Language*. New York: Humanities Press.

Schlesinger, I. M. 1977. *Production and Comprehension of Utterances*. NJ: Lawrence Erlbaum Associates.

Schlesinger, I. M. 1982. *Steps to Language: Towards a Theory of Native Language Acquisition*. NJ: Lawrence Erlbaum Associates.

Searle, J. R. 1972. Chomsky's revolution in linguistics. *New York Review of Books*. June 29.

Searle, J. R. 1976. The rules of the language game. *Times Literary Supplement*, 10 September.

Searle, J. R. 1980. Rules and Causation. *The Behavioral and Brain Sciences* 3, 37-39.

Strawson, P. F. 1970. *Meaning and Truth*. Oxford: Oxford University Press.

Strawson, P. F. 1974. *Subject and Predicate in Logic and Grammar*. London: Methuen.

Vygotsky, I. S. 1962. *Thought and Language*. Cambridge: MIT Press.

Wiggins, D. 1997. Languages as Social Objects. *Philosophy* 72, 499-524.

Wittgenstein, L. 1953. *Philosophical Investigations*. Oxford: Blackwell.

通讯地址：100191 北京航空航天大学 <ylin@bnu.edu.cn>

乔姆斯基对"日常语言"语言观的批评

林允清

提　要：有一个通常的语言观点，这个观点是 Wittgenstein, Quine, Strawson, Dummett, Searle, Putnam, Lewis, Wiggins 等人都持有的。这个观点就是：语言是约定俗成的，是受规则支配的，是学来的，人类大脑中有一些基本的学习机制，等等。我称此观点为"日常语言"语言观。乔姆斯基对这一观点一直持否定态度，他对此观点的摒弃是他发展自己的语言理论的一个重要动机。在本文中，我将回顾乔姆斯基对"日常语言"语言观的批评。我将阐明：（1）乔姆斯基的批评不足以摒弃"日常语言"语言观;(2)乔姆斯基的论证不能推出他对语言的结论;(3)"日常语言"语言观实际上为理解语言和心智指出了一条可行的道路。

关键词:"日常语言"语言观;乔姆斯基;约定俗成;规则

罗素论存在

德国海德堡大学哲学系 蒋运鹏

提　要：本体论的核心问题是"世界上究竟存在什么东西"？与该问题密切相关的另一个问题是"'存在'是什么意思？"本文仅仅关注第二个问题，限于讨论对存在概念本身的分析。准确地说，本文的主要任务在于澄清 Russell 关于存在概念的理论。这个任务将分为两个步骤来完成。首先，本文将转述 Russell 自己的理论。然后，着重处理 McGinn 对 Russell 的理论的三个批评。本文将证明，McGinn 的批评不对 Russell 的理论构成任何威胁。但是，这并不意味着 Russell 提供了一种十分理想的理论，因为（正如我们将要看见的）Russell 的理论至少有一个严重的弱点。

关键词：Russell；McGinn；存在；摹状词

1. 导言

存在的概念[1]是一个容易造成困难的概念，因此，它也是一个很让哲学家感兴趣的概念。如果存·在是一种所有存在的物体[2]所具有的性质，那么，不存·在看起来似乎也是一种所有不存在的物体所具有的性质。可是，不存在的物体如何能具有性质呢？这是一种困境。我们还可以换一种方式来描述同样的困境：在对句子"苏格拉底是聪明的"进行逻辑分析[3]的时候，我们会很自然地把该句子拆分为"苏格拉底"这个单项和"是聪明的"这个谓词。根据这种逻辑分析，该句子为真，当且仅当"苏格拉底"这一单称词项指称的物体包含在"是聪明的"这一谓词的外延之中。如果我们说出该句子，那么我们（在正常场合下）就针对苏格拉底作出了一个断言。我们断言，苏格拉底是聪明的。同理，在对句子

（Ⅰ）飞马不存在。

---

[1] 在德语或英语中，"existenz（existence）"在语法上是一个名词。我们可以说它指称一个性质，就好像"redness"指称红色这种性质一样。而"existiert（exist）"则是一个动词。在汉语中，这种名词和动词的区分无法在单个词汇上得到体现。为了方便起见，本文中做出以下规定：从现在起，"存·在"相当于名词"existenz（existence）"，而"存在"相当于动词"existiert（exist）"。但是，当"存在"这个词汇作为一个经常使用的专业术语的一部分出现的时候（比如"存在命题"），上述区分无效。

[2] 本文是在最广泛的意义上来使用"物体"这个词汇的。抽象的个体、抽象的共相、具体的个体和具体的共相在本文中都称为"物体"。

[3] 本文中所有的逻辑分析都基于传统的谓词逻辑。

进行逻辑分析的时候，我们也会很自然地将它拆分为"飞马"这个单称词项和"~（x 存在）"这个谓词（"x"的功能只在于标出可以填入单项的空位）。[1] 在此出现了类似的困境：（Ⅰ）不可能为真。因为根据我们的逻辑分析，（Ⅰ）为真，当且仅当"飞马"指称的物体包含在"~（x 存在）"的外延之中。而只有当"飞马"指称的物体（即飞马）存在的时候，该物体才能包含在一个谓词的外延之中。如果说出（Ⅰ），我们就针对飞马作出了一个断言。但这个断言也不可能为真。因为要使该断言为真，飞马必须存在。我们的困境在于：上述结论是不可接受的，因为我们中的绝大多数人不怀疑（Ⅰ）的真实性。许多否定的存在命题都面临该困难。另一个困境在于，任意一个肯定的存在命题不可能为伪。比如

（Ⅱ）飞马存在。

就不可能为伪。（Ⅱ）为伪，当且仅当（Ⅱ）的否定命题（Ⅰ）为真。而（Ⅰ）不可能为真。这个结论也是不可接受的，因为我们中的绝大多数人认为（Ⅱ）为伪。

针对上述困境，几乎每一个西方哲学史上的重要哲学家都提出过自己的解决方案。本文将不对它们进行综述。[2] 本文的主要目的在于考察 Russell 解决该问题的方案和当代哲学家 McGinn 对该方案的批评。

笔者将证明，McGinn 的批评完全建立在对 Russell 的误解之上。而对于 McGinn 的误解，Russell 自己也要负一部分责任。

2. 摹状词理论

Russell 关于存·在的理论可以分为两部分来考察。第一部分主要涉及对自然语言中的存在命题的逻辑分析，它构成了 Russell 的理论的形式基础。第二部分主要涉及对（经过逻辑分析之后的）存在命题的语义阐释以及由此引出的一些形而上学观点。在这一小节中，我们将考察第一部分。该部分与 Russell 的摹状词理论有密切关联。

Russell 的摹状词理论的核心可以用一句话来概括：对于任意一个包含有摹状词的、自然语言的命题 p 而言，p 可以被解释成一个不包含摹状词的命题 q。[3] 比如

（1）柏拉图的老师是秃顶的。

就可以被解释为

（1*）有一个物体，他是柏拉图的老师，并且他是秃顶的。

---

[1] "不存在"在谓词逻辑中不是一个谓词，所以（Ⅰ）的逻辑结构是"~（飞马存在）"。其中"~"是否定符号。
[2] 对这些理论的一个极度概括性的综述见 Miller, 2002。对分析哲学史上关于存在问题的理论的详细介绍可以在 Rosefeldt 教授的教授资格论文中找到，见 Rosefeldt, 2006。
[3] Russell 的摹状词理论见 Russell, 1905a。

在命题（1*）当中，作为摹状词的"柏拉图的老师"不再出现（我们只有一个逻辑上不可再拆分的谓词"是柏拉图的老师"）。（1*）的更形式化的版本：

（1**）E_x（x 是柏拉图的老师 ∧ x 是秃顶的）。[1]

Russell 希望用摹状词理论来解决的主要问题当中，有一个是由自然语言中那些包含了没有指称对象的摹状词（比如"当今法国国王"）的命题造成的。毫无疑问，这类命题当中有一些命题为真。而如果我们将这些命题所包含的摹状词看作逻辑个体常项（一个自然语言的命题 p 中包含的单位 x 是一个逻辑个体常项，当且仅当在对 p 的逻辑分析中，x 被当成一个个体常项来对待），那么，我们无法解释这些命题如何可能为真。因为在传统谓词逻辑的语言中，一个包含特定个体常项的命题为真或者为伪（或者说，该命题有意义），当且仅当那个特定的个体常项有指称对象。Russell 解决该问题的方法是：不再将摹状词看作逻辑个体常项。他将每一个自然语言的、包含摹状词的命题 p 解释成一个不包含摹状词的命题 q，并且声称，相对于在命题 p 当中而言，命题 p 的真实逻辑结构在命题 q 当中得到了更好的展现。由此可得，p 中包含的摹状词根本不是 p 的逻辑组成部分，因为它在 q 中没有出现。因此，p 中的摹状词自然也就不再是逻辑个体常项。

根据 Russell 的理论，我们也可以将自然语言中任意一个具有"a 存在"（"a"可以是任意一个摹状词）这种形式的存在命题解释成一个不再包含摹状词的命题。比如命题

（2）柏拉图的老师存在。

就可以被解释为

（2*）E_x（x 是柏拉图的老师）。[2]

命题（2*）不再包含摹状词，代替它的是谓词"是柏拉图的老师"。按照罗素的意见，自然语言中任意一个具有"a 存在"这种形式的存在命题都应当被解释成具有"Ex（Fx）"这种形式的命题。其中"F"代表一个谓词。

到目前为止，还有一个问题没有解决：自然语言中有些存在命题不包含摹状词，而包含一个专有名称，比如"苏格拉底存在"。这些命题应当如何解释？Russell 的解决方案分两个步骤。首先，Russell 声称，任何一个专有名称都是一个摹状词的缩写。简便起见，我们常常使用这种缩写方式。比如"苏格拉底"

---

[1] "Ex"在本文中作为存在量词来使用。严格而言，根据 Russell 的理论，当（1）包含的摹状词"柏拉图的老师"是用来指称并且仅仅指称一个特定物体的时候（在英语或德语中，这个条件可以用在摹状词前面加定冠词的方式来表达），（1**）不是（1）的正确解释。因为在 命题（1**）里，摹状词指称对象的唯一性没有得到相应的表达。不过，这点在以下的论述中不会造成实质性的影响，所以我们可以对它忽略不计。

[2] 见 Russell, 1918, 第 204-205 页和第 212-213 页。也请比较 Quine, 1964a, 第 7 页。

就可以是"柏拉图的老师"的缩写。¹然后,在此基础上,只要把每个专有名称替换成它对应的摹状词,我们就可以使用上面已经提到过的解释模式。因此,按照 Russell 自己的看法,他的摹状词理论也间接适用于包含专有名称的存在命题。

3. Russell论存·在及存在命题

  Russell 关于存在命题的形式理论我们可以总结如下:任何一个自然语言中的、具有"a 存在"("a"可以是一个摹状词,也可以是一个专有名称)这种形式的命题的真正逻辑结构都是"$E_x(Fx)$"。下面,我们来考察 Russell 对具有这种逻辑结构的命题进行的语义阐释以及他对存·在的本质的看法。Russell 写道:

  "When you take any propositional function and assert of it that it is possible, that it is sometimes true, that gives you the fundamental meaning of 'existence.' You may express it by saying that there is at least one value of x for which that propo-sitional function is true. Take 'x is a man,' there is at least one value of x for which this is true. That is what one means by saying that 'There are men', or that 'Men exist.' Existence is essentially a property of a propositional function. It means that that propositional function is true in at least one instance. If you say 'there are unicorns,' that will mean that 'there is an x, such that x is a unicorn' [...] It is perfectly clear that when you say 'Unicorns exist,' you are not saying any-thing that would apply to any unicorns there might happen to be [...] [RZ1]

  紧接着上面一段话,Russell 继续写道:

  "It is of propositional functions that you can assert or deny existence [...] Existence-propositions do not say anything about the actual individual but only about the class or function。²[RZ2]

  在开始讨论之前,还有两点需要强调。首先,根据上面引用的段落,我们不能清楚地知道所谓"命题函项(propositional functions)"究竟是何种物体。Russell 著作中的有些地方使我们倾向于认为,对 Russell 而言,命题函项就是像"x is a man"一样的语言符号。³而他的著作中的另一些段落则表明他似乎有另外的看法:所谓命题函项不是像"x is a man"一样的语言符号本身,而是这些语言符号所指称的物体。⁴对于本文的讨论而言,我们没有必要深究 Russell 在此的真正观点。以下的讨论将从第二种观点出发。其次,引文 RZ1 开头的第一句话容易引起误解。Russell 不是在现代模态逻辑的意义上来使用"possible"

---

1 见 Russell, 1918: 213。笔者在此将不考虑 Russell 这个看法造成的种种困难。
2 Russell, 1918: 204-205。
3 比如 Russell, 1903: 13。
4 比如 Russell, 1984: 132-133。

一词的。在现代模态逻辑的意义上，只有句子表达的内容才是可能的或不可能的。由 "x is a man" 表达的内容既不是可能的，也不是不可能的。为了避免不必要的误会，笔者在以下讨论中将直接从 Russell 的另一个比较清晰的陈述（即 RZ1 中的 "You may express it... for which that propositional function is true"）出发。

笔者认为，根据 RZ1 和 RZ2，我们可以将 Russell 的观点转述如下：

R1. 存在本质上是命题函项的性质。

R2. 存在本质上是这样一个性质：一个物体具有存·在这一性质，当且仅当该物体是一个具有如下特性的命题函项 Φ：有至少一个 x 的值，对于这个值来说，Φ 为真（这种性质，即存·在，我们以下简称为 Ψ）。

R3. 存在命题本质上是关于命题函项的命题，不是一个关于个体的命题。

R4. 以下情况是由存在命题的本质决定的：一个存在命题总是断言一个命题函项有（或没有）Ψ。[1]

Russell 不认为像（2）一样的、属于自然语言的存在命题没有意义。Russell 认为（2）为真。但是，Russell 认为，在说出（2）的时候，我们并没有断言柏拉图的老师这个个体具有存·在这一性质。因为（2）所表达的真正内容应当由（2*）来更好地表达。（2*）读作 "至少一个变项 x 的值，对于这个值来说，命题函项 'x 是柏拉图的老师'[2] 为真"。（2*）中的 "Ex" 这一部分指称 Ψ（即 Russell 意义上的存·在）。如果我们说出（2*），我们就针对 "x 是柏拉图的老师" 这个命题函项作出了一个断言。我们断言它具有 Ψ 这一性质。[3] 以上是 Russell 在逻辑分析的形式基础上对存在命题的语义阐释。该阐释同时也是一种关于存·在的本质的形而上学理论。

---

[1] Russell 关于存·在和存在命题的形而上学本质的看法与 Frege 非常接近。对 Frege 来说，存·在是一个二级概念，即一级概念的性质。存在命题是关于一级概念的命题。在这样一个命题中，我们断言一个一级概念有或没有存·在这一性质。见 Frege, 1988: 46, 53 和 Frege, 2002: 54。只要做一些小改动，R1—R4 也可以用来转述 Frege 的观点。

[2] 笔者十分清楚，用 "'x 是柏拉图的老师'" 来指称 "x 是柏拉图的老师" 所指称的命题函项是不妥当的。因为，严格来说，"'x 是柏拉图的老师'" 指称 "x 是柏拉图的老师" 这个语言符号本身。就此笔者请求读者谅解。在本文中，具有 "'Fx'" 这一形式的符号有时用来指称 "Fx" 指称的命题函项。但在大多数情况下，它还是用来指称 "Fx" 自身。遇到具体实例的时候，读者可以很容易地根据上下文区分两种用法。

[3] 在一篇早期的论文中，Russell 曾经认为 "存·在" 这个词汇有两种意义。根据其中一种意义，存·在（作为一种性质）只能赋予集合（或命题函项）。而根据另外一种意义，存·在可以赋予个体（见 Russell, 1905b, 第 398 页）。这种观点当然与 RZ1 和 RZ2 不符合。在 RZ1 和 RZ2 中，Russell 并不承认 "存·在" 还有第二意义，更没有声称根据第二种意义，存·在可以是个体的性质。我们可以推断，Russell 在写作 RZ1 和 RZ2 的时候改变了他早期的看法。由于 Russell 哲学思想的发展历史不是本文的考察对象，笔者将不对上述的观点转变进行更仔细的研究。笔者将把 R1—R4 当作 Russell 关于存·在和存在命题的唯一理论来对待。同时笔者十分清楚，这是一种简化了的阐释。

4. McGinn的批评以及笔者的反批评

McGinn在他的著作中将Russell称为"关于存·在和存在命题的正统理论的主要建筑师",并针对Russell的理论提出了一系列批评。[1] 其中第一条批评意见直接指向R2。McGinn认为,R2并未真正解释存·在是什么。他写道:

"The notion of existence is presupposed in the analysis, so the analysis does not settle what kind of notion it is(存在的概念在分析中被先设了,因此分析本身不能告诉我们它是一个什么样的概念)"。[2][MZ1]

他的论证的具体步骤笔者转述如下[3]:在性质Ψ中包含了一个部分,根据我们的直觉(intuition),该部分本身就是存在。该部分是由"有……一个(there is)"来指称的。由此可得,Russell对存在的解释是循环的,不是一个真正意义上的解释。根据R2的解释,存在就是Ψ。但是,除非我们已经知道(由"有……一个"指称的)存·在是什么,否则我们无法知道Ψ是什么。

无论如何,上述反驳不是毁灭性的。原则上讲,Russell至少可以作出以下回复:"存在"有两种意义。第一种是在R2中解释过的意义。按照R2的解释,存在就是Ψ。而就第二种意义而言,"存在"与"有……一个"指称同一个对象。让我们将"有……一个"的指称对象称为"Σ"。为了解释"存在"的第一种意义,我们先设读者已经知道Σ是什么,这并无不妥之处。这种回复的缺点在于我们必须承认"存在"有歧义,而正如RZ1和RZ2所显示的,Russell并不打算承认这点。

有没有另一种不需要承认"存在"有歧义的出路呢?本文认为有。Russell可以(并且很有可能)将McGinn的批评性论证的前提,即Σ是存在,完全驳回。其理由是:**从Russell自己的定义出发**,Ψ是唯一可以被称为"存在"的性质。我们在直觉上或许会认为Σ是存·在,但在Russell的理论内部,它不是存在,只是存在的一部分。由于前提错误,McGinn的论证什么也不能证明。McGinn之所以认为R2作为一个解释是循环的,是因为他从一开始就不顾Russell自己给出的定义。总之,在Russell的理论内部,McGinn的第一个批评无效。

有很多关于上述回复的问题可以讨论。在此仅仅指出一点,即这种出路至少有一个缺陷。讨论进行到这一步,我们有一个很容易想到的针对Russell的批评:Σ是存在这一观点受到非常自然的直觉的支持。Russell关于存在的理论完全不考虑该直觉,所以,至少在这方面上,它是不尽人意的。换言之,为了声称Σ不是存在,Russell必须使用一种语言。在该语言中,"有……一个"和"存在"不指称同一个性质。但是,由于我们直觉上倾向于认为它们指称同一个性质,所以Russell使用的语言至少没有照顾到我们的直觉。如果Russell不打算更改R2

---

[1] 见McGinn, 2000: 18-19。

[2] 见McGinn, 2000: 21。

[3] 为确保术语的统一,笔者在转述过程中略微改变了McGinn的一些表述方式。对他的批评意见的核心的转述并未因此有任何偏差。

这一观点，同时又不承认 R2 是循环的解释，那么，上述缺陷就不可避免。这是 Russell 理论的一个弱点。

在第二条批评意见中，McGinn 尝试证明：即使第一个批评不成立，Russell 的理论仍然面临严重的问题：

"The second problem has more of the character of a proof that the orthodox view cannot be a general analysis of the notion of existence [...] Consider the existence of properties or propositionnal functions or predicate themselves. These exist in the same sense that other things exist, despite their being（presumably）abstract and non-individual. Thus we can say, 'the property of being a planet exists'-as we might if insisting（rightly or wrongly）upon the truth of realism as opposed to nominalism about universals. But how might this statement be analysed? On the orthodox view, we must make reference to some property that the entity said to exist is a instance of [...] [w]e are now launched on a vicious infinite regress, since we must ask what the existence of the higher-order property consists in, thus requiring a further property to be a property of that property [MZ3]

McGinn 继续写道：

"In fact, this difficulty about property existence acts back on the analysis of individual existence, since the property the individual instantiates must itself exist, and this cannot be explained in terms of the orthodox view. Individual cannot be said to exist if the property（or predicates）they instantiate cannot be said to exist, since the former requires the latter: for x to exist is for there to exist some proper-ty（or predicate）F such that x instantiates F。[1][MZ4]

在以下讨论中，笔者将证明 McGinn 的第二条批评意见对 Russell 也不构成任何威胁。因为它最多是针对 McGinn 自己发明出来的一种理论的反驳，而并非针对 Russell 的理论的反驳。

首先，我们需要澄清 McGinn 的第二条批评意见所针对的究竟是一个什么样的理论。在 MZ3 的开头部分，McGinn 看来持这样的观点：具体的个体具有存·在这一性质。并且，抽象的、非个体的物体（比如性质、命题函项等等）和具体的个体在同一种意义上具有存·在这一性质。由此出发，McGinn 使用所谓的"正统理论"来分析具体个体的存·在和抽象物体的存·在：声称某具体个体 x 具有存·在，也就是声称一个性质 F 具有存·在并且 x 体现（instantiate）F（见 MZ4。换言之：声称某个体具有存·在，就是声称该个体体现一个性质。而被体现的性质本身当然也必须具有存·在这一性质）。[2] 同理，声称一个抽象的、非个体的物体 X 具有存·在，也就是声称一个逻辑上级别更高的性质 F^+ 具有存·在并且 X 体现 F^+ 这一性质（从上下文看，McGinn 本人所采取的正是这种分析，虽然他在引用的段

---

[1] 见 McGinn，2000：24-26。
[2] 所谓一个个体体现一个性质，就是指该性质在该个体上得到体现。这只是"该个体具有该性质"的另一种说法。比如一匹红色的马就体现了红色这种性质。

落中没有明确表达这点）。[1] 在以下意义上，个体和非个体的抽象物体在同一种意义上具有存·在：具有存·在对它们而言都意味着体现某种性质（当然，这里指的不是存·在这个性质）。[2] 我们总结如下：

　　M1. 所有物体都可以具有存·在这一性质[3]，比如各种个体，各个逻辑级别的性质，各个逻辑级别的谓词，各个逻辑级别的命题函项等等。

　　M2. 普遍而言：一个 n 级别的物体 Y^n 具有存·在 $=_{Def}$ Y^n 体现一个 n+1 级别的性质 F^{n+1}，并且 F^{n+1} 本身也具有存·在。这是一个对存·在的普遍有效的概念分析。

　　M1 和 M2 加在一起构成一个称之为"T_m"的、关于存在的理论。本文认为，T_m 就是 McGinn 的第二条批评意见所针对的理论。根据 M1，个体可以具有存在。而根据 M2，要理解"一个个体具有存在"的含义，我们必须首先明白"一个 0+1 级别的性质 F^1 具有存在"的含义。而要理解"一个 0+1 级别的性质 F^1 具有存在"，我们又必须首先理解"一个 1+1 级别的性质 F^2 具有存在"的含义，由此继续无穷尽的倒退。在解释任意一个逻辑级别的物体的存在的时候，同样的无穷倒退都会出现。我们永远不能理解任何物体的存在。可见，T_m 存在严重问题。不过，McGinn 倾向于认为，问题的根源在 M2，不在 M1。

　　现在关键在于，不难看出，T_m 不是 Russell 的理论。Russell 不会同意 M1。因为 Russell 意义上的存在（作为一种性质）不能被任意的物体所具有。按照 Russell 的观点，命题函项是唯一的可以具有存·在这一性质的物体。[4] 除此之外，Russell 对存在的概念分析也和 T_m 有显著差别。按照 Russell 的看法，一个物体具有存在这一性质，当且仅当该物体是一个具有如下特性的命题函项 Φ：有至少一个 x 的值，对于这个值来说，Φ 为真。而根据 T_m，具有存在这一性质却意味着体现某种性质（这里指的当不是存在这个性质本身）。更重要的是，在 Russell 的理论中，一个命题函项（比如"x 是柏拉图的老师"）具有存在这一事态不是由"命题函项'x 是柏拉图的老师'存在"这样的句子来表达的，而是由自然语言中的句子（2）或者（2*）来表达的。[5] 如果 T_m 是 McGinn 实际上批评的理论，并且，如果对 Russell 的理论转述正确，那么，McGinn 的第二条批评意见就完全偏离了

---

[1]　举例说明逻辑上级别更高的体现关系：比如，由"是一种颜色"表达的性质就是一个逻辑级别更高的性质，它可以由红色这种性质来体现。在本文中，个体属于最低的逻辑级别，即第 0 级别。个体的性质（比如红色）属于第 1 级别。个体的性质的性质（比如由"是一种颜色"表达的性质）属于第 2 级别，依此类推。

[2]　McGinn 自己也提到过这一点。见 McGinn, 2000：28。他在那里写道："To exist is to be an instance of a property"。这句话实际上涉及到他针对 Russell 提出的另外一个反驳，我们随后会谈到它。

[3]　更为准确的表达是：没有这样一种物体 x：由于存·在这一性质本身的逻辑本质，声称 x 具有存·在是没有意义的。

[4]　当然，RZ2 表明集合也可以具有存·在。不过，粗略而讲，集合是命题函项的外延形式，命题函项是集合的内涵形式。它们的区别在此可以忽略不计。

[5]　McGinn 在 MZ3 中用"'是一个行星'这个性质存在"这个句子来表达"是一个行星"这个性质具有存·在。显然，他也会用"命题函项'x 是柏拉图的老师'存在"这个句子来表达命题函项"x 是柏拉图的老师"具有存·在。这与 Russell 的理论有明显差别。

目标。他想证明 Russell 的理论有严重问题,但实际上却最多证明了 T_m 有严重问题,而 T_m 完全不是 Russell 的理论。

有一点我们在此需要简短地解释一下。我们也可以这样来理解 Russell:对于一个命题函项而言,具有存在这一性质就是体现一个逻辑级别更高的性质(即性质 Ψ)。这看来似乎与那种(在 McGinn 看来)会引起无穷倒退的观点有些相似。Russell 的理论是否也会引起无穷倒退呢?要理解"一个命题函项具有存在"的含义,我们是否需要首先理解"性质 Ψ 具有存在"的含义呢?笔者认为不是。以(2*)为例。根据 Russell 的理论,在(2*)中,我们断言"x 是柏拉图的老师"具有存在这一性质,也就是说,它体现 Ψ。为了理解"命题函项'x 是柏拉图的老师'具有存在"的含义,我们当然必须理解 Ψ 是一个什么样的性质。但这就已经足够了。我们不需要理解"Ψ 具有存在"的含义(也就是说,不需要理解从逻辑和形而上学的角度来看,"Ψ 具有存在"表达了何种事态)。理解一个物体 x 是什么和理解从逻辑和形而上学的角度来看,"x 具有存在"表达了何种事态是两回事。一个没有受过哲学训练的地理学家知道世界最高峰是什么,但他完全不知道(也不需要知道)从逻辑和形而上学的角度来看,"世界最高峰具有存在"表达了何种事态(虽然他或许知道"世界最高峰具有存在"这个句子的真值条件,也可以判断该句子的真值)。Russell 的理论不会导致无穷后退。

虽然 Russell 明确清晰地表述了他对于存在这一性质的分析,并且同样明确清晰地说明了在他看来,什么样的物体可以具有存在这一性质,但 McGinn 仍然错误地把 T_m 当成了 Russell 的理论。从某种意义上讲,我们可以从这一事实本身引出一种对 Russell 的反驳:McGinn 非常顽固地曲解 Russell 的理论的原因在于后者过分古怪。Russell 认为只有命题函项能具有存在。并且,Russell 认为存在就是 Ψ。将存在这种性质赋予一个命题函项 Φ,就是将 Ψ 赋予 Φ。[1] 可是,我们的反驳是:这和我们从直觉出发对"什么是存在?"这个问题作出的回答相差太远。从直觉出发,我们希望断言很多物体(而不只是命题函项)具有存在这个性质。我们当然可以断言一个命题函项 Φ 具有性质 Ψ。但是,从直觉出发,我们不觉得这和断言 Φ 具有存在是一回事。按照我们的直觉,断言 Φ 具有存在应该相当于断言 Φ 是世界的一部分(虽然不一定是物理世界的一部分)。[2] Russell 关于存在和存在命题的理论完全不顾上述直觉。和直觉的冲突当然不足以构成放弃一个理论的理由,但它至少降低了该理论的可信度。

Russell 的理论还面临另外一个困难,在此将对其进行简略叙述:一方面,Russell 认为(2)为真。另一方面,他又认为柏拉图的老师不具有存在(因为他认为个体不能具有存在这一性质)。换言之,Russell 所持的观点可以由"柏拉图的老师不具有存在"这一句子来表达。我们称该句子为"(2*)"。假如我们将(2)和(2*)都看作自然语言的句子,那么困难就出现了:(2*)是"柏拉图的老师

---

[1] 见 Russell,1903:21。
[2] 请读者注意,笔者在此并不是在对存在概念进行严格的分析。笔者只是在用不太严格的方式来表达我们关于存·在的直觉。

具有存在"的否定命题,而"柏拉图的老师具有存在"和(2)至少具有逻辑等值关系(即 □(2)柏拉图的老师具有存在))。Russell 不能在遵守命题逻辑的法则的前提下声称 ⟵⟶(2)和(2*)同时为真。也就是说,在用自然语言来叙述 Russell 的理论的时候,我们会遇到困难。当然,笔者并不认为该困难无法克服。但在此将不考虑具体的解决方案。

McGinn 的第三条批评意见:在 McGinn 看来,Russell 对存·在的分析的另一个缺陷在于,按照 Russell 的分析,任何存在物都必须具有一些性质:

"This implies that nothing could exist that failed to fall under some property-other than existence, obviously. To exist is to be an instance of a property, so necessarily whatever exists has at least one property. This rules out, as a matter of the meaning of 'exist', the possibility of what we might call 'bare existence'-a thing that exists without having any (further) properties."[1][MZ5]

McGinn 认为,一个对于存·在的成功的分析必须在面对"有没有'赤裸的'存在物?"这样的形而上学问题时保持中立。而 Russell 的分析没有满足该要求。

这条反驳建立在类似的误解之上(因为 McGinn 在此仍然将 T_m 和 Russell 的理论混为一谈)。按照 T_m,任何存在物(仅仅因为"存在"的意义,或者说因为存·在的本质)除了存·在之外都还必须具有至少一个性质。但 Russell 的理论并不会造成该结果。第一,在 Russell 的理论中,只有命题函项原则上可以具有存·在。第二,任何一个(在 Russell 的意义上)存在的命题函项(因为存·在的本质)都只需要具有性质 Ψ。而按照定义,Ψ 就是存·在。所以,在 Russell 的理论中,就存·在的本质而言,一个存在物不需要除了存·在之外还具有其他性质。当然,那种除了(Russell 意义上的)存·在之外不具有其他任何性质的命题函项是很难设想的。但是,Russell 关于存·在的本质的理论本身并不声称具有存·在的命题函项必须具有其他性质(反过来,Russell 的理论也不声称具有存·在的命题函项可以不具有其他性质)。因此,如果从 Russell 对存·在的理解出发,就"赤裸的存在物是否可能"这一形而上学问题,Russell 的理论是中立的。而如果从正常的、直觉上的对存·在的理解出发,Russell 的理论也是中立的。因为从正常的存在概念出发,上述形而上学问题大概可以这样表述:一个没有任何性质的物体是否可能成为世界的一部分?而就该问题,Russell 的理论更是完全没有发表任何看法。

5. 结论

Russell 对本文导言中提到的困境的解决方案是:不对(Ⅰ)和(Ⅱ)进行符合其表面句法结构的逻辑分析,并且断言,根据它们的真正的逻辑结构,它们表

---

[1] McGinn, 2000, 第28页。

达的事态和"苏格拉底是聪明的"这样的句子表达的事态一样不会造成困境。"苏格拉底是聪明的"断言一个个体具有一种性质。当该个体的确具有该性质的时候，该句子为真。反之，该句子为伪。类似地，（Ⅰ）和（Ⅱ）也断言一个命题函项具有（或不具有）性质Ψ。如果情况属实，则它们为真，反之，则它们为伪。除了（Ⅰ）和（Ⅱ）表达的事态在逻辑上提升了一个级别这一事实之外，它们并不会比"苏格拉底是聪明的"造成更多的困难。

McGinn 在第一个批评中无视 Russell 自己关于存·在的定义。他的第二和第三个批评也纯属误解。误解的根源都在于他错误地将 T_m 当成了 Russell 自己的理论。McGinn 的批评本身没有为我们提供任何放弃 Russell 关于存·在的理论或者放弃他为本文导言中提到的困境提供的解决方案的理由。Russell 的拥护者可以保持其立场不变。但是，正如我们看到的，他们这样做的代价是必须放弃一种直觉，即 Ψ 不是存·在。并且，由于 Russell 的理论与该直觉冲突，它很容易被误解。

参考文献

Frege, G. 1988. *Die Grundlagen der Arithmetik*. Hamburg: Felix Meiner Verlag.

Frege, G. 2002. Über begriff und gegenstand. In Textor, M.(ed.), *Funktion-Begriff-Bedeutung*. Göttingen: Vandenhoeck & Ruprecht.

McGinn, C. 2000. *Logical Properties-Identity, Existence, Predication Necessity, Truth*. Oxford: Clarendon Press.

Miller, B. 2002. Existence. In: *Stanford Encyclopedia of Philosophy*. http://plato.stanford.edu./entries/existence.

Quine, O. 1964. On what there is. In *From a Logical Point of View*. Cambridge, MA: Harvard University Press.

Rosefeldt, T. 2005. *Was es nicht gibt*. Unpublished manuscript.

Russell, B. 1903. *The Principles of Mathematics. Vol. 1*. Cambridge: Cambridge University Press.

Russell, B. 1956. On denoting. In *Mind* 14.

Russell, B. 1905. The existential import of propositions. In *Mind* 14.

Russell, B. 1986. The philosophy of logical atomism. In *The Monist* 28.

Russell, B. 1956. *Logic and Knowledge. Essays 1901-1950*. London: Allen und Unwin.

Russell, B. 1984. *Principia Mathematica*. Wien Berlin: Medusa Verlag.

Russell, B. 1986. *The Philosophy of Logical Atomism and Other Essays 1914-19*. London: Allen und Unwin.

通讯地址：德国海德堡大学哲学系 <pathernon81@yahoo.com.cn>

Russell on Existence
Yun Peng Asher Jiang

Abstract: The characteristic question of ontology is "What do exist in the world?" There is another question, which is closely tied with the first one, namely: "What does 'exist' mean?" The present study is focused only on the second question, i.e. on the analysis of the concept of existence itself. More exactly, the task of this paper is the clarification of Russell's theory of the concept of existence. In the discussion below, this task will be carried out in two steps. At first, I shall reconstruct Russell's own theory. Then I shall consider McGinn's three critical remarks upon Russell's Theory. McGinn's remarks, as it will be proven, do not threaten Russell at all. However, this conclusion does not mean that Russell's theory is an acceptable one, because it has at least one serious weakness.

Keywords: Russell; McGinn; Existence; Denoting

由分析悖论引发的意义理论思考

浙江工业大学外国语学院　黄会健

摘　要：本文以分析悖论为主线，探索了以弗雷格、罗素和奎因等为代表的分析哲学家消解分析悖论的途径，阐述了他们对意义理论的贡献，进而对意义理论的研究作进一步思考。作者认为，哲学的问题大多来自悖论，哲学家的任务常常是从不同的视角去消解悖论，从而施展哲人的睿智；分析哲学对意义理论的贡献常与分析悖论的消解紧密联系在一起。因此，学习和研究语言哲学，从分析悖论入手或许是一种较理想的路径。

关键词：悖论；分析悖论；意义理论；思考

1. 引言

哲学本质上是一门思辨的学问，即用思想思想思想的一种方式。消解悖论是一种超出人们一般思维范围的思辨活动，因此，哲学与悖论有着内在的关联。悖论，是一种似是而非、似假而真、看似矛盾而实际上又有道理的陈述。在现实生活中，从某种意义上讲，发现问题者可能比解决问题者更聪明。因此，悖论表面上看起来有点近似于诡辩，如人们所熟悉的"先有鸡后有蛋，还是先有蛋后有鸡"或者"先有千里马还是先有伯乐"的问题。哲学家应对生活中出现林林总总的悖论，其意义不完全在于提出解决问题的答案，而在于由悖论而引发的有关对问题的思考，或者对原先人们习以为常的思维模式的颠覆。美国的大哲学家奎因曾经说过："历史上，悖论的发现，曾多次成为思维基础重新构建的关键"（Quine, 1997: 1）。

研究哲学，从悖论入手，可能是一条比较有效的途径；研究语言哲学，从分析悖论入手，可能是一种比较方便的方法。国内外学者中从逻辑的角度解析悖论的很多（黄斌，1999；Quine, 1997；韩林合，2003；苏珊·哈克，2003；陈嘉映，2004；陈波，2005；李大强，2008），但是，从分析悖论入手，研究由分析悖论引发的意义理论的文章却很少。在笔者看来，语言哲学的发展与分析悖论之间的联系十分密切。弗雷格的涵义理论，罗素的摹状语理论，奎因对经验主义两个教条的批判以及意义理论中的一些谜团（puzzles），无一不与分析悖论有关。因此，通过研究语言哲学家对分析悖论的分析，我们可以推开一扇智慧之窗，得到一片照耀语言哲学之路的光辉，探寻语言哲学的来龙去脉，理解意义理论的一些本质问题，进而对语言哲学作更加深入的思考。

2. 悖论与分析悖论的逻辑机理

悖论——"如果承认了命题 A，就会推论得出命题非 A，如果承认了命题非 A，就会推论出 A，于是就出现了悖论"（陈嘉映，2004: 42）。在西方哲学中，悖论往往围绕着真假、对错、因果、矛盾、存在与虚存等问题展开。典型的悖论有，"说谎者悖论"、"理发师悖论"、"迈农悖论"等。

在日常生活中，我们常常听到一些看似有理，但经不起逻辑检验的悖论。如谚语中的"金钱如粪土，朋友值千金"（胡军，2002: 210），如果我们以此为前提，推出的结论是，"朋友是粪土"，这与谚语的本意正好相反。曹操说，"宁可我负天下人，休叫天下人负我"。如果我们问曹操，他是否属于"天下人"之列，那么他将陷入悖论的泥潭。如果是，那么他将既负天下人，又不负天下人；如果不是，那么他就不可能负天下人，因为他不属于这个世界的"人"，不可能作出对我们有意义的言说。当然，罗贯中如此描写曹操，其目的是要揭示曹操心地狠毒的一面。在日常生活中或文学作品中，人们的语言里尽管有逻辑上矛盾的成分，一般不会受到追究，因为语言使用与逻辑虽说关系密切，但毕竟有差别。

事实上，哲学家的言说中也充满了逻辑上的悖论。维特根斯坦说过："搞哲学就是为了能够不搞哲学"（江怡，2009: 163）。他的语言游戏理论强调了游戏中遵守规则的问题，他说："语言游戏是在我们不了解规则的情况下进行的，而我们又只能在遵守规则的前提下才会从事语言游戏"（同上：154）。相传柏拉图曾把守过一座桥，所有想穿过大桥的人都得说一句柏拉图认为是真的话，才能放过，不然，过桥的人将被扔进湍急的河流中淹死。有一天苏格拉底来到桥边祈求过桥，于是，柏拉图就说，我对天发誓，如果你的下一句话为真，我就放行，否则，我就把你扔进河里。苏格拉底听了此话后思索了片刻，然后说，"你会把我扔进河里"（Clark, 2002: 28）。这样，柏拉图就立刻掉进了自己所设的陷阱里。不管历史上是否发生过此事，我们仍可以从哲学家们对悖论的思辨中体验哲学思辨的睿智。

就悖论的机理而言，奎因曾这样问过："我们能否说，一个悖论通常就是，初听起来结论荒谬，但却有论证支持它的呢"（Quine, 1997: 1）？对这个问题，奎因自己持肯定的态度。他举了一个这样的例子：一个人二十一岁了，但只有五个生日，因为他出生在二月二十九日。

分析悖论（the paradox of analysis）是悖论的一个变体，即当用一个或几个概念（分析项）去解释或分析另一概念（被分析项）时，会产生被分析项与分析项同义，然后又可推出被分析项等于被分析项的结论。这类似于 $2 = 1 + 1$ 和 $2 = 2$ 这两个算术表达式，前者有算术上的意义，后者却没有。语言上的表达式也是如此：从"昏星是晨星"这一分析语句可推出"昏星是昏星，晨星是晨星"这类无意义的语句。正如弗雷格所论述的那样，从 $A = B$ 中可以推出 $A = A$，但 $A = B$ 具有认知意义，而 $A = A$ 却没有意义。一个有认知意义的命题，可以推出等值且无意义的命题，这就是分析悖论。

分析悖论的产生与 G. E. Moore 有密切的联系，但最先论述分析悖论的是弗雷格（参见 Clark, 2002）。从对一般悖论的逻辑分析，到对分析悖论的反思，我们可见哲学的语言转向，本体论向知识论的转向之一斑。从悖论的分析到分析悖论的分析，就是这些转向的切入点。一般来说悖论的分析重逻辑分析，分析悖论的分析却基于逻辑又侧重于语言意义的分析，人们为了区分两者的关系，把后者称为谜团（puzzle）。

分析悖论的典型例子是：(1) A brother is a male sibling（兄弟即男性同胞）。(2) Lines have the same direction if and only if they are parallel to one another.（线条沿相同方向（伸展）当且仅当它们相互平行）。

从以上两个例句的汉英文对译可以看出，由于两种语言表达方式有差异，在汉语译句中英语原有的信息已经失去，如英文中不定冠词修饰的名词或名词复数形式表示通称，而非特指，这在汉语中是不大看得出来的。另外，用汉语"兄弟"对译"brother"也非完全对等。然而，我们现在所能做的只能是这样对译，仅此而已。现在，问题的关键是，我们要从这两个句子中看看分析悖论是如何产生的。例（1）在用"男性、同胞"这两个概念去分析"兄弟"这一概念时，似乎是在说"兄弟即兄弟"，即同语反复；例（2）是双重条件句，即"q iff p"，其中 p 与 q 同义，因此，该语句似乎是在说"线条沿相同方向（伸展）当且仅当线条沿相同方向（伸展）。这样，上述语句所表达的意义似乎是微不足道的，即无意义的。但是，事实上，知道"兄弟"这个概念的人并非都知道"男性、同胞"这两个概念。同样，知道"线条沿相同方向（伸展）"意思的人，未必知道"线条相互平行"的意思。简言之，在两个语句中，分析项与被分析项之间有认知意义上的信息差，即（1）、（2）是有意义的。在实际的哲学活动中，分析哲学家所从事的工作往往是在做类似的分析工作，所以，语言哲学家要为自己的工作正名。

3. 由分析悖论到意义理论

3.1 分析悖论所预设的意义理论问题

从上述对分析悖论的分析可以看出，仅仅从逻辑的角度去分析分析悖论，是看不出分析命题的意义的，相反，那只会混淆是非。在消解分析悖论时，首先要明确的是，分析悖论的产生是在于其被分析项与分析项概念的逻辑关系，还是词语意义关系，或是命题、语词与现实世界的关系。达米特（2005）在谈到哲学的语言转向时说过，分析哲学学派相信，通过语言的哲学说明可以获得对思想的一种哲学说明。他把是否坚持对语言的解释优于对思想的解释看成分析哲学的重要特性。在哲学的语言转向过程中，我们可以看到，众多的分析哲学家通过对悖论的语言分析，来消解悖论并推动了意义理论的发展。所谓意义理论，就是研究客观世界、语言和人的世界关系的一种理论。

从本质上讲，消解分析悖论就是为分析哲学家的工作正名，而消解分析悖论的主要障碍就是康德对"分析命题"和"综合命题"的区分，以及哲学上讲的"同一性"与"同一替代原则"。根据韩林合（2003）的观点，所谓同一性（identity）是指事物存在的必要条件。哲学上说，没有同一性就没有存在物（entity），因为所有的存在物分别与自身相同，但存在物之间彼此不同。我们是依靠同一性去理解世界的，一事物不可能同时在两个地方出现。一般来说，同一性是指事物在数方面的同一性，而非指质方面的同一性。两片树叶可以是同质的，但毕竟还是两片不同的树叶。强调"数"的同一性，本质上就是注重概念（名称）与存在物的同一关系，而"质"的同一性只是注重事物之间的相似性。

康德认为，概念的形成需要经验，概念的表达是由命题完成的，而命题是主词、谓词通过系词连接而成的形式。所谓分析命题是指，命题中的谓词是通过对主词内涵的分析而得到的。如"物体是有广延的"，主词"物体"本来就包含"有广延的"属性，谓词"有广延的"只不过把主词的内涵揭示出来而已，它并没有给主词增加什么新的东西。综合命题中的谓词并不包含在主词之中，两者没有必然的联系，谓词能扩大主词的内容。综合命题如"物体是有重量的"，谓词扩大了主词的内涵，提供了新的知识。对于分析命题和综合命题的区分，奎因作了强烈的批评。关于这一点，我们留在 3.4 节阐述。

3.2 分析悖论与弗雷格的涵义理论

弗雷格是分析哲学的奠基人，是推动哲学的语言转向的第一人。弗雷格对语言哲学的伟大贡献与他消解分析悖论有着紧密的联系。

在 On Sense and Nominatum（Martinich, 2001）一文中，弗雷格开门见山地指出：同一性观念令人深思（The idea of the Sameness challenges reflection）。他是怎么思考的呢？他思考同一性这一事物之存在的必要条件，给语言意义的研究带来的麻烦，或者说，他思考同一性使 A = B 这样的语句产生分析悖论这个难题。他应对分析悖论的路径不像其他哲学家那样绕着悖论兜圈子，被悖论牵着鼻子走，而是围绕同一性这个中心问题，改写分析语句。在这篇论文中，弗雷格指出："昏星和晨星虽然是同一个星辰，但这两个名称具有不同的涵义"（同上，200）。实际上，弗雷格在这里已经把原先的"A brother is a male sibling"改写为"The morning star is the evening star"了。在笔者看来，这一改写对于意义理论的发展具有重大意义。首先，从逻辑框架上看，这一改写并没有回避"a = b"与"a = a"具有相同的逻辑真值的问题，因为当用两个不同的符号指称相同的事物时，两个符号各自的指称意义是相同的，所以弗雷格没有回避悖论的关键点。但是，从原先悖论中带不定冠词的通称词项（general term）的语句，到改写后含定冠词的单称词项的语句，情况就发生了本质性的改变：弗雷格把语言与世界紧密地联系起来了，同时把意义的确定性与不确定性也区分开了，因为通称词项的指称是不确定的，因而它与现实世界的联系不够直接，其指称意义也就不那么确定了。更重要的是，他把指称意义与涵义区分开来了。因为，在弗雷格之前，许多哲学家一直把语言指称的对象看成是意义，而语言只是贴在事物上的标签。

弗雷格既是哲学家又是数学家，他在消解分析悖论时，用的重要工具常是数理逻辑。例如，设一个三角形 ABC，用三条线 a、b 和 c，分别从三个角与其对边的中点连接。这样，a、b 和 c 的交叉处汇合在同一个点上。对于这个汇合点，我们则可以用不同的方式来指称，如 a 和 b 的交点，或 b 和 c 的交点。以此类推，我们可以设一个圆，在圆周边上选任何一个点，由此出发，通过圆心画直径线。这样，我们可以画无数条不同的直径线，它们交于圆心，但各自的方向不同。如果这个圆是个圆球体，那么通过圆心可画的直径线就会更多。如果我们再设想一下，整个地球只有一个中心，但我们每个人可以认为地心在自己的脚下。这样，从每个人的角度去描述地心，尽管指称只有一个，但各自的描述含义是不同的。弗雷格把涵义（sense）定义为表达方式（manner of presentation, or mode of representation），这样，他使意义理论的内涵更加丰富了，把语言、世界和人紧密地联系起来了。

3.3 分析悖论与罗素的摹状语理论

在分析哲学的阵营里，罗素是一名紧随弗雷格之后的大将，他们都是走内涵意义之路的分析哲学家。不过，罗素认为弗雷格的把意义分为所指和涵义的做法不可取。但是，与弗雷格十分相似的是，在消解分析悖论时，罗素一方面不回避分析悖论的本质问题，即同一性问题；另一方面，他也改写分析语句："Scott is the author of Waverley"。这里，我们可以看到，罗素的版本已经引入了专名和单称词项。有关同一性问题，罗素认为，在 a = b 这个等式中，只有在符号 "a" 和 "b"，或者其中之一，是相关摹状语时，该命题才提供认知知识；如果 "a" 和 "b" 都是逻辑专名，那么或者是同语反复，或者是必然假。

罗素对意义理论的贡献主要在于他创建了摹状语理论。罗素（Russell, 1905）认为，Meinong 和 John Mill 的指称理论是最简单的意义理论，因为他们的理论把任何在语法上正确的指称词语看成是指称物的标签，语言的意义在于存在物。这有点像我们所说的"皮之不存，毛将焉附"的味道。但语言之毛，一旦长成，离开皮肤依然能活得好好的。例如，孔子离开这个世界已有 2400 多年了，我们照样可以建那么多的孔子学院，弘扬中国的传统文化！

罗素认为，"指谓的重要性不仅在于逻辑和数学方面，而且还在于知识论方面"（The subject of denoting is of very importance, not only in logic and mathematics, but also in theory of knowledge）（Martinich, 2001: 212）。这与弗雷格认为有关涵义具有认知知识是一致的。按照罗素的观点，在"Scott is the author of Waverley"中，我们用了专名和限定摹状语来指谓相同的指称，但不产生分析悖论。他说，"我们以不同的意义来确定指谓的同一"（We assert an identity of denotation with difference of meaning.）（同上：214）。在他看来，专名与限定摹状语的意义是不同的。Scott 独立地具有意义，而限定摹状语 "the author of Waverley" 是个不完全符号，独立地看没有任何意义，只有在命题的语境下，才会有意义。

分析哲学的重要性就在于从语言中分析出意义来，而意义在某种程度上与知识有关。要回答知识是如何被人所掌握的这一问题，首先要知道意义是如何从语言中分析出来的。语言分析是从概念分析开始的，在概念分析中，被分析的概念在系词（be）的左边，新的知识在右边，形成主语和谓语的句子结构联系，新知识就此产生。

3.4 分析悖论与奎因的实用主义整体理论

如果说弗雷格和罗素为分析哲学正名是在分析命题的框架内进行的，那么，奎因（Quine, 1953）的态度却更为激进些。在"经验主义的两个教条"（Martinich, 2001）檄文中，我们不难发现奎因有替分析哲学辩护的意图，其中的主题依然是分析悖论的消解问题。他认为，分析命题与综合命题没有绝对的界线，把命题中的语言成分和事实成分截然分开是一个值得反省的错误。

所谓的"教条"就是指康德的观点，即分析命题无需借助经验观察，是先天的；综合命题是后验的，它产生于经验观察。

奎因的理论体现在他的整体论和实用主义思想，而这种实用主义整体论，完全是表现在他对语言意义的分析上的。他说："依亚里士多德看来，事物有本质，但只是语言形式才有意义。当本质由所指对象分离出来而同语词结合时，它才变成了有意义"（Quine，1953：48）。他又说："一旦把意义理论和指称理论严格分开，就容易认识到只有语言形式的同义性和陈述的分析性才是意义理论要探讨的首要问题"（同上）。看来，奎因非常重视从语言中探讨事物本质（意义）问题。这是奎因的意义理论区别于指称理论的一大特征。从中也可看出奎因与弗雷格以及罗素有相同的观点，即不同的名称，即使冠以相同的对象，其意义是不同的。奎因在文章中举的几个典型的例子与分析悖论中的例子是相似的，如："人是有理性的动物。""单身汉是未婚男子。"

这里要讨论的是"甲就是甲"不同于用一个"同义词"替代另一个"同义词"。为什么呢？因为我们可以说，人是有理性的动物，但如果说"有理性的动物是人"，在某些情况下就行不通。如植物人已经丧失理性，但人们还是将其当作人来照料。

单身汉是未婚男子，但未婚男子未必就可以称为单身汉，因为在不同的社会文化背景中，单身汉的标准是不一样的。例如在中国的家庭中，家长绝不会把自己年满18岁的儿子叫做"单身汉"。"这表明，根据本质（意义）的规定性所下的定义或所确定的同义词，总是依据一定的语境的，总是取决于人们在一定文化共同体中如何使用这个词"（张庆熊等，2005: 292）。"甲就是甲"与分析命题中的同义词替换是不同的，前者可以不思考命题意义，后者必须考虑语词的意义和语词使用的语境。这里可以看出奎因的实用主义倾向，同时，我们也知道分析命题的意义与逻辑真值命题是有区别的。

分析悖论的语句与定义语句是相同的，前者由被分析项和分析项组成，后者由被定义项和定义项组成。奎因认为被定义项和定义项有三种方式的关系，即定义项可以是用范围较窄的一套记号来忠实地为被定义词释义……；或者定义词可以按照解释的本旨，把被定义词的先前用法加以改良；或者，最后，被定义项可以是一个新创造的记号,是此时此地新近地赋予意义(Martinich,2001: 50)。从这里我们可看出,奎因又回到分析悖论的句式:"a brother is a male sibling"——"a bachelor is an unmarried man"。我们没有必要担心这种语句会产生分析悖论,因为按照整体论的观点,"人们始终应该将新知识看成是从旧的知识中生长出来的"(张庆熊等,2005: 285)。而且,不同的社会文化背景对于"未婚男子"和"单身汉"的定义是不同的,因而不会出现同义反复。

总之,在我看来,奎因在批评经验主义的两个教条时,所围绕的一个中心话题仍然是分析悖论的问题。要摆脱架在分析哲学家身上的桎梏,首先是要说清楚本体论上的同一性与分析命题中的同义词关系是不一样的;分析命题并非必然真,它有其认知价值。奎因在谈论分析语句是带有实用主义整体论的思想,即把语句分析与语境结合起来,把分析命题与知识系统结合起来,只是与弗雷格和罗素消解分析悖论的方法不同罢了。

4. 分析悖论的消解给我们留下了什么

钱冠连先生在谈到哲学的语言转向的特征时说:"意义是哲学的语言转向以后的中心之题。英美分析哲学家认为:第一,研究人的思维活动和认识能力应让位于探究语言表达式的意义,因为后者才有公共性、客观性和直接性;第二,传统哲学大多是形而上学思辨的产物,揭露其谬误的最有效方法是指出其对语言的误用;第三,即使对语言的地位、功用有不同的看法,最低限度可以同意,把语言所代表的对象的存在论地位搁置一旁,就大家有一致用法的语言加以比较,是避免无谓争论、有效探讨哲学问题的可取方法"(钱冠连,2005: 65)。钱先生的这一论述充分而又深刻地概括了分析哲学的特点,也非常适合概括分析哲学家在消解分析悖论过程中采取的方法。从弗雷格的涵义理论到罗素的摹状语理论,再到奎因的实用主义整体论,他们都涉及如何消解分析悖论的问题,并为分析哲学的发展作出了巨大的贡献。

分析哲学到了20世纪80年代似乎发展到了高峰。现在看来,分析哲学有许多局限性,如弗雷格和罗素都想改造日常语言,以形式语言来代替。另外,把意义研究只局限在句子水平上,并把精力全部放到了对名词意义的静止研究上,这也是分析哲学中几个主要人物的理论上的缺憾。尽管如此,在我看来,早期的分析哲学家的研究大大推动了哲学的语言转向,使本体论向知识论转变,功不可没。而作为后来居上者,奎因对意义理论的发展具有划时代的意义。当然,语言哲学发展到今天,我们完全可以多角度地透视分析悖论问题,如从逻辑、语义、认知、隐喻以及不同文化内涵等方面来考察它。

例如,汉语中有如下表达式:战胜就是战败;改正就是改错;打是亲,骂是爱。

怎样理解上述含有分析悖论的分析语句?明明是反义词,怎么就成了同义词了呢?逻辑上说不过去,语义上也说不过去,但认知上却行得通。为什么呢?因为"胜"和"败",是双方"战"的结果,说话者可以从胜的一方的立场言说,也可以从败者的角度言说。这就像一个装有半瓶水的瓶子,我们可以说半瓶空,也可以说是半瓶满,各自的凸显和背景情况是不一样的;"改正"可以是结果或目的,"改错"可以是过程,两者的功能是一样的,所以我们可以说"短文改正、校对、改错、勘误",即改错为正。但是,"改错"并不完全等于"改正",因为"改错"可以是将错的改对,也可以将错的改错,也可以将对的改错。至于"短文改错"到底是什么意义,我们参加一场有"短文改错"内容的考试就知道了!最后一例可以多种分析。"打"和"骂"是物理行为,"亲"和"爱"是情感上的东西,两者不能相提并论,需要一点隐喻与文化内涵的知识。当然也可以按因果关系来分析,不过,这样一来,悖论就又产生了:为什么"亲"和"爱"却要"打"和"骂"呢?

庄子说:"筌者所以在鱼,得鱼而忘筌"(《庄子·外物》)。我想,此"鱼"乃是我们探求的"意",此"筌"乃是我们的指称对象或叫"形"。设"筌"为得"鱼",得"鱼"者得"意",得"意"者而忘"形"。这就是语言哲学家,特别是分析哲学消解分析悖论、发展意义理论的共同特点。

陆游有诗,"天机云锦用在我,剪裁妙处非刀尺"。将有形的存在物暂时搁在一边,坚持物为我用,语义上行,这就是语言哲学之妙处。分析悖论成了意义理论发展的一个源头,哲学家在消解它时展示了各自的智慧。我们可以从中得到些启发,厘清分析哲学的发展脉络,沿着前人踏过的足迹,一步一个脚印地往前走下去。

参考文献

陈　波,2005,《逻辑哲学》。北京:北京大学出版社。
陈嘉映,2004,《语言哲学》。北京:北京大学出版社。
韩林合,2003,《分析的形而上学》。北京:商务印书馆。
胡　军,2002,《分析哲学在中国》。北京:首都师范大学出版社。
黄　斌,1999,《语言逻辑哲学——难题与解析》。重庆:重庆出版社。
李大强,2008,分析悖论的分析,反思与奠基,http://www.pftheory.org/index.jsp。
达米特著,2005,《分析哲学的起源(王路译)》。上海:上海译文出版社。
江　怡,2009,《分析哲学教程》。北京:北京大学出版社。
钱冠连,2005,《语言:人类最后的家园》。北京:商务印书馆。
苏珊·哈克,2003,《逻辑哲学(罗毅译)》。北京:商务印书馆。
张庆熊,周林东,徐英瑾,2005,《二十世纪英美哲学》。北京:人民出版社。
Clark, M. 2002. *Paradoxes from A to Z*. London: Routledge Taylor & Francis Group.
Frege, G. 1892. On sense and nominatum. In A. P. Martinich (ed.), *Philosophy of Language*. Oxford: Oxford University Press, 199-211.
Quine, W. V. 1953. Two dogmas of empiricism. In A. P. Martinich (ed.), *Philosophy of Language*. Oxford: Oxford University Press, 47-60.

Quine, W. V. 1997. *The ways of paradoxes and other essays*. Massachusetts: Harvard University Press.

Russell, B. 1905. On denoting. In A. P. Martinich (ed.), *Philosophy of Language*. Oxford: Oxford University Press, 212-227.

通讯地址：310014 浙江工业大学外国语学院 huanghj@zjut.edu.cn

Some Reflections on the Paradox of Analysis and the Theory of Meaning

Huang Huijian

Abstract: With the paradox of analysis as a main thread, this paper is intended to trace back to the ways in which some major representatives of the School of Analytic Philosophy, i.e. Gottlob Frege, Bertrand Russell and W. V. Quine attempted to dissolve the paradox of analysis, and states their contributions to the theory of meaning. On this basis, the author shows some reflections on the study of the theory of meaning. The author holds that most philosophical problems come from paradoxes, and that the task for philosophers tends to be dissolving paradoxes from different perspectives so as to display their wisdom, and that the contributions made by the analytical school to the theory of meaning are often associated with the dissolution of the paradox of analysis. Therefore, doing research into the philosophy of language via the paradox of analysis might be an ideal approach.

Keywords: paradox; paradox of analysis; theories of meaning; thinking

● 语言哲学与教学实践

"西方语言哲学"与外语学科博士研究生理论创新能力的培养

广东外语外贸大学 霍永寿

提 要：通过"西方语言哲学"课程的开设培养外语学科博士研究生理论创新能力需要摆正三种关系：知识与智慧，"照着讲"与"接着讲"，语言哲学与语言学。课程教学涉及知识的传授，但其真正目标是培养学员的理性智慧；课程强调"照着讲"旨在了解西方语言哲学，而"接着讲"才是课程的真正目的；学习西方语言哲学是为了更好地把握、认识当代语言学发展脉络，从而更好地进行创新型语言学研究。

关键词：语言哲学、语言学博士研究生、理论创新能力、培养

1. 引言

近年来，国内外语学科研究生阶段课程设置中出现了这样一个趋势：哲学类课程正在得到培养单位的重视，带有哲学字眼的新课程（如："语言哲学"，"翻译哲学"等）正在悄然进入外语学科研究生阶段的课程结构。与此相关的是，哲学（尤其是语言哲学）逐渐为外语界学人所熟悉，对语言哲学的研究正在兴起。由外语界主办的语言哲学讲习班、研讨会等学术活动日益频繁，规模也日渐扩大，其中最值得一提的是中西语言哲学研究会的成立暨首届西方语言哲学研讨会的召开（2008年1月，广东外语外贸大学，广州）。

应该说，这是外语界的大事，它标志着一个新的研究思路（甚至可以说，外语界学术研究新阶段）的涌动和到来。这一思路不是改革开放三十余年来外语界学术研究的继续，而是一种突破，其结果或许可以使我国外语界的语言研究摆脱对西方语言学的单纯依赖，从而逐步走上自主创新的健康道路。

围绕这一趋势需要考虑的问题是：如何使"西方语言哲学"课的教学和学生创新能力的培养有机地结合起来，从而更好地培养出既有创新意识又具备创新能力的外语学科研究者。

《中华人民共和国学位条例》（1980年2月）明确将博士研究生的学术水平定位为"在本门学科上掌握坚实宽广的基础理论和系统深入的专门知识；具有独立从事科学研究工作的能力；在科学或专门技术上作出创造性的成果"。这里，"在

科学上作出创造性的成果"显然是对博士研究生理论创新能力的要求。

本文围绕外语学科博士研究生理论创新能力的培养,思考和报告近年来笔者为广东外语外贸大学国家文科重点研究基地"外国语言学及应用语言学"专业博士研究生开设的"西方语言哲学"课程的初步尝试。

2. 知识与智慧

哲学是追求知识的学问,哲学课的教学自然离不开知识的传授。哲学也是追求智慧的学问,哲学课的教学当然也是培养智慧的活动。这样一来,如何摆正二者之间的关系成了哲学课程必须考虑和解决的一个问题。

我们的做法是把课程内容分为三个模块:西方(语言)哲学史,现、当代语言哲学理论与经典哲学名篇解读以及哲学研究方法。西方(语言)哲学史的内容主要包括西方哲学自苏格拉底以来各阶段发展史的简要梳理和介绍,其中最为重要的是西方哲学对语言问题的关注,包括本体论阶段对语言问题的关注,认识论阶段对语言问题的关注以及分析哲学阶段对语言问题的关注。大致说来,这部分内容主要采取课堂讲授的方式完成,而且这种讲授也不是系统、完整地一次性完成的,而是分散在后面两个模块中以零散的方式进行。

现、当代语言哲学理论是本课程教学中的重要内容。一个学期(十六周)中,我们从20世纪哲学发展各阶段语言哲学家之最有成就者中选取最有代表性的哲学家,同时为每一位哲学家选取一篇代表作供学生研读。本部分内容的教学主要以读书汇报的方式完成。具体做法是由一名(或数名)学生提前准备,然后在课堂上汇报对所读文章的理解和读书心得,并组织学员就文章内容进行讨论。

本模块的第二部分内容,是教师对上述文章内容的进一步解读。解读内容包括文章的哲学史背景(文章研究内容的历史定位及其所代表的哲学流派和研究课题),作者的哲学观点和文章的内容以及文章的研究对(语言)哲学史乃至于其他学科(如语言学、心理学、认知科学等的研究)所产生的重大推动作用。

哲学研究方法(课程内容模块之三)是本课程内容的核心。我们始终不忘记,"西方语言哲学"是为"外国语言学及应用语言学"专业博士研究生开设的基础课,不是专业方向课。这就是说,我们的课程是为学生目前和将来的专业研究服务的。那么,课程内容中哪一部分和学员的专业创新能力发展关系最为紧密呢?答案是:哲学研究方法。

哲学研究方法是哲学理性智慧在认识层面上的体现,它反映了认识主体认识世界、建立关于世界的科学理论模型和知识体系的思维运作过程。从元思维的层面上来看,这一过程包括①认识到问题的存在;②定义问题的性质;③表征问题的信息;④形成解决问题的策略;⑤分配解决问题的资源;⑥监控解决问题的方案;⑦评估解决问题的反馈信息七个步骤(Sternberg, 2003)。我们认为,这七个步骤也反映了科学研究创新能力在元思维层面上的运作过程。当然,由于课程本身的限制，我们教学一般只涉及上述①至④个步骤。

那么，如何在哲学课的教学中进行哲学研究方法的教学，从而培养学生学科研究的创新能力呢？我们认为，这一方法及其步骤就体现在课程经典哲学名篇的篇章组织过程中。基于这样一种认识，我们在名篇解读中一直坚持以下列方式分析每一篇文章。首先，我们对每一篇文章的解读都以上述（语言）哲学史以及作者的哲学观点为背景，并以此为基础找出文章试图解决的理论问题。同时，我们要讨论，为什么在这样的背景下作者会提出相应的研究问题？提出这样的问题于当时的背景有什么重要的学术价值？哲学论文的一个特点是作者一般不会对相关文献作详细综述，而经常是开宗明义、直奔主题。这样一来，文章的哲学史背景经常是必不可少的。通过多次的讨论，学生会逐步明白什么是研究中的真问题，以及真问题是如何找出来的。我们认为，选题能力是学生学科研究创新能力的一个重要组成部分。

确定研究问题后的下一步是作者对文章研究问题的性质的定义或界定。对问题的定义或界定反映了作者对研究问题所持的观点或视角，以及作者基于当代和特定时期学科研究现状和研究水平对研究问题的理解和把握，是作者智慧和眼界的重要体现。

与此相关的是作者在文章中对研究问题的表征或表述。研究问题的表述反映了作者从哲学的角度出发认识研究问题的路径。西方语言哲学研究的一个重要路径是采用语义上行（semantic ascent，见 Quine, 1960），把关于哲学问题的争论简化为对语词（或语词表征的概念）问题的讨论（亦称哲学的语言相关性, the linguistic relativity of philosophy）（Losonsky, 2006）。这样一来，对哲学问题的表述就可以体现为在语词层面上对研究问题的分析和讨论。同样，这里的讨论也反映了文章作者对上述问题的深刻理解和把握，也体现了其独特的视角和智慧。

既然问题是语词层面上的问题，解决问题的策略也是在语词层面上形成的。在这一层面上，哲学家解决问题的策略就体现为新概念的提出、区分和讨论。实际上，哲学问题的解决（或消解）正是通过这些策略得以完成的。新概念的提出反映了哲学家对研究问题的独特认识，概念的区分使研究问题得到了更为清楚、明确的认识。而这一过程中策略的选择和动用正是上述哲学理性智慧的体现。

以分析哲学创始人弗雷格的名篇《内涵义与指称义》（分析哲学奠基之作）为例。意义理论（语言哲学核心论题之一）的基本假设是：语词的功能是对实在的对象加以命名，语词的意义也来自于其对实在对象的指称（正因为这个原因，指称理论是意义理论的重要内容）。但英国哲学家穆勒（J. S. Mill）却发现这一观点无法解释同一性陈述（identity statement）现象（Chapman, 2000）。以"Sophroniscus is the father of Socrates"为例。既然"Sophroniscus"（命题的主项）和"the father of Socrates"（命题的谓项）指称同一个对象，二者意义相同，命题应为重言式，不传递任何意义。但事实是，上述命题是可以被理解的，因而是有意义的。何以如此呢？

解读《内涵义与指称义》时，我们发现，弗雷格首先以数学等式 $a = a$ 和 $a = b$ 介入对上述问题的讨论（弗雷格的例句为"The morning star is the evening star")。以此为基础,他区分了符号使用时涉及的两个层面:符号指称的对象和符号本身。在指称对象层面上,上述语句的数学表达式为 a = a,因为此时语句的主项和谓项指称同一个对象;在符号层面上,上述语句的数学表达式为 a = b。他把语句主项和谓项间的差异称作内涵义(sense),并将语词内涵义的差异归结为呈现方式(mode of presentation)或认识价值(cognitive value)的差异。应该说,这是在数学层面上发现、认识和表述哲学问题的典范。

基于对问题性质的上述认识,弗雷格形成了自己解决上述问题的思路。首先,他区分了三个主要概念,即符号(包括专名、语词的组合以及字母)、指称义和内涵义,并联系符号(如专名)出现的语篇类型(如宗教语篇和文学语篇)对指称义和内涵义的各种情形(如转述情形)以及二者间的关系(如指称义和内涵义的通常性和间接性,以及二者间的转换关系)作了明确的界定和说明。在上述概念区分和概念关系讨论的基础上,弗雷格开始讨论语言符号(即语词、直陈语句和复合语句)的内涵义(文章的研究重点)。研究发现,直陈语句的内涵义表现为一个思想(thought),而复合语句的内涵义则表现各异:有时一个复合语句只表达一个思想(如条件复合语句中从句的主语为非定指名词时);有时复合语句的主从句各表达一个思想(如条件复合语句中从句的主语为定指名词时);有时一个主从复合语句表达三个思想(如因果复合语句,此时一个思想为隐含信息)。这样一来,原来穆勒留下的问题有了一个很好的回答。更为重要的是,弗雷格为意义问题(语言哲学的根本问题,当然也是语言研究的重要问题)的研究发现、开辟了更大的空间,并由此开启了语言哲学研究的新时代——分析哲学。

从问题的提出、界定和表述到解决策略的形成,我们看到了哲学理性智慧在元思维层面上的运作与体现,而这一过程的推进又是在上述哲学史、哲学理论这一背景上展开的。问题的选定既反映了哲学家对哲学史的理解,也反映了哲学家对当代哲学发展走向的深刻认识和把握。在这里,知识与智慧有机地结合,并成为学科研究创新能力的元成分。

这一结合正好体现了我们以知识教学为背景,以智慧培养为旨归的教学原则。

3. "照着讲"与"接着讲"

"照着讲"和"接着讲"是我们确定课程内容时始终坚持的总原则。

"西方语言哲学"体现了西方语言文化的特殊性质,反映了西方哲学家(甚至还包括科学家)在认识世界的过程中构建起来的知识体系以及形成的思想方法和智慧,是西方学者(包括人文科学学者和自然科学学者)科学研究的元成分。身处不同的语言文化环境中,我们的学员当然不可能自然获得这种能力。因而,"照着讲"是必须的,而且我们只有老老实实、认认真真地"照着讲","照着学",才能把隔壁人家的东西搞清楚、弄明白。

"西方语言哲学"内容安排中"照着讲"对于外语学科博士研究生还有一层同样重要的意义。从近代哲学开始,西方哲学家在讨论哲学认识论问题的过程中逐步把目光投向与人类认识过程关系密切的语言问题。自洛克开始,对语言问题的系统关注成了西方哲学的一大"副业"。哲学家们从不同的研究兴趣出发对语言问题进行了深入的思考。虽然哲学家关注语言问题其根本原因是要解决哲学问题,但这种关注的后果之一是促成了普通语言学学科地位的确立。这是语言学史上的大事,这一事件为西方语言学20世纪的蓬勃发展奠定了坚实的学科基础。我们的学员既然是外语学科博士研究生,当然要熟谙西方语言学。而把握西方语言学的哲学渊源正是深入了解西方语言学的最佳路径。这样一来,"照着讲"便具有学科能力发展的重要意义。

但"照着讲"是不够的,还要"接着讲"。何以要接着讲?原因有二。首先,如前所述,我们培养的是既有创新意识又具备创新能力的外语学科研究者。对于外语学科研究工作,创新型研究者"既要重视向西方学习,又要立足于自己的理论建构"(钱冠连语)。要立足于自己的理论建构,当然要提出自己的真问题,这样的真问题当然不能从西方学者的书本上照搬过来,而是从本民族的语言文化以及研究者自身的专业特点和研究兴趣中来的。从这个意义上来说,"接着讲"就是从西方学者研究的尽头处入手,以本民族语言文化的特点为基础,提出自己的研究问题,并从自己研究的需要出发界定、表述问题,进而形成自己的解决策略。这是创新意识培养的重要一步。

重视"接着讲"的原因之二来自西方语言哲学本身可能具有的特点和缺陷。作为西方哲学中的一个分支学科,西方语言哲学来自于西方哲学家(当然也是西方人)从哲学研究(如本体论、认识论研究)的需要出发对语言问题的思考。这样一来,西方文化、西方哲学的特点(甚至是不足)必然会在其语言哲学中体现出来。[1] 而我们的学员所面对的是汉语及其在汉文化语境中的使用。在这样的情况下,把西方语言哲学作为基础来考察汉语的语言、语用问题就必然会出现这样的结果,即西方语言哲学以及在此基础上形成的西方语言学理论不一定都切合汉语语言研究的需要。[2] 这里,强调"接着讲"意在使学员在领会、吸收西方语言哲学研究成果的同时,也要明白,西方的语言哲学理论也不是万能的,只有合理吸收,才能使课程的学习对自己的研究有助益。

那么,如何才能做到既"照着讲",又"接着讲"呢?我们认为,既然课程的目的是讲授西方语言哲学,西方语言哲学当然是课程内容的主体,但在授课过程

---

[1] 英国量子理论物理学家玻姆(Bohm, 1980)认为,西方思想中的分析性传统(即任何事物最终都由一组有固定本性的基本粒子构成,因而对事物的认识便是将其分割、分解为不同层面的构成成分)以及由此而建立起来的各门科学认为世界是破碎的(fragmented)。在他看来,世界只有在显析(explicate)层面上是可分析的,而在隐性层面上是隐缠的(implicate)、整体的。值得注意的是,玻姆认为,在使世界破碎化的过程中,西方的语言起了推波助澜的作用。而玻姆关于世界整体性的观点来自于东方哲学(具体说来,是印度哲学)。

[2] 美国心理学家尼斯贝特(Nisbett, 2003)认为,西方人的世界是由孤立的、没有联系的物体构成的,而东方人的世界是由相互联系的事物组成的。与此相关的是,西方人眼中的世界是由名词构成的,中国人眼中的世界是由动词构成的。这种形而上学层面上的差异势必会在语言结构中反映出来。关于这方面的心理学实验,可参阅该书的相关章节。

中我们也适时注意介绍中国语言哲学对相关问题的解释。例如，讲到语言的命名、指称功能以及语词的指称义时，我们总会有意识地引导学员思考中国哲学的相关问题，如荀子的正名理论、公孙龙的名学思想、墨子的名辩学思想，同时也注意向学员介绍现代学者的研究，如胡适《先秦名学史》、周云之《名辩学论》等研究成果。这些研究是基于汉语的哲学思考，其对汉语研究的启发是自不待言的。有了国学的语言哲学基础，学科的创新才能有所依归。

通过对比与阐发，逐步使学员在领会西方语言哲学理论的同时，也接触到了中国语言哲学，进而通过中西互释、中西互补、扬长避短，形成自己的看法。我们相信，课程内容的这种安排对于强化学员的理论创新意识，培养学员的学科研究创新能力，是大有益处的。

4. 语言哲学与语言学

与上述"西方语言哲学"课程定位相关的是，在授课过程中应该如何处理语言哲学与语言学的关系。这即是说，在为"外国语言学及应用语言学"专业的博士研究生讲授"西方语言哲学"课程时要不要涉及语言学内容？答案当然是肯定的。但问题是，该讲什么？又怎么讲呢？

根据学员的专业特点和课程的性质，我们主要从两个方面处理语言哲学与语言学的关系。首先，作为课程内容的一部分，在介绍语言哲学研究论题时，我们始终提醒并鼓励学员从语言学角度对这些论题作进一步的思考。如在解读弗雷格《内涵义与指称义》时，我们一直提醒学员注意弗雷格对内涵义（尤其是语句的内涵义或思想）的定义及其生成机制的考察和分析。弗雷格对语句内涵义（思想）的考察始终不离语句所处的语境（即上述复合语句和语篇），这一思考意义问题的进路对语用学研究肯定有不少的启发。罗素在解决困扰哲学家的存在问题和同一性问题时引入有定描述语（definite descriptions）和命题函项（propositional function）这两个概念，并论述了有定描述语作为不完全符号以及命题函项中变元（variable）的指称对象对语境的依赖和敏感性。奎因对翻译不确定性也作了不少论述，等等。诸如此类的问题原本是哲学问题，但哲学家的讨论却并不止于哲学，同时还可以对语言研究提供深刻的洞见。认真、细致地理解经典哲学文章，准确把握哲学家的观点，同时又引导学员以此为基础进一步思考和发现语言学的研究论题，是充分发挥语言哲学"营养钵"作用的一条路径。

其次，厘清语言学的哲学根源是本课程内容中的重要组成部分。西方语言学在20世纪获得了空前的发展，其研究范围的广度以及研究所达到的深度，均远胜此前的任何一个时代。但是，这种发展不是凭空而来的，而是源自西方哲学（尤其是近代以来的认识论哲学）长期以来对语言问题的持久甚至是系统的关注。当然，哲学家关注语言问题并非是要研究语言或解决语言问题，而是要解决哲学（形而上学或认识论）问题。但这种关注却在近代引发了语言研究的兴趣，促成了普通语言学的诞生以及20世纪语言学的大发展。这是当前国内语言学研究中必须注意、也必须解决的一个问题。

那么，在教学中如何引导学员关注和认识语言学的哲学根源呢？鉴于目前课程选读的经典文章中尚未列入近代哲学的相关文献，在课堂教学层面我们在哲学史部分有意识地介绍近代哲学对语言问题的关注，特别是关注的论题、方式及深度。西方哲学在近代经由认识论转向之后，转向对知识问题（知识体系的基础和知识体系的建构）的深切关注和研究。作为这一研究的延伸，哲学家（如霍布斯、洛克、休谟、莱布尼茨、孔狄亚克等）逐步介入对语言问题的思考，并逐步形成了思考语言问题的两个主要路向：洛克倡导的经验主义路向和莱布尼茨提倡的理性主义路向（Losonsky, 2006）。前者把语言作为一种行为，主张从对人类行为的观察入手，用归纳法介入对语言系统的研究；后者把语言作为一个体系，主张从建立公理系统入手，借用演绎法介入对语言潜在的逻辑形式的分析。这两条路向经过不断发展逐步形成了现代语言研究的两个主要发展趋势：基于逻辑实证主义的语言描写和基于理性主义的语言解释。

何以如此？经验主义于19世纪与自然科学研究结合并发展为实证主义，20世纪上半叶由维也纳学派进一步发展成为逻辑实证主义（一种科学哲学思想）。20年代，在这一科学哲学思潮的影响下，出身于人类学的语言学家萨丕尔、布龙菲尔德等建立了美国描写语言学（或称结构主义语言学）派，这一学派的语言描写方法（如著名的发现程序）和语言观（如对意义问题的态度）在第二次世界大战期间和行为主义（同样源自逻辑实证主义的心理学流派）结合，形成了语言学习和语言教学的重要流派——听说法，对当时的语言学和语言教学研究产生了广泛、深刻的影响。值得一提的是，上世纪三四十年代，我国语言学家吕叔湘等应用美国描写语言学派的研究方法研究汉语，取得了重要的成就。钱冠连（2004）将以吕叔湘为代表的这一研究路向称为"实证派"。

与此相对的是，笛卡儿的理性主义经过莱布尼茨发展成为对人类语言逻辑形式的分析以及对普遍语法形式的探求。19世纪中期，德国语言学家洪堡特在这一哲学理念的影响下建立了普通语言学（不过洪堡特关注的是对人类语言音系结构的形式分析），穆勒用自然主义的理论框架分析了人类语言的逻辑形式，之后的弗雷格把自然语言的逻辑形式从穆勒的心理主义桎梏中解救出来，从数学函项出发解释语言的逻辑形式，从而使逻辑形式成为语言哲学的中心论题（Losonsky, 2006）。弗雷格的努力在罗素的逻辑主义研究中得到进一步的发展，语言逻辑形式的研究与数学的结合更加紧密了。20世纪50年代中期，美国语言学家乔姆斯基在这一思想的影响下，创立了转换生成语法学派，借用数理逻辑的理念和概念解释人类语言的形式特征，从而使形式语言学的研究得到了巨大的发展。

语用学情形如何？语用学是研究会话含意（语言使用意义之一种）的语言学分支学科。哲学史上，中西哲学家对语言使用过程中的含意问题多有论述。先秦时期，中国哲学家庄周就曾有"意有所随者不可以言传也"（《庄子·天道》）的论断。20世纪20年代，维特根斯坦提出"意义在于使用"的口号，把语词的意义放到语言游戏和生活形式中考察。30年代初，英国哲学家奥斯汀开始思考语言的施事功能，并在50年代形成较为系统的言语行为理论（语用学基础理论之一)。30年代末,美国哲学家莫里斯(Morris, 1938)第一次把语用学引入其符号学体系中,作为符号学体系中的一个专司研究符号与其使用者关系的子学科。50年代中期,哲学家格赖斯(Grice, 1957)区分了自然意义和非自然意义,60年代又提出合作原则及其准则,为会话含意推导机制的研究指出了一个明确的方向。进入70年代后,上述哲学家对语言使用问题的思考,逐步进入语言学家的视野,并逐步演化为20世纪后半叶轰轰烈烈的语用学研究,成就了语言学研究的新气象。可以说,带有学科原创性质的语言学问题多半是哲学家发现的。

除课堂教学层面之外,我们还在课程管理层面上鼓励学员从语言哲学出发思考本专业的问题。按照课程的要求,学员在课程结束时必须撰写一篇学期论文,论文在期末成绩中占60%。在论文选题阶段,我们引导、鼓励学员在语言哲学层面上思考自己专业的问题,并尝试从语言哲学层面出发,发现和讨论本专业的研究课题。这样一来,论文的写作既深化了学员对语言哲学的理解,也加深、拓展了其对本专业研究问题的认识。更为重要的是,这一做法为学员基于本学科的创新型研究找到了一个锚定点,这个锚定点同时也可能是学员学科研究的生长点。一个具体学科的生长点往往不在本学科内,而是存在于比本学科高一个等级的学科上。对于"外国语言学及应用语言学"专业的博士研究生来说,这个学科便是语言哲学。

从语言哲学层面眺望、展望语言学领域,从语言哲学角度考察语言学发展的历史,这种"上蹿下跳"、"瞻前顾后"式的教学思路有助于学员更加清楚地认识语言学的学科本质。我们相信学员通过学习应该明白:语言学从何而来,将向何而去。这是学科研究创新的原点,也是学科研究创新能力的起点。

5. 结束语

外语学科博士研究生阶段"西方语言哲学"课程虽然不完善,属探索性质,但它绝不是哲学专业语言哲学分支学科内容的简单复制,而是以创新型语言学研究为指向的学科基础课程。作为基础课,"西方语言哲学"的授课内容既要兼顾学科本身的内容,同时也要考虑学员的专业特点,学员的专业特点是多样的,课程的内容和管理也是动态的。以上所述,仅是近年授课心得,希望有更多的老师参加讨论,从而把外语界语言哲学的教学推向前进,为外语界语言学研究者理论创新能力的培养打下基础。

参考文献

Bohm, D. 1980. *Wholeness and the Implicate Order*. London/New York: Routledge & Kegan Paul.

Chapman, S. 2000. *Philosophy for Linguists: An Introduction*. London & New York: Routledge.

Grice, H. P. 1957. Meaning. *Philosophical Review*(66): 377-388.

Losonsky, M. 2006. *Linguistic Turns in Modern Philosophy*. Cambridge: Cambridge University Press.

Morris, C. W. 1938. *Foundations of the Theory of Signs*. Chicago/London: The University of Chicago Press.

Nisbett, R. 2003. *The Geography of Thought*. New York: The Free Press.

Quine, W. V. O. 1960. *Word and Object*. Boston: The MIT Press.

Sternberg, R. J. 2003. *Wisdom, Intelligence and Creativity Synthesized*. Cambridge: Cambridge University Press,

钱冠连，2004，以学派意识看汉语研究，《汉语学报》(2)：2-8。

通讯地址：510420 广东外语外贸大学 <huoys63@yahoo.com.cn>

"Western Philosophy of Language" and the Development of Linguistics PhD Students' Theoretical Originality

Huo Yongshou

Abstract: In teaching "Western Philosophy of Language" to Chinese PhD students of linguistics, we have attempted to balance knowledge against wisdom, "teaching what has been said" against "teaching what has not been said", and philosophy of language against linguistics. In this foundation course, the teaching of knowledge is aimed to develop the students' rationalized philosophical wisdom, the teaching of "what has been said" in Western philosophy of language is purported to help the students to go beyond this and become aware of "what has not been said", and the teaching of philosophy of language itself is to help the students to have a better command of linguistics. All of these attempts aim to develop the students' theoretical originality in their linguistic studies.

Keywords: philosophy of language; linguistics PhD students; theoretical originality; development

《语言哲学研究》稿约

《语言哲学研究》欢迎以下稿件：

一、为了逐步形成《语言哲学研究》的独特风格与路径，来稿无论是以分析哲学为基础的分析，还是以欧陆哲学为基础的阐释，都应以语言分析为入口，以世界与人的思想为出口，允许多样化风格，重视汉语语料。

二、论文务必有创见，批评文章必须有真知灼见，介绍或翻译的对象必须是西方语言哲学的精品。

三、《语言哲学研究》的栏目分为：论文（60% 分量）、评论、书评、西语哲的经典与名著翻译、学术活动。（拟在"论文"栏目之内，每一辑都刊登一篇英文稿，以便将来向英文版过渡。）

四、如有高水平的专著文稿，可出版专著特辑。这将另有评审办法，以保证质量。

五、来稿如采用电邮方式，电子邮件的主题栏内请以以下方式填写（便于电邮识别，不与垃圾邮件相混）："投稿"三字加上投稿人全名（如"投稿刘玉梅"、"投稿刘辉"等等）

对适用稿件与不适用稿件，均会收到通知。

投稿请寄　王爱华　wang_diana2003@yahoo.com.cn

中西语言哲学研究会　《语言哲学研究》编辑部　2010-6-29

Journal of the China Association for the Philosophy of Language (CAPL)
Calling for Papers

Contributions on the philosophy of language both in the analytic tradition and in the hermeneutic tradition are invited for the journal of CAPL.

Articles with original and insightful viewpoints are welcome. Papers concerning introduction of Western philosophy of language or translation of classics are also accepted.

Whether your contributions will be accepted or not will be notified.

E-mail: wang_diana2003@yahoo.com.cn

郑 重 声 明

高等教育出版社依法对本书享有专有出版权。任何未经许可的复制、销售行为均违反《中华人民共和国著作权法》，其行为人将承担相应的民事责任和行政责任，构成犯罪的，将被依法追究刑事责任。为了维护市场秩序，保护读者的合法权益，避免读者误用盗版书造成不良后果，我社将配合行政执法部门和司法机关对违法犯罪的单位和个人给予严厉打击。社会各界人士如发现上述侵权行为，希望及时举报，本社将奖励举报有功人员。

反盗版举报电话：(010) 58581897/58581896/58581879
传　　真：(010) 82086060
E - mail：dd@hep.com.cn
通信地址：北京市西城区德外大街4号
　　　　　高等教育出版社打击盗版办公室
邮　　编：100120

购书请拨打电话：(010)58581118